# And Then There Were ~~None~~ Some

## A ~~Murder~~ Survival Mystery



Jay D. Clark

First edition 2024

*Dedicated to my daughter, Dana, whose thesis on Edgar Allen Poe incubated the idea for this review.*

# Acknowledgments

Profound appreciation goes to Stephen C. Meyer whose seminal work, *Return of the God Hypothesis,* revealed the scientific basis for "the mind behind the universe;" to Eric Metaxas who provided insightful details on atheism's demise; to Ante-Nicene Fathers, historians, chroniclers, scientists, explorers, professors, prophets, and other disciples who enlightened us on the nature of the Godhead and the practice of early Christianity; to the Prophet Joseph Smith who introduced the biblically prophesied dispensation of the fulness of times with apostolic succession down to the present day; and to Christians worldwide who merit heartfelt admiration for their deep love of Jesus Christ, in spite of inheriting doctrines and ordinances that have been corrupted through the ages.

# Contents

# And Then There Were ~~None~~ Some

## A ~~Murder~~ Survival Mystery

# TEN LITTLE SOLDIER BOYS

TEN little Soldier Boys went out to dine;
One choked his little self and then there were nine.

NINE little Soldier boys sat up very late;
One overslept himself and then there were eight.

EIGHT little Soldier Boys travelling in Devon;
One said he'd stay there and then there were seven.

SEVEN little Soldier Boys chopping up sticks;
One chopped himself in half and then there were six.

SIX little Soldier Boys playing with a hive;
A bumble-bee stung one and then there were five.

FIVE little Soldier Boys going in for law;
One got in Chancery and then there were four.

FOUR little Soldier Boys going out to sea;
A red herring swallowed one and then there were three.

THREE little Soldier Boys walking in the Zoo;
A big bear hugged one and then there were two.

TWO little Soldier Boys sitting in the sun;
One got frizzled up and then there was one.

ONE little Soldier Boy left all alone;
He went and hanged himself and then there were None.

# Preface

In Rogers and Hammerstein's 1956 motion picture, *Carousel,* Billy Bigelow, who had died during an attempted robbery to provide for his forthcoming child, is permitted to return from the Spirit World to help his struggling, fifteen-year-old daughter. Everything he tries to do for her backfires, and time is running out before he must return. The dialogue between Billy and his guardian angel is poignant:

Billy: "But my little girl, my Louise...I gotta do something for her."

Angel: "So far you ain't done much."

Billy: "I know, I know. Time's running out. But it ain't over yet. Look...I want an extension."

Billy is granted his requested extension to see his daughter's graduation. The commencement speaker's words give Billy the opportunity to encourage her:

Speaker: "I can't tell you any sure way to happiness. I only know that you've got to go out and find it for yourselves. You can't lean on the success of your parents. That's their success...and don't be held back by their failures."

Billy (whispering to Louise, who can't see him): "Listen to him! Believe him!"

Speaker: "...makes no difference what they did or didn't do! You just stand on your own two feet. The world belongs to you as much as to the next fellow. So, don't give it up. And try not to be scared of people not liking you. Just you try liking them...and just keep your faith—and your courage—and you'll turn out alright! It's like what we used to sing every morning when I was a boy at school. Maybe you still sing it...'When you walk through a storm, hold your head up high....' Do you know that one?"

All (standing and singing except Louise): "...and don't be afraid of the dark..."

Billy (to Louise): "Believe him, darling! Believe!"

Although Louise cannot see her father, she draws strength from his words...stands, smiles, and joins in singing: "At the end of the storm is a golden sky, and the sweet silver song of a lark. Walk on through the wind, walk on through the rain though your dreams be tossed and blown. Walk on, walk on, with hope in your heart and you'll never walk alone. You'll NEVER walk alone!"

Billy's return visit to the world of mortals was a success.

Recently, I was reminded of this heartwarming scene as I heard a newscaster report that life expectancy in the United States had fallen from 79 years in 2019 to 76 years in 2022. Since turning 77 in 2023, I thought my life was "on extension." I have outlived all of my paternal ancestry and, like Billy, I want to reach out to the Louises of the world who have lost their faith because they feel that "the world has gone mad." However, getting listened to when you're old can be tricky, like coming back from the dead was for Billy. Sometimes, youth chatter around and through us old folks as though we were dead. Maybe this is life's way of preparing us for death...slowly through aging. On one occasion, when I was in a crowd, I pinched a nearby youth on the arm who yelped, "Why did you do that?"

Relieved, I responded, "Thank you! I thought I was dead!"

What do I want to say to all the Louises and Louises of the world after pinching them to get their attention? I want them to be open to positive claims in spite of how much more interesting negative ones might sound. It isn't always possible to recognize the truth or error of a claim at first. For example, in October of 2022, Bloomberg reported that 100% of U.S. economists predicted a recession in 2023. The recession didn't happen and, in fact, the S&P 500 rose 24% that year. False claims like this one are not uncommon but are hard to ignore when they come from "authorities" who speak with conviction. However, getting a recession wrong isn't catastrophic like getting a worldview wrong.

Everyone is born with a brain, free and clear, with far more capability to resolve problems than artificial intelligence. And yet, many people choose to follow the conclusions of think-tanks that delude them into believing they are "doing their own thing." French entomologist Jean Henri Fabre illustrated this principle through an experiment in which he placed a line of caterpillars, nose to tail, onto the rim of a large flowerpot, forming a circle without end or beginning. Through sheer force of habit and, of course, instinct, the ring of caterpillars circled the flowerpot for seven days and seven nights. An ample supply of food was close at hand and plainly visible, but it was outside the range of the circle, so the caterpillars continued along the beaten path until they all died from exhaustion and starvation.[1]

People often behave similarly to caterpillars. Habit patterns and ways of thinking become deeply established, and it seems easier and more comfortable to follow them than to cope with change, even when that change may represent freedom, achievement, and success. A hard thing to understand is that even people in large numbers can be wrong. So, sometimes, it's a good idea to step out of the line and look around to see if the line is going where we want it to go. If it isn't, it might be time for a new direction. General George S. Patton once said, "If everyone is thinking alike, then somebody isn't thinking."

As important as it is to know what to believe...is to know what not to believe. We're bombarded, all our lives, with claims that can sound so convincing as to make us feel guilty for questioning them. Sometimes, claims are attributed to sources which, upon careful scrutiny, are found to deny the claims outright or modify them so much as to render them completely worthless. It is critical to learn how to evaluate claims properly so they can be prioritized and judged as to how much we will let them control our lives.

There are five general categories of claims: fact, definition, cause, value, and policy.

1) A fact claim asks: "Did it happen?" "Does it exist?"

2) A definition claim asks: "What is it?" "How should I describe it?"

3) A cause claim asks: "What caused it?"

4) A value claim asks: "How good or bad is it?" "What criteria will help me to decide?"

5) A policy claim asks: "What should I do about it?" "What should be my course of action?"

Claims are debatable and require evidence. This is what separates claims from facts that are not open to debate by reasonable people. Sadly, claims are often confused with facts. Properly understood claims stimulate discussion by those who are unafraid of facts. Claims are thought-provoking and ask important questions about the world that can help us form, reinforce, or change our worldview. Inasmuch as our judgment is no better than our information, this book invites you to investigate for yourself the major claims competing for your worldview.

# Introduction

I became a good reader early in life thanks in part to children's mystery novels...Nancy Drew, the Hardy Boys, Judy Bolton.... The author and characters didn't matter as long as clues were provided, leading me to the criminal. The scene of the crime was typically where everything began. All details (samples, motives, weapons, locations, times, witnesses, etc.) were relentlessly pursued. No clue was overlooked since even the most subtle evidence could make a difference in solving the case. With sufficient time and patience, the criminal was ultimately identified and apprehended. There was no perfect crime...only imperfect crime detection.

While my childhood friends were collecting marbles, toys, and baseball cards, I usually found myself mulling over evidence from the most recent episode of *Alfred Hitchcock Presents*. Among the collections of my adolescent friends were girlfriends, animals, and sports. Although I was similarly inclined, my primary pursuit was seeking evidence, leading to a fulfilling discovery. In adulthood, I *collected* education, a wife, six children, twenty-three grandchildren, two great-grandchildren, hobbies, investments, etc. In the midst of these, my search for evidence continued. Today, questions from my younger years have been largely answered and replaced by newer ones. However, my quest for new and confirming evidence continues unabated. It is a delight to which I awaken each morning.

My most compelling childhood mystery discovery was Agatha Christie's *And Then There Were None,* which the author described as her most difficult novel to write. Composed in 1939, it went on to become the world's best-selling mystery as well as one of the best-selling books of all time. Publications International lists it as the sixth best-selling title, with over 100 million copies sold. In 1943, a stage production of the novel was made, and the first movie version followed in 1945. Since that time, the plot has been used in numerous stage and movie adaptations with settings that include a mountaintop chalet, an Iranian desert, and even an African safari. However, the original setting was Soldier Island, an isolated rock cut off from the mainland near the Devon coast of southwest England.

The story begins with eight strangers arriving together by boat in the late 1930s as Europe teeters on the brink of World War II. Each guest has received a weekend invitation tailored to personal circumstances, such as an offer for employment or a late summer holiday. When they arrive on the island, they are greeted by a butler and a cook-housekeeper who state that their host, whom they have not yet met in person, has not arrived but left instructions. Of course, this strikes all the guests as odd. An ethnic variation of an old English nursery rhyme, “Ten Little Soldier Boys” (later adapted to other ethnic characters, monkeys, roosters, strangers, etc.) hangs in every guest’s room. The nursery rhyme version of the poem goes as follows (see also page xi):

The poem becomes self-fulfilling as guests begin to die, one by one, in the exact manner stated in the poem. Ten figurines sitting on the dining room table begin to break simultaneously with each death to keep score.

Although the poem and novel title suggest the story's end, there is an interesting twist in the movie, adding intrigue to the plot. The butler and housekeeper are actually guests, making the total island count ten. The seemingly generous hosts, disguised as Mr. and Mrs. U.N. Owen (a play on words for "unknown"), leave a recorded message for the butler to play after a delicious dinner their first night on the island. The recording accuses each guest of murder, naming the victim and the date of the guest's purported crime. After listing the crimes, the recording asks if anyone has something to say in defense. All are left speechless, realizing there is no escape for them unless they identify their hosts and prevent them from carrying out the poem's fulfillment.

Guests become distrustful of each other and begin to die. Common to all guests is an overwhelming desire to learn as much as possible about their host. Clues are left to enable them to gain an understanding of their host's character, the relationship among them, and their destiny. These questions are almost everything they think about, talk about, and study on the island. In the words of the author: "There was something magical about an island—the mere word suggested fantasy. You lost touch with the world—an island was a world of its own. A world, perhaps, from which you might never return."

## SPOILER ALERT

Two of the guests suspect that the murderer might be the judge, one of the ten guests who had feigned his own death when it was his turn in the poem. Although uncertain about the innocence of each other, the last two survivors (Phillip and Vera) decide to trust each other and pretend to play along with their host's plot. They fake their own deaths on the poem's cue so that the judge, supposing he is the last person alive on the island, takes his own life. Phillip and Vera's ability to weigh the evidence correctly and trust one another in the face of danger and uncertainty saves them in the end.

Part of the appeal of *And Then There Were None* can be traced to its striking parallel to life. Agatha Christie's guests on a not-so-paradise island were motivated by a desire to live. The success of the survivors depended on their discovery of the identity of their host, along with someone they could trust. It is a fascinating plot that plays itself out in life...in one form or another. Our survival instinct leads us, sooner or later, to the question, "What is the purpose of mortality?" And that question prompts our pursuit of evidence for life's host.

As mortals, we have been invited to a "weekend" on planet Earth. Born into amnesia, most of us have a natural curiosity to know why we are here and whether our host wants to kill us or exalt us. Others dismiss the question with the platitude that life has neither host nor purpose. Rather than looking for clues, they spend their time enjoying the abundant amenities of their island paradise or commiserating over the scant supplies of their island prison until their time is up. Does either of these viewpoints have any basis in reality? According to evolutionary thinking, that depends on whether your primary pursuit is truth or survival.

Notre Dame professor Alvin Platinga points out that if our belief-forming tendency is derived from evolution, it must affect our behavior in a way that influences our prospects for survival or reproductive success. "Natural selection favors behaviors that enhance survival. However, it doesn't 'care about' whether the beliefs associated with the behaviors are true or not."[2] University of Texas philosopher Robert Koons amplifies this idea that, from an evolutionary point of view, belief-forming mechanisms that might have helped early human beings survive by enabling them to spear mastodons or avoid saber-toothed tigers might not be suited to forming reliable beliefs about particle physics, cosmology, or the evolution of life on earth.[3]

In his autobiography, Charles Darwin wondered how we could trust the reliability of our cognitive faculties if they had evolved from the minds of lower animals. In a letter to a friend, he wrote, "But then with me the horrid doubt always arises whether the convictions of man's mind, which has been developed from the mind of the lower animals, are of any value or at all trustworthy. Would anyone trust in the convictions of a monkey's mind, if there are any convictions in such a mind?"[4] Evolutionary biologist Richard Dawkins acknowledges that survival value and truth are not necessarily correlated. For example, he grants that it is "perfectly plausible" that religious belief "could indeed have highly beneficial effects upon health."[5] Yet he also argues that belief in God is false and delusional. So, he tacitly concedes that natural selection can preserve false beliefs.[6]

If evolutionary-derived naturalism [atheism] depicts reality, then human beings have failed to perceive this fact.[7] Even though belief in God has declined in the increasingly secular West, especially among college-educated millennials, a recent Pew Research study shows that 84 percent of the world's population identifies with religious systems of belief, most of which contradict strict naturalism and many of which affirm some form of theism. Multiple studies across many populations indicate that human beings are hardwired for religious belief.[8] Acceptance of the supernatural appears to be deeply built into the foundations of our cognition, evident even among young children. As Berkeley psychology professor Alison Gopnik observes, "By elementary-school age, children start to invoke an ultimate God-like designer to explain the complexity of the world around them—even children brought up as atheists."[9]

A Pew Research model projects that over the next three decades, religiously affiliated populations will increase in comparison to religiously unaffiliated populations.[10] Evidently, religious belief correlates with higher reproductive rates—precisely what evolution favors— but, again, that means it selects human populations with false beliefs...at least as defined by evolutionary naturalists. British historian Paul Johnson has said, "The existence or non-existence of God is the most important question we humans [can ever ask]."[11] Indeed, a rigorous search for our Host is conducive to both truth and survival.

# What is Abduction?

In childhood, we learn to process information through our senses. If we see rain, we know that the family car parked in the driveway must be getting wet. This is *deduction* from direct, personal observation or experience. If A is true, then B follows. A is true. Therefore, B is certain.

However, the really important decisions we make in life are often based on evidence outside the reach of deduction. Time and space severely limit what we are able to see, hear, smell, taste, or touch. Like Phillip and Vera on Agatha Christie's island of crime, our success and survival depend upon our ability to think backward (from the scene of the "crime"). This is *abduction*. If B is true, then A might follow. B is true. Therefore, A is a possibility, which should be investigated.

For example, if we awaken from an afternoon nap to discover that the car is wet, we might at first assume that it has rained. However, as we look further, we see that the street isn't wet. We wonder if the sprinklers might have sprayed the car, but the grass is dry. Our eyes then catch the sight of a bucket on the driveway. At this point, we conclude that someone must have washed the car. Other possibilities, such as a drive-by water attack or a neighbor's water bucket being blown by the wind onto our driveway, don't occur to us because they aren't the most likely explanation. This is an example of **Ockham's razor**, a type of abductive reasoning in which the most plausible working hypothesis is favored unless evidence directs us to a more complex scenario. Ockham's razor does not always lead us to the correct answer. But it works more often than not and is, at the very least, a good starting point for our research.

In criminology, investigators rarely deduce anything firsthand. They abduce conclusions from clues. As they encounter new evidence, they themselves are sometimes challenged by discoveries that they might find disturbing—discoveries that perhaps implicate a loved one or upset a hoped-for outcome. When this happens, thinking can become biased and lead to an incorrect conclusion.

The science of crime detection is built primarily around motive. The detective takes clues and works backward to find the motive. If the motive can be determined, the criminal can usually be identified. Religion is crime detection in reverse. It starts with motive and works forward to a result. If the right motive can be established and sufficiently stimulated, a positive outcome can be virtually guaranteed. Repenting of unworthy motives changes thoughts. As thoughts grow into deeds, deeds become habits, habits ripen into character, and character determines destiny.

Any long-range planning invariably begins with the question, "Is there a God?" How we answer this question forms our worldview, directs our lifestyle, and charts our future. Like Agatha Christie's island guests, true belief and well-placed trust improve our chances for survival. Inasmuch as deductive evidence of God is outside the scope of science and many people are either unable or unwilling to accept the experience, wisdom, and word of others, beginning with an abductive approach can lead to an evidence-based worldview with the highest probability of reality.

# How Can Science Contribute to Our Worldview?

In his book, *Return of the God Hypothesis*, Stephen Meyer identifies four fundamental worldviews:

1. **Naturalism** (materialism) views matter, energy, and the laws of nature as the foundational realities from which all else comes. This is the worldview of *atheism,* which holds, in the words of Carl Sagan that "the cosmos is all that is or was or ever will be."
2. **Pantheism** asserts an impersonal deity present in the matter and energy of the cosmos as the prime reality. Eastern religions (*Hinduism, Buddhism, Taoism*, etc.) are notable adherents to this worldview.
3. **Deism** affirms a personal, transcendent (independent of the universe), intelligent God who produced the first matter and then ceased to

intervene within the created order after its origin. *Theistic evolution* is an example of deism in which God began the process of life, implanting within the creation an order from which evolution followed.

4. **Theism** affirms a personal, transcendent, intelligent God who continues to intervene within the creation. *Christianity, Judaism,* and *Islam* are theistic worldviews.

Significant twentieth-century scientific discoveries can help us establish guideposts for navigating through these worldviews. They include: 1) Evidence from cosmology that the material universe had a beginning, 2) Evidence from physics that, from the beginning, the universe has been "finely tuned" to facilitate life, and 3) Evidence from biology that, since the beginning, large amounts of new functional genetic information have arisen in our biosphere to make new forms of life possible.[12]

These discoveries have led to powerful abductive conclusions to the following questions:

1) Does God exist? Naturalism says "no;" pantheism, deism, and theism say "yes."

2) If so, is God personal or impersonal? Pantheism says "impersonal;" deism and theism say "personal."

3) If personal, does God act only at the beginning of the universe or also afterward...within the created order? Deism says "only at the beginning;" theism says "also afterward within the created order."

Studied objectively, a personally rewarding worldview can be embraced that conforms to evidence-based reality. For such an exploration to be effective, incorrect definitions need to be set aside. For example, *theism* is not synonymous with *fideism*—a tenet that affirms the sufficiency of faith without either reason or evidence—or "faith in faith alone." Returning to our example of the wet car in the driveway with a nearby water bucket, evidence plus abductive reasoning by inference to the best explanation leads to the most plausible working conclusion that someone had washed the car.

In the final analysis, science cannot think for us. It provides no deductive proof of anything, but it can offer evidence, weak or powerful, from which we can make abductive inferences. The conclusion is determined by us. It is a test, of sorts, of our capacity to analyze the data. More importantly, it extracts from us our personal worldview selection based on our interpretation of evidence. Three scientific questions invite us to weigh and formulate our personal worldview choices.

## Question #1: Did the Universe Have a Beginning?

In the 1820s, German astronomer Heinrich Olbers recognized that an infinitely large universe with a roughly uniform distribution of stars should exhibit a completely bright sky. That is, if the universe is infinite in time and space, any line of sight would lead to a star that should shine brightly (Olbers' paradox).[13] This mystery of the dark night sky had been debated for centuries. Proposals that had been offered included light exhaustion from distant stars, a finite number of stars within infinite space, and light-absorbing dark objects that obscured the view of distant stars.

It wasn't until 1848 that Edgar Allen Poe, in his last major work (also his longest non-fiction work), wrote what he considered to be his greatest masterpiece. In *Eureka: A Prose Poem,* he proposed that the universe was not old enough for light from the most remote regions of the night sky to reach the Earth.[14] That same year, Austrian physicist Christian Doppler discovered that sound from a train's whistle rises in pitch (shortens in wavelength) as the train approaches and lowers in pitch (stretches out in wavelength) as the train recedes. This principle was also found to apply to light waves. The shorter wavelength of approaching light appears blue, whereas the longer wavelength of receding light appears red.

In 1912, American astronomer Vesto Slipher discovered that light from distant nebulae (clouds of dust and gas from outer space) looked red or exhibited a "redshift," indicating that the universe was expanding. In 1924, astronomer Edwin Hubble confirmed Slipher's observation, adding that distant galaxies beyond our Milky Way were also redshifted. Shortly afterward, Belgian priest and physicist Georges Lemaître developed a model to show the beginning of the universe's expansion from a "cosmic egg." The farther away a galaxy is, the faster it is moving away from the Earth. This "farther—faster" observation was later called Hubble's Law. However, it was Lemaître who first formulated it and became known as the "father of the Big Bang theory." Poe's "Eureka" moment had preceded the scientific discovery of the universe's beginning by three-quarters of a century!

The creative implication of the **Big Bang** ran counter to the worldview of science naturalists. Physicist Robert Dicke explained that a finite universe produced a widespread knee-jerk philosophical opposition among many scientists. An infinitely old universe "would relieve us," he said, "of the necessity of understanding the origin of matter at any finite time in the past."[15] On the other hand, a finite universe would force scientists to confront uncomfortable questions about the beginning of the material universe. It also raised the possibility that the universe had been created by a cause that existed independently of matter, space, time, and energy. British astrophysicist Sir Arthur Eddington found the discovery "repugnant" and remarked: "I should like to find a genuine loophole. I simply do not believe the present order of things started off with a bang. The expanding universe is preposterous...It leaves me cold."[16]

During the remainder of the twentieth century, physicists and cosmologists formulated many alternatives to the Big Bang Theory. Seeking to preserve a static universe, Albert Einstein altered his own equation by arbitrarily assigning a precise "fudge factor" to counter the effect of gravitational contraction with a balancing expansive force. To his credit, he later announced that his "cosmological constant" was not merely an error, but "the greatest stupidity of [his] life."

He knew that if he had not acted out of fear of the scientific consensus in reaction to what smacked of faith, he could have been the one credited for discovering that the universe was expanding years before anyone else had done so.[17]

Cosmological models were offered as loopholes to defend the idea of an uncreated universe. The **steady state theory** posited that, as the universe expands, new matter is generated spontaneously in the space between galaxies so that the density of the universe always remains constant. This theory was the Big Bang's greatest rival until two scientific discoveries laid it to rest in the 1960s: 1) The steady state required that galaxies have a wide range of different ages, which was not found to be the case as observational astronomy became more advanced. 2) Cosmic microwave background radiation (CMBR), discovered at a Bell Laboratory in 1965, confirmed the existence of radiation left over from the hot, high-density plasma state resulting from the Big Bang. According to the steady-state theory, CMBR should not have existed.

Following the demise of the steady-state model, an **oscillating universe theory** envisioned a universe that would expand and contract by some unknown mechanism *ad infinitum*. While this model preserved the notion of an eternal self-existing universe, it ran into difficulty with the second law of thermodynamics, which says that the disorder (entropy) of an isolated system of matter and energy increases over time. This means that less energy would be available with each contraction and expansion cycle. Like a ball that bounces to a smaller and smaller height until it can bounce no more, the universe would have reached heat death, leaving no energy to do the oscillating.

By the 1970s, most astronomers had come to accept the Big Bang over its rivals. The universe as well as space and time—or spacetime—had a beginning. This presented a problem for **standard naturalism,** which held that only the matter and energy in this universe are the entities from which all else comes or that "the cosmos is all that is or was or ever will be." In order to explain the beginning of spacetime without a creative event, the existence of "foreign" universes, **exotic naturalism,**[18] was developed by the mathematics of quantum mechanics to describe possibilities in which our universe might be the product of a vast number of unknown universes beyond our own—a **multiverse**. Inasmuch as *95 percent* of our observable universe is invisible to us and *100 percent* of any unobservable universes are invisible to us,[19] exotic naturalism was an imaginative attempt to explain naturalistic phenomena within our own universe, such as its beginning and fine-tuning.

Two leading models emerged:

1) **Inflationary cosmology** proposed that an inflation field produces an infinite number of bubble universes (of which ours is one). Each new bubble universe is produced by an older one. This concept moves the beginning of spacetime and matter beyond the Big Bang. New universes could have different configurations of mass and energy,

making their events and structures different from our universe.

2) **String theory** proposed one-dimensional strings or filaments of energy whose properties led to a "theory of everything," not through a unique solution corresponding to the laws of physics but through infinitely many solutions from unobserved physics. Adherents to this model proposed that each solution to the equations of string theory corresponds to a different universe, which, like inflationary cosmology, has different physical laws and constants of physics.

Over the years, key predictions of the multiverse theories either failed to materialize or were contradicted by new evidence. In 2003, the **Borde-Guth-Vilenkin (BGV) theorem** showed that if one follows a spacetime trajectory back in time, any expanding universe, including one expanding as a consequence of a multiverse, must have had a starting point to its expansion, indicating a beginning.[20] Eventually, some leading physicists dismissed the multiverse hypothesis as a speculative metaphysical hypothesis, not a scientific one.[21]

Prize-winning theoretical physicist Gerard 't Hooft explained: "I would not even be prepared to call string theory a 'theory,' rather a 'model,' or not even that: just a hunch. After all, a theory should come with instructions on how...to identify the things one wishes to describe, in our case, the elementary particles, and one should, at least in principle be able to formulate the rules for calculating the properties of these particles, and how to make new predictions for them. Imagine that I give you a chair, while explaining that the legs are missing, and that the seat, back, and armrests will be delivered soon. Whatever I gave you, can I still call it a chair?"[22]

Over a century ago, a children's book was written with the interesting title of *The Chance World.*[23] It pictured a make-believe world in which everything happened by chance. The Sun might come up in the morning or not. If you jumped up in the air, you might come down or keep on going. If water ran out to the edge of a cliff, it might fall down or up. If you planted your field with wheat, you would have no way to determine in advance whether it would grow, but if it did, it might be wheat, barley, asparagus, rosebushes, or apple trees, and there would be no way to tell which in advance. Children loved the book because it was so silly.

However, science is not based on a chance world, chance universe, or chance multiverse. It is based on observed laws. Water freezes at 32 degrees Fahrenheit. If 20 percent salt is added, it freezes at 2.4 degrees. Alcohol will not freeze until the temperature reaches 30 degrees below zero. It is possible to know in advance when water freezes and that when it does, it will expand with a power so tremendous that it is capable of shattering the strongest steel.

We don't understand why these laws are so. Isaac Newton discovered and explained gravity, but no one understands it to this day. We might think water would be better off if it did not freeze until 32 degrees below zero. How does water know when it is cold enough to freeze? It never makes a mistake. It never forgets. It never alters its course because of someone's opinion, influence, or need. If it did, it would eliminate our ability to predict future events and it would destroy science. And that is what today's multiverse theories attempt to do since they are not based on laws that have been observed. Speculating on a different set of unobserved laws for each universe is analogous to proposing "chance universes." Such proposals are science-destroying attempts to explain away a beginning of our own universe...and extreme efforts to dismiss God.

The discovery of the Big Bang is a powerful blow to naturalism's worldview. Science popularizers have tried to obfuscate the implications of the universe's beginning, before which the known laws of physics break down. Does the Big Bang suggest to you as it does to evolutionary biologist Richard Dawkins that "the universe as we observe has precisely the properties we should expect if there is, at bottom, no design, no purpose, no evil, no good, nothing but blind, pitiless indifference?"[24]

Or, are you more inclined to agree with Arno Penzias, Nobel Prize-winning physicist for his discovery of the cosmic background radiation? He said: "The best data we have are exactly what I would have predicted, had I nothing to go on but the first five books of Moses, the Psalms, the Bible as a whole."[25] In making this connection, Penzias might have had in mind any of a number of Biblical references...

...to a beginning of time:

- "In the beginning God created the heaven and the earth" (Genesis 1:1).
- "...before the world began" (2 Timothy 1:9).
- "In hope of eternal life, which God, that cannot lie, promised before the world began" (Titus 1:2).

...or to an expanding universe:

- "God...who stretches out the heavens like a curtain" (Psalm 104:1-2).
- "I have made the earth, and created man upon it: I, *even* my hands, have stretched out the heavens, and all their host have I commanded" (Isaiah 45:12).
- "The burden of the word of the Lord for Israel, saith the Lord, which stretcheth forth the heavens, and layeth the foundation of the earth, and formeth the spirit of man within him" (Zechariah 12:1).

Theism and deism affirm a personal, intelligent, transcendent God as the cause (creator) of the universe. Returning to our model of abductive reasoning....

Major premise: If theism or deism is true, then we would have reason to expect evidence showing that the universe had a beginning.

Minor premise: We have convincing evidence that the universe had a beginning.

Conclusion: We have reason to think that theism or deism might be true.

The Big Bang is incompatible with the worldview of naturalism. Hubble astronomer Allan Sandage remarked, "If God did not exist, science would have to...invent the concept to explain what it is discovering."[26] Dr. Sandage's statement was made after a lifelong career as a naturalist and agnostic with little interest in questions about the existence and nature of God. Scientific evidence of a creation event contributed to a profound change in his worldview. Although the Big Bang is not proof of the existence of God, it is the most plausible explanation for the cause of the universe as well as a compelling reason to look for additional evidence.

While the Big Bang points to a beginning of spacetime, it does not tell us where matter and energy came from. Naturalists Stephen Hawking and George Ellis have reflected: "The creation of the universe out of nothing [creation *ex nihilo*] has been argued, indecisively, from early times; ...The results we have obtained support the idea that the universe began a finite time ago. However, the actual point of creation, the singularity, is outside the presently known laws of physics."[27] The "singularity" to which Hawking and Ellis refer doesn't mean "nothing." It means an unimaginably dense, hot mass. French chemist Antoine Lavoisier determined in 1789 that matter cannot be created or destroyed in a chemical reaction. Moreover, the Law of Conservation of Mass states that in a closed system, the mass of the system must remain constant over time.

Gary Rendsburg, professor of History and Jewish Studies at Rutgers University, points out that the Book of Genesis provides an insight into the question of matter at the creation of the universe. A truer translation is found in the original Hebrew syntax of the first three verses, which say: "When God began to create heaven and earth, the earth being unformed and void with darkness over the surface of the deep and a wind from God sweeping over the water, God said, 'Let there be light.' And there was light."[28] These verses provide us with a description of the state of the Earth before God does any creative work. Professor Rendsburg goes on to say that, "Contrary to what most people might assume or believe, the world is not created *ex nihilo*... Instead, the earth begins as a mass of pre-existing matter, characterized by chaos, unformed and void with darkness... these findings pre-existed God's creative activity."[29]

Although the origin of matter is unknown, as well as its mass and density, the original rendering of Genesis teaches that the world is created *ex materia*—out of pre-existing material. Later translations of the first three verses of the Bible into three independent sentences led the whole of Christianity, Judaism, and Islam to believe in creation *ex nihilo,* which Professor Rendsburg says is exactly the opposite of the Genesis account in original Hebrew. This refutes the allegation that God was the creator (from nothing) of evil as well as good. The Pearl of Great Price confirms a creation *ex materia.* In the Lord's words to Moses: "...in the beginning I created [organized] the heaven, and the earth upon which thou standest. And the earth was without form, and void" (Moses 2:1-2).

In C.S. Lewis' classic book, *The Screwtape Letters*, the senior demon, Screwtape, writes some advice to his junior demon, Wormwood, on how to keep mankind from becoming theistic. Screwtape writes, "Keep pressing home on him the ordinariness of things. Above all, do not attempt to use science (I mean the real sciences) as a defense against Christianity. They will positively encourage him to think about realities he can't touch and see. There have been sad cases among modern physicists."[30] The "sad cases" to which he refers are scientists who, like Allan Sandage, were honest with the evidence they saw...and humble enough to acknowledge the implications of that evidence.

The Big Bang is not only incompatible with naturalism but also with pantheism, which asserts that an impersonal deity is present in matter and energy. In the words of Dr. Meyer: "God as conceived by pantheists cannot act to bring the physical universe into being...since such a god does not exist independently of the physical universe. If at some point in the past the physical universe did not exist, then a pantheistic god would not have existed either. If the pantheistic god did not exist before the universe began, it could not have caused the universe to begin to exist. Thus, pantheism [like naturalism] does not meet the test of causal adequacy."[31]

Only a personal God, acting independently, was capable of creating our universe. Understanding this fact alone should direct every one of us to the same conclusion as Daniel Webster (1782-1852): "The greatest thought that has ever entered my mind is the consciousness of my individual responsibility to God."[32]

## Question #2: Has the Universe Been "Fine-Tuned" for Life?

On a beautiful day in 1966, I was walking with my missionary companion down the streets of Pôrto Alegre, Brazil. Our eyes caught a newsstand prominently displaying the red cover of the latest *Time* magazine with the heading, "IS GOD DEAD?" Wanting to know how the cover story might affect the minds and hearts of people we would be teaching, we bought and read a copy. The article said practically nothing about God but presented the cultural narrative that He is obsolete...that, as science progresses, there is less need for a "God" to explain the universe.

The same year, *Time* also featured astronomer Carl Sagan, who announced that there were two important criteria for a planet to support life: the right kind of star and a planet the right distance from that star. This suggested that the universe contained a trillion trillion planets that were candidates for supporting life.

With such spectacular odds, the Search for Extraterrestrial Intelligence (SETI) project was launched. Funded initially by public and private funds, the search was met with deafening silence from the rest of the universe. Congress finally defunded SETI in 1993, but the search continued with private funds. So far, no life outside our earth has been found. However, science did learn that Sagan's two parameters later grew to ten, twenty, fifty, and then to hundreds—all of which must be precisely met to support life. As the number of requirements grew, the number of possible life-supporting planets dropped to zero, and then science concluded that we shouldn't be here. In fact, the degree of fine-tuning required for life on our planet makes our own existence hyper-exponentially remote.

We live on a planet called Earth, in a galaxy called Milky Way, and in a universe called Cosmos. Conditions for life on Earth were established when it was formed roughly 4.5 billion years ago. But far more intricate conditions had first been established 13.8 billion years ago when the universe was formed. By a series of remarkable "coincidences," many properties of the universe fall within extremely narrow and improbable ranges that turn out to be absolutely necessary for any conceivable form of life to exist. This delicate fine-tuning is referred to as the **anthropic principle**, after the Greek word *anthropos*, meaning *human being*. We live in a "Goldilocks Universe" with characteristics so precisely conducive to life that even the most outspoken naturalists, such as Richard Dawkins and Christopher Hitchens, acknowledge the **fine-tuning problem** as the most formidable threat to New Atheism.[33]

Ten examples of Earth's innumerable prerequisites for life include the following:

1. **Earth's Distance from the Sun**—The presence and size of the Sun, along with its distance from the Earth, were two known requirements for life in 1966. Had Earth not been 93 million miles away from the Sun, we wouldn't be here. Slightly closer to the Sun, Earth's water would have evaporated. Slightly farther away, Earth's water would have frozen. Let's look at a few things that were unknown or overlooked in 1966.

2. **Earth's Size**—Prior to Earth's formation, roughly 4.5 billion years ago, a smaller "proto-earth" existed that scientists refer to as Theia. A Mars-sized body with just the right composition collided with Theia at the perfect angle and speed to explode Theia's super-thick atmosphere into outer space, never to return. Suddenly, the new atmosphere was much, much thinner. Some of the Mars-sized body's parts became part of Theia, increasing it to Earth's size today. The quantity and composition of mass added to Theia were crucial. If our Earth were any smaller, our weaker magnetic field would permit solar wind to strip away our atmosphere to a lifeless planet like Mars. Earth's ideal size enables its magnetic field ("magnetosphere") to deflect solar wind from stripping away our water-making hydrogen and oxygen. If Earth were larger, its more powerful gravity would prevent water, methane, or carbon dioxide from escaping the atmosphere, which

would be so thick we couldn't breathe. Earth needed to be eight thousand miles in diameter.[34]

3. **Moon**—Part of the mass that split away from Theia's collision congealed to form the Moon at just the right distance, 240,000 miles away. Since that time, the Moon has steadied the earth on its axis, provided the right seasonal variation compatible with life, and controlled our ocean tides, crucial to the ecosystems of our coasts. If the Moon-Earth gravitational interaction were excessive, tidal effects on the oceans, atmosphere, and rotational period would be lethal. If it were too little, orbital changes would cause lethal climatic instabilities. Compared to other moons, ours is very large—two thousand miles in diameter, 1/400th the size of the Sun, and 1/400th the distance from us as the Sun. This unique size/distance relationship makes it possible for the Moon to become superimposed on the Sun during an eclipse. The two appear to be the same size, obliterating all of the Sun except for its corona. A number of measurements have been made during eclipses, such as solar flash spectrum, prominences, starlight deflection, Earth's rotation, as well as discovery of the element, helium.

4. **Oxygen Level**—Today, the Earth's atmosphere is comprised of 21% oxygen but this was not always so. The "Great Oxygenation Event" (GOE) 2.33 billion years ago produced the first irreversible influx of oxygen into our atmosphere. It took place within a relatively short period of time (one to ten million years) and set off a cascade of events

leading to the advent of multicellular life. A big question that science would like to know is: "Why do we have 21% oxygen in the Earth's atmosphere that is stable?"[35] What we do know is that if our atmospheric oxygen level were slightly higher or lower, life on Earth would be impossible.

5. **Carbon Dioxide Level**—The oxygen we breathe requires photosynthesis from plants consuming carbon dioxide. If the level of atmospheric carbon dioxide were too high, a runaway greenhouse effect would burn us up. If it were too low, we'd freeze.

6. **Earth's Crust**—If the Earth's crust were thicker, too much oxygen would be transferred to it to support life. If it were too thin, volcanic and tectonic activity would be destructive to life.

7. **Earth's Rotation**—If the rotation of the Earth took longer than 24 hours per cycle, day/night temperature differences would be lethal. If the rotation period were shorter, atmospheric wind velocities would be deadly.

8. **Earth's Axis**—If the Earth's 23-degree axil tilt were altered slightly either way, surface temperatures would be too extreme for life.

9. **Atmospheric Discharge**—If the lightning rate were greater, fire destruction would threaten life. If it were less, there would be insufficient nitrogen fixation in the soil.

10. **Seismic Activity**—More seismic activity would exacerbate the loss of life on Earth. Less would

prevent nutrients from the ocean floors and river runoff from being cycled back to continents through tectonic uplift. Even earthquakes are necessary to sustain life.[36]

The list goes on. However, as demanding as Earth's fine-tuning requirements are, Cambridge physicist Sir John Polkinghorne pointed out that the fine-tuning necessary for the universe to sustain life is far more complex than the fine-tuning required for life to exist on a planet. He illustrated this by asking his students to imagine a "universe-creating machine" with numerous dials, knobs, and adjustable sliders, each representing one of many cosmological fine-tuning parameters, fixed to a specific setting out of a vast number of possible settings. One click this way or that would result in catastrophic consequences to prevent the universe from sustaining life.[37]

The universe's fine-tuning even caused Hawking to say: "It would be very difficult to explain why the universe would have begun in this way, except as the act of a god who intended to create beings like us."[38] For the rest of his life, he backpedaled from this statement with naturalistic explanations for fine-tuning. However, some things don't just happen; the universe is one of them! Ten examples of the universe's exact calibrations necessary for life include the following:

1. **Earth's Location in the Universe**—Back to *Carousel*, when Billy learns he is about to become a father, he says to his wife, Julie: "I don't need you. I don't need anybody helpin' me. Well, I got it

figured out for myself. We're not important. What are we? A couple o' specks with nothin'. Look up there. There's a hell of a lotta stars in the sky, and the sky's so big, the sea looks small. And two little people, you and I, we don't count at all." What Billy didn't know was that he and Julie were among "specks" for whom our solar system was formed on the inner edge of the Orion Arm of our galaxy, about twenty-six thousand light-years from the center. This zone is a rare galactic habitable location for life. If we were closer to the galaxy's center, the density of stars would expose us to lethal radiation. If we were farther out from the center, our atmosphere and plate tectonics would be non-survivable.

2. **Jupiter and Saturn**—Like cosmic magnets, Jupiter and Saturn's enormous mass and gravity enable them to protect Earth from being pelted endlessly by meteorites and asteroids. Acting as veritable bodyguards, they pull most speeding objects away from us by either deflecting them into outer space or absorbing them into themselves. Sixty-six million years ago, a single asteroid only seven miles in diameter hit Earth and wiped out 75% of animal life, including all dinosaurs. In 1908, an asteroid only 300 feet in diameter flattened eighty million trees in Siberia and caused so much atmospheric disturbance that the effects were noticed as far away as London. If Jupiter and Saturn weren't where they are, we wouldn't be here.[39]

3. **Carbon**—Crucial to all forms of life is the presence of carbon, which is essential for forming stable, long, chain-like molecules capable of storing and processing genetic information as well as the energy that living cells need to survive. Astrophysicist Sir Fred Hoyle was shaken from his atheism when he discovered numerous fine-tuning parameters linked to carbon's production from nuclear reactions inside stars.[40] Carbon-based life is the only known form of life.

4. **Four Fundamental Forces**—The universe and all its atoms are held together by four fundamental forces: 1) Gravity, 2) The weak nuclear force, 3) The electromagnetic force, and 4) The strong nuclear force. These precise forces were determined less than one millionth of a second after the Big Bang and their values have not changed for almost fourteen billion years.[41] The laws governing these forces did not exist prior to the Big Bang and nature could not have created them. Not only must each of these forces be kept within extraordinary accuracy, their ratios to each other must also be kept incredibly accurate. For example, if the ratio of the strong nuclear force to the electromagnetic force had been altered by one in 400 quadrillion, stars (the elemental building blocks of everything we observe) could not have been formed.[42] Following is a brief summary of the four fundamental forces in ascending order of power:

- Gravity, or the gravitational force, is the attractive force between all matter in the universe. It is the weakest of the four forces and exists between any two objects possessing mass. It is what brings us back to Earth when we jump and what holds our solar system, galaxy, and universe together. If the value of the gravitational constant were different by one part in 10 to the 34th power, the universe wouldn't have any planets capable of sustaining life.[43]

- The weak nuclear force, unlike the other three forces that hold things together, plays a greater role in things falling apart. It is the mechanism of interaction between subatomic particles that is responsible for the radioactive decay of atoms and is 10 to the 32nd power times stronger than gravity.
- The electromagnetic force is what keeps electrons in orbit around their nuclei. It is perfectly calibrated to enable electrons to leap from their orbit to the orbit of other atoms in order to form molecules necessary for life. The electromagnetic force is 10 to the 37th power times stronger than gravity and its reach is infinite. If it were slightly weaker, electrons would leave their orbits too easily, but if it were slightly stronger, they would never budge from their original orbits.[44] In either case, essential elements would be missing and there would be no life.
- The strong nuclear force is what holds protons and neutrons together in the nucleus of every atom. It is the strongest of the four forces, 10 to

the 39th power times stronger than gravity. If the strong nuclear force were 2 percent weaker, protons and neutrons would drift apart, leaving us with a universe consisting entirely of hydrogen. If it were 0.3 percent stronger, protons and neutrons would attract each other to the point of creating only large nuclei and leaving no hydrogen. Both scenarios would be incompatible with life.[45]

5. **Atmospheric Transparency**—The degree of transparency of the atmosphere must be precise for life on Earth to exist. If the atmosphere were less transparent, not enough solar radiation would reach the Earth's surface. If it were more transparent, we would be bombarded with lethal solar radiation.

6. **Centrifugal Force**—If the centrifugal force of planetary movements did not precisely balance gravitational forces, nothing could be held in orbit around the sun.

7. **Laws of Physics**—The laws of physics are a function of the velocity of light. Even a slight change in the speed of light would alter other constants and preclude the possibility of life on Earth.

8. **Water Vapor**—If atmospheric water vapor levels were too high, a runaway greenhouse effect would elevate temperatures too high to sustain life; if they were too low, temperatures would be too low to sustain life.[46]

9. **Mass of the Universe**—The mass of our observable universe in kilograms is 1.5 times 10 to the 53rd power. It is a small fraction of the total

universe that includes dark matter and dark energy. Science thinks it even knows the total number of atoms in the universe—10 to the 80th power or one followed by 80 zeros. Our universe contains 2 trillion galaxies, each of which contains 100 billion stars, most of which are comparable to our own Sun. Had the universe's mass been infinitesimally less, essential life-compatible elements like nitrogen, oxygen, and carbon would not have existed. Had it been greater, gravity would have been too much to have allowed the universe to expand. *Right after the Big Bang, the universe would have been destroyed if its mass had been either greater or less . . . by the weight of a dime.*[47] If the universe had expanded at a rate one millionth more slowly than it did, gravity would have caused it to collapse on itself before any stars could have formed. If it had expanded faster, galaxies would not have formed.

10. **Energy Density of the Universe**—Perhaps the most finely-tuned constant yet reported came from American Nobel Prize-winning physicist Steven Weinberg. An atheist with a particular disdain for religion, Weinberg said that if the energy density of the universe, often referred to as the "cosmological constant," were different by just one part in 10 to the 120th power (one followed by 120 zeros), life could not exist.[48] As unfathomable as this number is, in order to get a closer idea of the chance of life occurring randomly in our universe, we would need

to know enough to be able to add all of the universe's life-sustaining constants together!

Of course, none of the "constants" quoted above should be understood as absolutes. The point is that their precision and relationship to each other are required for life. English physicist Paul Davies (not a man of faith) wrote: "Scientists are slowly waking up to an inconvenient truth—the universe looks suspiciously like a fix. The issue concerns the very laws of nature themselves. For forty years, physicists and cosmologists have been quietly collecting examples of all too convenient 'coincidences' and special features in the underlying laws of the universe that seem to be necessary in order for life, and hence conscious beings, to exist. Change any of them and the consequences would be lethal."[49]

The fine-tuning problem has been publicly acknowledged by naturalists as the best argument for a designer of the universe. Causally inadequate explanations for the origin and fine-tuning of the universe have made many scientists question their default commitment to scientific materialism and consider a new natural theology. Science historian Frederic Burnham has observed that the God hypothesis "is now a more respectable hypothesis than at any time in the last one hundred years."[50]

Victor Hugo once said, "Nothing is as powerful as an idea whose time has come... One resists the invasion of armies; one does not resist the invasion of ideas." You and I are the ones who determine when the time has come for us to open our minds to the God hypothesis. Thereafter, our mind's appetite develops by what we feed it.

**Question #3: Have New Life Forms Been Added to the Biosphere?**

When I was a freshman at the University of Washington, an eye-catching book attracted my attention one day. The year was 1965 and the book was Time-Life Nature's *Early Man.*[51] It contained an illustrated foldout portraying a series of ape-like creatures that became more human-like as they marched across the page. This "March of Progress" picture by painter Rudolph Zallinger would later become the most famous icon of evolution. Since I would be entering full-time missionary service within a few months, I studied the book in preparation for naturalistic viewpoints I might encounter.

This famous figure's caption cautioned readers that the artistic representations were based upon "fragmentary fossil evidence." The book went on to confess: "Although protoapes and apes were quadrupedal, all are shown here standing for the purpose of comparison." There was no compelling evidence to suggest that protoapes evolved into man. Transitional forms existed only in the artist's mind, the most powerful form of evidence for many people. Most people ignored the fine print because it was overshadowed by the persuasive image. Almost forty years later, a review of the influence of Zallinger's March of Progress picture was written:

"This parade has been one of the most successful tools ever used to promote human evolution. It is constituted as a powerful visual 'proof' for human evolution that even a small child could grasp... There were few social studies classrooms and school library bulletin boards where this parade was not prominently displayed. Because of its graphic power, it is still indelibly etched into the minds of billions of people worldwide... That visually powerful parade was so successful in advancing human evolution because it received a far greater distribution and viewing than did the Early Man book. Worldwide mailings for advertising purposes were made of the particular pages featuring the parade. The posting of these pages in classrooms and libraries meant that far more people saw the parade than possessed the book. Perhaps less than five percent of those who had the book actually read it, but they would have seen the parade. Thus, the visual image of the parade sold the concept of human evolution even though the book revealed that the parade was fictitious."[52]

In 1859, Charles Darwin theorized that all advanced life on earth had evolved from one-celled organisms by a process of natural selection acting on random variations slowly and gradually—a theory that came to be known as **Classical Darwinism**. Darwin hoped the mystery of missing fossils in his day would be solved by future geological discoveries documenting the gradual transitions his theory predicted. During the

1930s and 40s, evolutionary thinking was modified by **Neo-Darwinism,** in which natural selection acted on a particular variation known as genetic mutation. According to Neo-Darwinism, which became the predominant thinking in biology, small-scale microevolutionary changes within species could be extrapolated indefinitely to project macroevolutionary development across species lines.

But the opposite of what Darwin had hoped for was actually discovered. Very few people are aware that *virtually every reputed "ape-man" bone has been contested by experts in the field.* Fossil evidence is both fragmentary and self-contradicting. Contrary to what is widely believed, the fossil evidence is weak and does not provide compelling evidence for human evolution.[53]

In the 165 years since the publication of *Origin of the Species*, paleontologists have combed strata worldwide for precursors to modern organisms. What they found was the abrupt appearance of fully developed life forms in the fossil record without precursors. This **Cambrian explosion** occurred about 530 million years ago with the sudden emergence of diverse forms of complexity without relationships that would be expected to fit the pattern of biological evolution. The first winged insects, birds, flowering plants, mammals, and many other groups appeared suddenly with no connection to lower-order organisms—a phenomenon referred to as the **"Biological Big Bang."**

Evolutionists were compelled to concede that there is no single universal common ancestor.[54] Darwin's evolutionary tree turned out to be an orchard of fully developed, independent life forms (Genesis 1:11-12, 21, 24-25). The probability of unintended production of even a single functional protein compatible with life—with a modest length of at least 150 amino acids—by chance alone in a prebiotic environment stands at less than one chance in a trillion trillion.[55] The complexity of the events that origin-of-life researchers need to explain exceeds the probabilistic resources of the entire universe. In other words, the universe itself does not possess the resources necessary to render probable the origin of biological information by chance alone.

During the 1960s, computer programs showed that random changes in sequence inevitably degrade and destroy the function of the existing program long before a new program could emerge through the process.[56] Decades later, geneticists confirmed that mutations cause birth defects, cancer, and aging. Aside from rare temporary adaptations, they are overwhelmingly destructive.[57] Mutations do not create us. They kill us.[58] We are not evolving. We are devolving along with every other major organism. A huge hiatus exists between *Homo sapiens* and every other form of life.

Paleo-expert Jonathan Marks explained: "It is not difficult to tell a human from an ape, after all. The human is the one walking, talking, sweating, praying, building, reading, trading, crying, dancing, writing, cooking, joking, working, decorating, shaving, driving a car, or playing football. Quite literally, from the top of our head (where the hair is continually growing, unlike gorillas) to the tips of our toes (the stoutest of which is non-opposable), one can tell the human part from the ape part quite readily if one knows what to look for. Our white eyes, small canine teeth, evaporative heat loss, short arms and long legs, breasts, knees, and of course, our cognitive communication abilities, and the productive anatomies of our tongue and throat are all dead giveaways."[59]

Evolutionist Juan Arsuaga added: "We are unique and alone in the world. There is no other animal species that truly resembles our own. A physical and mental chasm separates us from all other living creatures. There is no bipedal mammal. No other mammal controls and uses fire, writes books, travels in space, paints portraits, or prays. This is not a question of degrees. It is all or nothing; there is no semi-pedal animal, none that makes only small fires, writes only short sentences, builds only rudimentary spaceships, draws just a little bit, or prays just occasionally."[60]

Paleo-expert Ian Tattersall, emeritus curator of the American Museum of Natural History, concurred: "Even allowing for the poor record we have of our close extinct kin, *Homo sapiens* appears as distinctive and unprecedented. . . there is certainly no evidence to support the notion that we gradually became who we inherently are over an extended period, in either the physical or intellectual sense."[61]

Evolutionist Jacob Bronowski added: "Man is a singular creature. He has a set of gifts which make him unique among the animals: so that, unlike them, he is not a figure in the landscape—he is shaper of the landscape."[62] This statement comes as no surprise to anyone who has read: "And God blessed them, and God said unto them, Be fruitful, and multiply, and replenish the earth, and subdue it: and have dominion over the fish of the sea, and over the fowl of the air, and over every living thing that moveth upon the earth" (Genesis 1:28). So, God gave mankind dominion over everything...including himself.

Naturalists like to point to abductive evidence of anthropoid life hundreds of thousands or even millions of years ago to suggest that the Bible's presumed timeline of a few thousand years invalidates its content. However, any cognitive dissonance that a theist might experience in trying to understand the metaphoric meaning of the word "day" in the poetic Hebrew rendering of the six creative periods of the Earth pales in comparison to that which a naturalist experiences in trying to understand the universe's Big Bang, its ongoing fine-tuning, and Biology's Big Bang.

A Google search for the earliest known writings identifies the Semitic people of Sumer (Shinar) in Mesopotamia in the 4th millennium B.C.—the cradle of civilization where and when the biblical record begins. No physical evidence exists of *civilized* mankind with a writing system prior to that time. What does "civilized mankind" really mean? Adam and Eve marked the beginning of God's covenant relationship with mankind on Earth—a relationship that encompassed marriage and children as the nuclear family.

What about life prior to that time? In the words of Hugh Nibley: "Do not begrudge existence to creatures that looked like men long, long ago, nor deny them a place in God's affection or even a right to exaltation—for our scriptures allow them such. Nor am I overly concerned as to just when they might have lived, for their world is not our world."[63] In other words, don't let yourself get lost in abductive blind alleys that prevent you from acting on your own individual responsibility to God.

# Which Worldview is Most Compatible with Science?

In *Return of the God Hypothesis*, Dr. Meyer describes the irony of theologians who deny that scientific evidence supports a belief in God. An ultimate beginning of the universe has profound theological implications. Despite herculean attempts to circumvent a cause for the Big Bang, no explanation has been adequate to reject the notion of a creator god or someone else with god-like skills.

**Naturalism** (atheism) fails all three tests of causal adequacy to explain 1) The universe's beginning, 2) Its ongoing fine-tuning, and 3) New functional genetic information arising in the biosphere billions of years after the universe's beginning. In a 2008 movie, *Expelled*, Richard Dawkins proposed the possibility that an alien civilization evolved somewhere in the cosmos and then designed and seeded the first life on Earth. However, the Search for Extraterrestrial

Intelligence concluded that the existence of alien life anywhere in the observable universe is extremely remote. This includes any aliens responsible for seeding life on Earth (panspermia). Even if aliens were discovered, they, like us, would be byproducts of the Big Bang. There is neither claim nor evidence that aliens created the universe.

Like Naturalism, **Pantheism** fails all three tests of causal adequacy. The god of pantheism exists within and is coextensive with the universe. Thus, it could not have brought the universe into being since such a god does not exist independently of the physical universe. Prior to the Big Bang, there could have been no pantheistic god to 1) Create the universe, 2) Maintain its ongoing fine-tuning, or 3) Provide new functional genetic information after the universe's beginning. Pantheism's chief tenet, reincarnation, the belief that all forms of life undergo recurring rebirth into mortality, is the prime reality of the heavily populated Eastern religions. If reincarnation were true, it would have had to have been orchestrated by the creator of the universe—not by the god of pantheism who is the universe itself. There is no claim or evidence that the creator of the universe has authored reincarnation.

Although pantheism does not meet causal adequacy for the god of the universe, its worldview has taught worthwhile principles that have led to much good. One of the most compelling of today's pantheistic worldviews, practiced by 70-100 million people in China, is **Falun Dafa** (also called Falun Gong), a path of Buddhism teaching that *the great way* to divinity is by embracing three fundamental qualities underlying all of existence: truth, compassion, and tolerance.[64] One would think that such admirable virtues wouldn't offend anyone. However, when the main text (*Zhuan Falun*) of this spiritual practice became a national best seller in China in the 1990s, the Chinese Communist Party officially banned Falun Dafa in July of 1999. As one of eighty-four thousand avenues to enlightenment spoken of in Buddhist thought,[65] Falun Dafa continues to thrive underground throughout China and the rest of the world.

If a non-threatening, principle-based worldview like Falun Dafa (believing in a pantheistic god who dies if the universe dies) is capable of provoking such ire from a materialistic government, imagine the threat of a theistic worldview that honors the creator and host of the universe! Like employees who recognize the source of their paycheck, all theists want to do is perform to the right audience…the founder and CEO of the universe.

**Deism**, like theism, posits a transcendent, personal, free agent—a causally adequate explanation for the origin of the universe from a discrete beginning of time. However, deism conceives of God as acting only at the beginning of the universe, who, after creating the universe, follows a "hands-off" approach. Evolutionary creationists are deists who hold that god brought about the Big Bang and, at the same time, stacked the deck to produce life billions of years later. Like an expert billiards player, he sank all the balls into the pockets on the first shot. Ironically, many adherents to this worldview are not true deists since they believe that god actively sustains the orderly concourse of nature on a moment-to-moment basis and hears personal prayers.

Science has never discovered a law that was deterministic to generate future events such as ongoing fine-tuning or new biological information. Physical laws are highly regular, repetitive, and periodic. “Front-loading” (deism) can explain the fact that the material universe had a beginning. However, deism fails two tests of causal adequacy since it cannot explain the universe’s ongoing fine-tuning nor the large discontinuous increases in functionally specific information that has entered the biosphere since the beginning.

**Theism**, the belief in a transcendent, personal, free-will god who acted to bring time and space into existence, fine-tune the universe for life, and bring large discontinuous increases of functionally genetic life into the biosphere, is the only worldview consistent with scientific evidence. It is where facts align with claims to offer the best worldview corresponding to reality. Theism provides a springboard from which its adherents can launch into a search for understanding the nature, character, and personality of their host.

Our aloneness in the universe naturally prompts a search for companionship somewhere...anywhere. It is what evoked entertainer Ellen DeGeneres to say: “The only thing that scares me more than space aliens is the idea that there aren’t any space aliens. We can’t be the best that creation has to offer. I pray we’re not all there is. If so, we're in big trouble." Science popularizer Arthur C. Clarke quipped: "Two possibilities exist: either we are alone in the universe or we are not. Both are equally terrifying."

British biologist J.B.S. Haldane said, "If mental processes are determined wholly by the motions of atoms in my brain, I [would] have no reason to suppose my beliefs are true...and hence no reason for supposing my brain to be made of atoms."[66] Haldane's humorous illustration shows the circular thinking we can get ourselves into by following abductive leads, ending up spending all our lives in rabbit holes. If an eyewitness to a fire, when asked about the cause of the fire, answers, "It was oxygen in the air," that person is probably not the best source of information for establishing a worldview based on causal adequacy.

All of us have a far greater reason for learning about the personality, character, and design of our life's host than Agatha Christie's guests on Soldier Island. If it was important for them to hear from their host, it is of paramount importance for us to hear from ours. **The creator/host of Earth, Milky Way Galaxy and Cosmos went to a lot of trouble to fashion this uniquely inhabitable universe and planet for us. He couldn't have created it all just to have us fail...or to accuse us** (James 1:5).

Our host is also a master fine-tuner who communicates effectively with all who are willing to reciprocate. To the Prophet Moses, God said: "The heavens, they are many, and they cannot be numbered unto man; but they are numbered unto me, for they are mine. And as one earth shall pass away, and the heavens thereof even so shall another come; and there is no end to my works, neither to my words. For behold, this is my work and my glory—to bring to pass the immortality and eternal life of man" (Pearl of Great Price 1:37-39). Indeed, God's work and glory requires that there be "no end...to [His fine-tuning] words."

# Which Form of Theism is Most Compatible with the Evidence?

Throughout my life, I have come to know and admire people from all worldviews. I studied their books, tried to "walk a mile in their shoes," and learned something worthwhile from each to live by. The most serious errors I have discovered in assessing relative strengths and weaknesses of worldviews have been: 1) Imputing a worldview claim that it did not make itself, and 2) Discounting the validity of a worldview due to the fault of one or more of its spokespersons. The stereotype that "all churches claim to be the true church" or "all churches claim authority from God" can be easily refuted by fact-checking their own claims. When a claim is confirmed to have come from an authoritative source, a search for substantiating evidence can then be made. Personal pitfalls of pastors, priests, popes, and prophets do not disqualify legitimate claims.

## Judaism

As a word, ***Judaism*** first appeared during the second century B.C.[67] However, its roots date back to the early patriarchs of the third millennium B.C. with the birth of Jacob's fourth son, Judah (Genesis 29:35). As a tribe of Israel, Judah's claim to God's authority came through Moses and other Israelite prophets. What was that claim?—A covenantal relationship with God. If they kept God's commandments, they would become a "holy people unto the Lord" who had "chosen [Israel] to be a special people unto himself, above all people that are upon the face of the earth" (Deuteronomy 7:6).

Such a bold claim was by no means exclusionary. Metaphorically, Israel was a bride, bound exclusively to God, the bridegroom, who was free to establish covenantal relationships with other brides (people willing to commit to His covenant).[68] According to Jewish Sifre Deuteronomy 343, Israel was not God's first choice. After offering His covenant to many other nations who were unwilling to accept the responsibility of the covenant, "God scraped the bottom of the barrel and offered [His covenant] to the Israelites. They immediately accepted without even asking about the contents."[69] However, Israel's status as the Lord's chosen people was not permanent; it was conditional upon keeping *her* covenants with the Lord, who could be confidently relied upon for keeping His.

Did Israel keep her covenants? Not according to the Prophets Isaiah (Isaiah 5) and Jeremiah (Jeremiah 11). The Old Testament describes the Assyrian destruction of Israel (2 Kings 17:7-23) and later Babylonian destruction of Judah (2 Kings 24:1-4) as a result of their apostasy (breaking their covenants). Notwithstanding, Jews believed in a utopian future, led by a messiah, wherein their nation would one day be restored to the grandeur it had once enjoyed under David and Solomon. Jesus of Nazareth was not that messiah for whom organized Judaism had awaited. Furthermore, the destruction of the Jerusalem Temple in A.D. 70 extinguished their immediate messianic hope and radically changed Jewish history.

Over the centuries, Jews suffered tremendous persecution, which peaked during World War II. The Roman Catholic Church's Second Vatican Council of 1962-1965 repudiated antisemitism and the charge that Jews were collectively responsible for the crucifixion of Jesus. The council went so far as to officially recognize that God's covenant with the Jewish people remained intact...and there was no need for Jews to convert to Christianity to achieve salvation.[70] This well-intended edict from the Catholic Church discouraged antisemitism and promoted peace in a troubled world. Notwithstanding, the same Vatican Council acknowledged that the Catholic Church's position to speak on behalf of God was tenuous, at best.[71]

Professor Isaiah Gafni of the Hebrew University of Jerusalem provides a good overview of Judaism's fundamental change after the destruction of the Temple: "The Temple and its priesthood ceased to function.... Some felt that life without a Temple was meaningless, and embarked on a life of perpetual mourning or ascetic abstinence.... When Rabbi Joshua asked how sins would be atoned without Temple sacrifice, his mentor Yohanan ben Zakkai replied that acts of loving kindness would be as effective."[72] However, the remnant of the (Wailing) Western Wall, a sacred site of prayer closest to the former Holy of Holies of the Temple, stands as a witness today that acts of even the most loving kindness are not a substitute for an enriching covenantal relationship with God in His Holy Temple.

Professor Gafni goes on to say: "How and when did the synagogue come to replace the Temple? Who is responsible for instituting prayer as an alternative to sacrificial worship? How did the study of the Torah under rabbis become so central to the Jewish tradition, when rabbis are not even mentioned in the Bible? The answer to these questions lies in the character and frameworks of rabbinic Judaism, which Jews gradually came to embrace after the destruction of the Second Temple."[73] In remembering "the travails, and the labors, and the pains of the Jews, and their diligence unto [God], in bringing forth salvation unto the Gentiles" through the Bible, the Lord lovingly referred to the Jews as "mine ancient covenant people" (2 Nephi 29:4).

During His mortality, Jesus declared that because the Jews had rejected His covenant, they would lose it to another people. In a parable to the chief priests and Pharisees, He said:

> "There was a certain householder, which planted a vineyard, and hedged it round about, and digged a winepress in it, and built a tower, and let it out to husbandmen, and went into a far country: And when the time of the fruit drew near, he sent his servants to the husbandmen, that they might receive the fruits of it. And the husbandmen took his servants, and beat one, and killed another, and stoned another. Again, he sent other servants more than the first: and they did unto them likewise. But last of all he sent unto them his son, saying, They will reverence my son. But when the husbandmen saw the son, they said among themselves, This is the heir; come, let us kill him, and let us seize on his inheritance. And they caught him, and cast him out of the vineyard, and slew him. When the lord therefore of the vineyard cometh, what will he do unto those husbandmen? They say unto him, He will miserably destroy those wicked men, and will let out his vineyard unto other husbandmen, which shall render him the fruits in their seasons. Jesus saith unto them, Did ye never read in the scriptures, The stone which the builders rejected, the same is become the head of the corner: this is the Lord's doing, and it is marvellous in our eyes? Therefore say I unto you, The kingdom of God shall be taken

from you, and given to a nation bringing forth the fruits thereof" (Matthew 21: 33-43).

The chief priests and Pharisees who heard this parable "perceived that [Jesus was speaking] of them" (Matthew 21:45). God was the householder; the chief priests and Pharisees were the husbandmen; the servants were the prophets who had been sent; and Jesus was the son. The chief priests and Pharisees recognized that they were the wicked who would be destroyed, and, consequently, would lose the vineyard to other husbandmen. Jesus confirmed to them that the gospel kingdom (covenant) would be taken from them [Judah] and given to a nation worthy of the covenant.

## Islam

As the second largest faith in the world, ***Islam*** has over a billion followers (Muslims) who live in some 56 countries. The word *Islam* means "submission" or "surrender." Muslims seek to submit and surrender to the will of God (Allah), both individually and as members of a worldwide community of "believers, God ordained and guided, to spread an Islamic order to create a socially just society."[74] Like Judaism and Christianity, Islam traces its ancestry to Abraham. Muslims trace their ancestry to Abraham through Sarah's Egyptian handmaid, Hagar, and her son, Ishmael. Jews and Christians trace their ancestry to Abraham through Sarah and her son, Isaac.

Abraham loved both Ishmael and Isaac. God told Abraham that Ishmael would be multiplied and become a great nation (Genesis 17:20). At the same time, God made it clear that the everlasting covenant would be established through Isaac (Genesis 17:19). All who accept the gospel become part of the covenant lineage of Abraham. In Galatians, we read: "For as many of you as have been baptized into Christ have put on Christ...for Ye are all one in Christ Jesus. And if ye be Christ's, then are ye Abraham's seed, and heirs according to the promise" (Galatians 3:27-29). Thus, everyone on earth, including Muslims, can become heirs to the covenant, if not by birth, then by adoption.[75]

According to Islamic tradition, the prophet **Muhammed** (A.D. 570-632) began to receive revelations at the age of forty from the angel Gabriel atop one of the mountains in the vicinity of Mecca.[76] This prompted major reforms in the tribal Arabian society of the early seventh century A.D. Muhammad's preaching called for the end of polytheism and idolatry; emphasis on membership in the faith community rather than tribal affiliation; the implementation of social justice, particularly for women and poor; and limitations on materialism, corruption, and avarice. At first, his reforms were met with persecution and resistance at Mecca, prompting Muhammed to move to Medina, where he established his base.

At Medina, relations with local Jewish tribes steadily worsened. Muslims began to pray in the direction of the Meccan Ka'bah rather than toward Jerusalem, as was the Jewish practice. This was a period in history when neither Judaism nor Christianity claimed ongoing divine revelation. Muhammed's assumption of influence and power began at Medina, followed by his subjugation of Mecca and the ultimate consolidation of Muslim rule over the rest of Arabia through a combination of diplomatic and military means. Thereafter, he served as prophet, political ruler, military commander, chief judge, and lawgiver.[77]

Beginning in A.D. 610 and extending over a 22-year period, the Quran was revealed to Muhammad as Islamic scripture, believed to reflect and correct earlier revelations in the Torah and New Testament and to be the final revelation of God to mankind.[78] Such a bold claim merits study of the Quran, which can be read in less time than it takes to read the New Testament. It comprises only 114 chapters and 6,000 verses—shorter in length than the New Testament.

Critics of Islam point out that, centuries before Muhammed, the name "Allah" was used in Arabia to designate the highest god among 360 gods worshiped by Arabian polytheists. Muslims counter that Allah was always the true god whose name had been intermingled with idols by false worshippers. Muhammed was God's messenger who proclaimed the monotheism of Allah. According to the Quran: "The Messiah, Jesus, son of Mary was only a Messenger of Allah, and (a fulfillment of) His word which He communicated to Mary, and a mercy from Him. Believe, therefore, in Allah and in all His messengers, and do not say, '(There are) three (Gods).' Refrain (from following this doctrine) it will be better for you.

Verily, Allah is the One and only worthy of worship. He is Holy. Far above having a son."[79]

Muslims honor Jesus as one of the prophets but not as the Son of God. In fact, conversion to Islam requires one to make a two-fold declaration of faith (*Shahada*) that is incompatible with accepting Jesus as the Son of God. A Muslim bears witness that 1) *There is no true god except Allah*, and 2) *Muhammad is Allah's [final] messenger*. Like rabbinic Judaism and post-apostolic Christianity, Islam does not believe in ongoing revelation; no "fine-tuning" from the God of the universe who might want to call a prophet (messenger) to proclaim His word as it becomes misunderstood through the ages.

Historically, Muslims once accepted the principle of ongoing revelation. Eighth-century B.C. writer Amos (honored by Jews, Christians, and Muslims alike as a prophet) stated: "Surely the Lord God will do nothing, but he revealeth his secret unto his servants the prophets" (Amos 3:7). Amos went on to prophesy, "Behold, the days come, saith the Lord God, that I will send a famine in the land, not a famine of bread, nor a thirst for water, but of hearing the words of the Lord: And they shall wander from sea to sea, and from the north even to the east, they shall run to and fro to seek the word of the Lord, and shall not find it" (Amos 8:11-12). Three centuries earlier, such a famine had been observed by the Prophet Samuel as "the word of the Lord was precious in those days; there was no open vision" (1 Samuel 3:1). Similar famines, of hearing the words of the Lord, have been evident many times throughout history when mankind was unreceptive to a covenantal relationship with God. The seventh century A.D. was one of those periods.

Muhammed's death in June of A.D. 632 provided for no arrangement of his succession, provoking a major dispute over the future leadership of the community he founded. Of today's many denominations of Islam, two have emerged as the most prominent. **Sunni Islam,** comprising around 85% of the Muslim world, was first led by four democratically elected caliphs who were succeeded by a hereditary dynastic rule until the fall of the Ottoman Empire in 1923. Since that time, Sunnis have had no caliph but have been divided into competing schools of Islamic ideology. **Shia Islam,** the second largest denomination of Islam, comprises 10-15% of the total Muslim population. Shias believe that Muhammad's family, including his descendants known as imams, have distinguished spiritual and political authority over the community. They believe Ali ibn Abi Talib, Muhammad's cousin and son-in-law, was the first of those imams and the rightful successor to Muhammad, and thus reject the legitimacy of the caliphs.[80]

## Christianity

***Christianity*** is the largest faith in the world. **"Christ"** is the Greek form of the Hebrew title "Messiah," meaning the "anointed one." Christians revere Jesus of Nazareth as the anointed one, chosen by God to rescue all mankind from permanent death while offering eternal life to everyone willing to accept His covenant. According to Bill O'Reilly, "To say that Jesus of Nazareth was the most influential man who ever lived is almost trite. Nearly two thousand years after he was brutally executed by Roman soldiers, more than 2.2 billion human beings attempt to follow his teachings and believe he is God. That includes 77 percent of the U.S. population, according to a Gallup Poll. The teachings of Jesus have shaped the entire world and continue to do so."[81]

Unique to Jesus of Nazareth are prophecies from antiquity foretelling details of His birth and mission. The Book of Matthew contains numerous references to Old Testament prophecies about Jesus that were fulfilled. A careful reading of the Old Testament opens one's view to an almost ubiquitous source of prophecies and types of Jesus as the Messiah. Sixth century B.C. American Prophet Jacob also declared, "all the holy prophets...believed in Christ and worshipped the Father in his name" (Jacob 4:4-5).

Other non-Biblical references attest to the historicity of Jesus of Nazareth, as well. Jewish historian **Flavius Josephus** (A.D. 37-100) wrote: "Now there was about this time Jesus, a wise man, if it be lawful to call him a man, for he was a doer of wonderful works, a teacher of such men as receive the truth with pleasure. He drew over to him both many of the Jews, and many of the Gentiles. He was the Christ. And when Pilate, at the suggestion of the principal men amongst us, had condemned him to the cross, those that loved him at the first did not forsake him; for he appeared unto them alive again on the third day; as the divine prophets had foretold these and thousand other wonderful things concerning him. And the tribe of Christians, so named from him, are not extinct at this day."[82]

This is a remarkable statement coming from an aristocratic Sadducee who did not believe in the resurrection. Some modern scholars reject the authenticity of Josephus' testimony. However, they do acknowledge a second Josephus reference to Jesus, as well as other independent sources, Roman governor Pliny the Younger, Roman historian and senator Tacitus, Roman historian Suetonius, and Greek satirist Lucian of Samosata whose hostility toward Jesus, His crucifixion, and "misguided" Christian followers provide unbiased evidence of Jesus' historicity.

During Jesus' lifetime, two hundred and fifty persons claimed to be the Messiah. None were successful in gathering many people except Jesus, who attracted thousands to see Him even though many could not get close enough to hear Him. Historical records show that informants (spies) working independently for the Jewish Sanhedrin and the Roman Empire, both unsympathetic sources, reported witnessing Jesus performing miracles. It was the wide circulation of their reports that attracted large crowds from all over to see Jesus.[83]

In Mesoamerica, sixteenth-century Spanish chroniclers compiled legends of the visit of a white god whom many called Quetzalcoatl (feathered serpent).

Others called him Hueman because of his great virtues and the prints or stamps in his hands.[84] The dual symbolism of the quetzal bird ascending to heaven and the serpent descending below all things as a sacrifice so all who "looketh upon [Him] shall live" (Numbers 21:8) is as meaningful to Mesoamericans as the Crucifix is to Christianity. Schoolchildren in Mexico study the role of Quetzalcoatl, and quetzal is the national bird as well as the basic currency of Guatemala.

**Juan de Torquemada** (1557-1664) wrote a history of Mexico in which he described legends of Quetzalcoatl, the white god who wore a white robe.[85] **Bernardino de Sahagun** (1499-1591) taught that the name Quetzalcoatl came about because of the advent of Christ in America, who promised to return in the future.[86] **Fernando de Alva Ixtlilxochitl** (1578-1650), considered by many to be the Josephus of Mexico, said Quetzalcoatl was born of a virgin, taught His people, prophesied of future events, ascended to heaven, and then came to America at the time of the great destruction at the death of Christ. Quetzalcoatl also taught that His children would become lords and heirs of the earth.[87]

Quetzalcoatl's name later became paganized when a tenth-century ruler (Topiltzin) took upon himself the title of Quetzalcoatl. Heathen attributes began to replace the original symbolism of Christ, whose divine attributes, as described by Spanish writers, had included: 1) creator of all things, 2) performer of miracles, 3) teacher of the ordinance of baptism, 4)

Lord of disciples who taught His word, 5) infant whose birth was associated with a new star, 6) God of the universe, etc. Like today's use of the given name "Jesus," Quetzalcoatl the god became confused with Quetzalcoatl the man.[88]

South American Spanish chroniclers also documented legends of the visit of a white god whose virtues were so numerous that he had no official name except for dozens of different metaphors. When Francisco Pizzaro landed on the Peruvian shores in 1532, native populations mistook the bearded white men for gods, addressing the first Spanish they met as Wiracocha (in Quechua), the white god who had lived with them anciently for a time and then, leaving by sea, promised to return one day.

**Pedro Cieza de León** (1520-1554) explained that Viracocha (in Spanish) meant "foam on the sea," which signifies the manner in which the white god walked on the water like sea foam.[89] Cieza added that "where ever there were sick, he healed them, and to the blind he gave sight by simply speaking."[90] **Alonso Ramos Gavilán** (1570-1639), who called Viracocha "Tunupa" (in Aymara), said He performed "miracles and great wonders, and made a great effort to persuade them to build a temple to the true god. There they worshipped him with a special religion and ritual service."[91] **Pedro Sarmiento de Gamboa** (1532-1592) described Viracocha as "creator of all things." However, early Andeans did not believe in a universal creation *ex nihilo* [out of nothing]. They believed in the energizing of matter that already existed,[92] consistent with scientific findings and the original Hebrew account of the creation.

Many additional descriptive titles were given to Viracocha. A few of them included: 1) Splendor and firmament, 2) Creator, son of the creator, 3) Perfect, complete, He who finishes, 4) He who controls or owns all things, 5) Jesus Christ, 6) Infinite, invisible, all-powerful, 7) All-wise, 8) Person coming from the sky—supreme god, 9) Originator of all things, divine origin, 10) Eternal light, sacred origin, 11) God of the Old Testament, 12) The most high god who gives life and being to the universe, etc.[93]

Since it was impossible for chroniclers not to link Viracocha to the Lord Jesus Christ, they had to conceal their description of Him. To acknowledge native American legends as anything more than folklore, showing they were already Christians, would have subjected chroniclers themselves to the Spanish Inquisition. Santa Cruz and Domingo de Santo Tomás were the only priests actually brave enough to equate this god with the name of Jesus Christ or the Christian God.[94] However, like Quetzalcoatl, confusion about Viracocha was introduced in the fifteenth century when the man, Viracocha, reigned as the eighth Inca sovereign of the Hanan dynasty in the Kingdom of Cusco.

Archeologist **L. Taylor Hansen** (1897-1976) spent twenty-five years researching Indian legends from tribes all over the Americas. By consulting museums, libraries, ancient ruins, and experts on folklore, she correlated her findings of a Fair God who visited numerous locations almost two thousand years ago, healing the sick, raising the dead, and teaching in the same words as Jesus Himself. She discovered local legends descriptive of Christ in Peru, Brazil, Guatemala, Mexico, Georgia, Oklahoma, West Virginia, Mississippi, Missouri, New York, Michigan, South Dakota, Canada, Wyoming, Washington, Oregon, California, Arizona, and Polynesia.[95] Although the highest concentration of legends came from Mexico and Peru, the real question that begs to be asked is: "How many legends of Christ have been lost?"

Evidence of Jesus' post-resurrection appearances is by no means confined to America. In the Garden Vestibule of the Mikhailovsky Palace at St. Petersburg hangs a 9' x 7' masterpiece painting by Russian painter Mikhail Nesterov entitled "The Holy Rus." According to the Metropole Peterim of the Russian Orthodox Church, Nesterov's painting was inspired by an ancient folktale...that after the resurrection, Christ visited the Slavic people, ancestors of the Russians, to bring His gospel. The people who listened to Christ were the humble and lowly in the farms and countryside. Those who believed in Him took upon themselves the name, "Kristianya" [Christians], which is also the word for "peasants" in Russian.[96]

*Holy Rus*: a picture by the Russian painter Mikhail Nesterov, circa 1900

The accuracy of the legends is not the point. Generational oral traditions would be expected to become corrupted as they are passed along. Experiences that parents might want to emphasize to their posterity can become lost over time. This can even happen in a single generation! What is important to remember is that the legends exist. They are strongly repetitive, correlative, and supportive of the New Testament account of the resurrection of Jesus Christ. They are also powerful evidence of the fulfillment of Jesus' word to His disciples at Jerusalem: "And other sheep I have, which are not of this fold: them also I must bring, and they shall hear my voice; and there shall be one fold, and one shepherd" (John 10:16).

When the resurrected Lord appeared to the Nephites, a branch of Israel in America, He declared to them: "...ye are they of whom I said: Other sheep I have which are not of this fold; them also I must bring, and they shall hear my voice; and there shall be one fold, and one shepherd" (3 Nephi 15:21). While visiting them, He told them: "I have other sheep, which are not of this land, neither of the land of Jerusalem, neither in any parts of that land round about whither I have been to minister. For they of whom I speak are they who have not as yet heard my voice; neither have I at any time manifested myself unto them. But I have received a commandment of the Father that I shall go unto them, and that they shall hear my voice, and shall be numbered among my sheep, that there may be one fold and one shepherd; therefore I go to show myself unto them." (3 Nephi 16:1-3).

Should it be of any surprise for us to hear of these widespread legends of Christ's post-resurrection visits? Fortunately, we have more than just legends and references to His visits. At least one recorded account of His visit has been preserved for us by way of commandment from the Lord, in case the other records of His visits became lost. To the Nephites, the Lord said:

> "And I command you that ye shall write these sayings after I am gone, that if it so be that my people at Jerusalem, they who have seen me and been with me in my ministry, do not ask the Father in my name, that they may receive

> a knowledge of you by the Holy Ghost, and also of the other tribes whom they know not of, that these sayings which ye shall write shall be kept and shall be manifested unto the Gentiles, that through the fulness of the Gentiles, the remnant of their seed, who shall be scattered forth upon the face of the earth because of their unbelief, may be brought in, or may be brought to a knowledge of me, their Redeemer. And then will I gather them in from the four quarters of the earth; and then will I fulfil the covenant which the Father hath made unto all the people of the house of Israel. And blessed are the Gentiles, because of their belief in me, in and of the Holy Ghost, which witnesses unto them of me and of the Father. Behold, because of their belief in me, saith the Father, and because of the unbelief of you, O house of Israel, in the latter day shall the truth come unto the Gentiles, that the fulness of these things shall be made known unto them" (3 Nephi 16: 4-7).

What other worldview furnishes claims, as well as evidence of a host with prophecies antedating His birth, a life of miracles, a resurrection from the dead, and post-resurrection appearances that have been witnessed and testified of all over the world? Christ's domain is vast, but He oversees all of it personally. In 1832, He described the nature of His ongoing visits to His children by way of the following parable:

“I will liken these kingdoms unto a man having a field, and he sent forth his servants into the field to dig in the field. And he said unto the first: Go ye and labor in the field, and in the first hour I will come unto you, and ye shall behold the joy of my countenance. And he said unto the second: Go ye also into the field, and in the second hour I will visit you with the joy of my countenance. And also unto the third, saying: I will visit you; And unto the fourth, and so on unto the twelfth. And the lord of the field went unto the first in the first hour, and tarried with him all that hour, and he was made glad with the light of the countenance of his lord. And then he withdrew from the first that he might visit the second also, and the third, and the fourth, and so on unto the twelfth. And thus they all received the light of the countenance of their lord, every man in his hour, and in his time, and in his season—Beginning at the first, and so on unto the last, and from the last unto the first, and from the first unto the last; Every man in his own order, until his hour was finished, even according as his lord had commanded him, that his lord might be glorified in him, and he in his lord, that they all might be glorified. Therefore, unto this parable I will liken all these kingdoms, and the inhabitants thereof—every kingdom in its hour, and in its time, and in its season, even

> according to the decree which God hath made" (Doctrine and Covenants 88:51-61).

In contrast to every other person in history, Jesus of Nazareth cannot be simply regarded as a sage, guru, master, teacher, wise man, or prophet. C.S. Lewis wrote:

> "We can all understand how a man forgives offenses against himself. You tread on my toes and I forgive you, you steal my money and I forgive you. But what should we make of a man, himself...who announced that he forgave you for treading on other men's toes and stealing other men's money? ... Yet this is what Jesus did. He told people that their sins were forgiven, and never waited to consult all the other people whom their sins had undoubtedly injured. He unhesitatingly behaved as if He was the party chiefly concerned, the person chiefly offended in all offenses. This makes sense only if He really was the God whose laws are broken and whose love is wounded in every sin. In the mouth of any speaker who is not God, these words would imply what I can only regard as a silliness and conceit unrivaled by any other character in history...
>
> "... Yet (and this is the strange, significant thing) even His enemies, when they read the Gospels, do not usually get the impression of

silliness and conceit... Christ says that He is 'humble and meek' and we believe Him; not noticing that, if He were merely a man, humility and meekness are the very last characteristics we could attribute to some of His sayings...

"... I am trying here to prevent anyone saying the really foolish thing that people often say about Him: 'I'm ready to accept Jesus as a great moral teacher, but I don't accept His claim to be God.' That is the one thing we must not say. A man who was merely a man and said the sort of things Jesus said would not be a great moral teacher. He would either be a lunatic...or else he would be the Devil of Hell. You must make your choice. Either this man was, and is, the Son of God: or else a madman or something worse. You can shut Him up for a fool, you can spit at Him and kill Him as a demon; or you can fall at His feet and call Him Lord and God. But let us not come with any patronizing nonsense about His being a great human teacher. He has not left that open to us. He did not intend to."[97]

To Lewis's point, the resurrected Lord appeared to His Apostle John on the isle of Patmos and confirmed to him: "I am he that liveth, and was dead; and, behold, I am alive for evermore, Amen; and have the keys of hell and of death" (Revelation 1:18). The keys to which the Lord refers are solely His to employ...however, whenever, and for whomsoever He chooses.

Jesus' bold claim not only distinguishes Christianity, but defines other worldviews as well. Atheists do not believe Jesus was the Son of God, the Messiah, or a prophet. Some go so far as to say that He never existed. Organized Judaism does not accept Jesus as the Son of God, the anticipated Messiah, or a prophet—but views Him as an imposter of Jehovah, who is the one and only true God. Islam claims that Allah is the one and only true God and that Jesus was a prophet born of the Virgin Mary, the only woman mentioned in the Quran. Ironically, the same angel, Gabriel, who declared to Muhammed in the Quran that Jesus was not the Son of God, declared to Mary in the Bible that her child *was* the Son of God (Luke 1:32, 35). The vast majority of today's Christians hold the belief that Jesus is not only the Son of God—but also God the Father and God the Holy Ghost—constituting one god in substance. Christians who hold this view of a triune god or Trinity contend that they are monotheists. Muslims and Jews do not agree.[98]

Jesus made it clear that the most important investigation we can ever conduct in life is to find God. More than any other invitation, He beckoned us to "ask, seek and knock" (Matthew 7:7). There is urgency in His appeal. What should we ask, seek, and knock for? While lifting up His eyes to heaven, He said to His Father, "And this is life eternal, that they might know thee the only true God, and Jesus Christ, whom thou hast sent" (John 17:3). Since knowing God is of such critical importance, why doesn't God just show Himself to us? At least two reasons include: 1) Agency and 2) Accountability.

1. **Agency:** In his *Parable of a King and a Maiden*, Danish philosopher, Soren Kierkegaard, poses the question, "'How can the king (God) reveal his love to a woman (us) of humble parentage—given the huge disparity of rank, status and wealth between them—without coercing and crushing her? 'Not to reveal oneself,' he writes, 'is the death of love, to reveal oneself is the death of the beloved.' The only real choice open to the king is to court his beloved indirectly, by descending to her station, by taking on the character of a servant. So, he disguises himself. God, Kierkegaard says, wants us to love him freely because we come to know him as lovable, not because he's powerful, terrifying or overwhelming. And we have abundant reason to do that. Similarly, though, He wants us to develop faith and trust in him, He doesn't seek a compelled belief. He doesn't desire an assent that has been forced upon us because we had no rational alternative or escape."[99] For this reason, "[Christ] took upon himself the form of a servant, and was made in the likeness of men" (Philippians 2:7). He doesn't want us to just obey God, but to agree with Him.

2. **Accountability:** Our creator knows our capabilities. Like parents with open arms standing a few feet away from their toddler who is learning to walk, our Heavenly Father beckons us with open arms to walk to Him on our own accord without being carried. However, each toddler has to want to walk. Mortality is our time and space to think about what we want in eternity, whether it is to live with God in His kingdom in conformance with His laws and covenants or to "enjoy that which [we] are willing to receive, because [we] were not willing to enjoy that which [we] might have received" (Doctrine and Covenants 88:32).

As we learned from science, God's *modus operandi* is to 1) Create, 2) Fine-tune, and 3) Add new information. This was true of His creation of the universe, the Earth, and mankind. Oddly, many of His children today believe that God created instructions for His children—the Torah for the Jews, the Quran for the Muslims, and the Bible for the Christians—and then withdrew from providing any additional information. In essence, the majority of today's major worldviews believe that God front-loaded His commandments and covenants into scripture deistically and then stepped back from offering ongoing revelation or prophetic guidance.

When we were children, many of us can remember playing a game called "telephone" in which we whispered a secret from person to person around a circle and compared what the first person said with what the last person understood, which usually turned out to be a far cry from the original message. On the contrary, God, who fine-tunes the mass of the universe down to the weight of a dime, intervenes to correct misunderstandings His children pass along from generation to generation, providing they are willing to listen.

# What Did Early Christianity Say About the Nature of God?

In order to get a correct understanding of God, the first step is a scriptural study of the life, teachings, and acts of His Son, Jesus Christ. Water is purer at its source than it is downstream. However, one of the challenges of Biblical reading is distinguishing literal from figurative descriptions. The Godhead spoken of in the Bible (Acts 17:29, Romans 1:20, Colossians 2:9) is a literal depiction of three separate personages, the Father, the Son, and the Holy Ghost, which Christianity later came to perceive as one person. Here are ten (out of hundreds of) clarifying references to the three persons of the godhead:

1. "Then said Jesus, Father, forgive them; for they know not what they do" (Luke 23:34). Was Jesus praying to Himself to forgive others?
2. "And he said, Abba, Father, all things are possible unto thee; take away this cup from me: nevertheless not what I will, but what thou wilt" (Mark 14:36). Did Jesus have two conflicting wills?
3. "... Jesus cried with a loud voice, saying,... My God, my God, why hast thou forsaken me?" (Matthew 27:46). Why would Jesus make this plea to Himself if the Father was also on the cross?
4. "...my Father is greater than I" (John 14:28). Would Jesus make this declaration if He and His Father were the same person?
5. "... I seek not mine own will, but the will of the Father which hath sent me" (John 5:30). Does this sound like a mission to which Jesus commissioned Himself?
6. "If I bear witness of myself, my witness is not true. There is another that beareth witness of me; and I know that the witness which he witnesseth of me is true" (John 5:31). Wouldn't this declaration be disingenuous if Jesus were bearing witness of Himself under a different name?
7. At Jesus' baptism, John the Baptist "...saw the Spirit of God descending like a dove, and lighting upon him: And lo a voice from heaven,

saying This is my beloved Son, in whom I am well pleased" (Matthew 3:16-17). In this setting, all three members of the Godhead are present, each distinguished from one another. Jesus is in the water about to be baptized, the Father's voice from heaven bears witness of His Son, and the Holy Ghost descends and lights upon Jesus.

8. "Jesus saith unto [Mary], Touch me not; for I am not yet ascended to my Father: but go to my brethren, and say unto them, I ascend unto my Father, and your Father; and to my God, and your God" (John 20:17). Is it consistent with Jesus' character to make an excuse to leave Mary so He could ascend unto Himself?
9. "Then saith [Jesus] to Thomas, Reach hither thy finger, and behold my hands; and reach hither thy hand, and thrust it into my side: and be not faithless, but believing" (John 20:27). "...have ye any meat?" (John 21:5). "Jesus saith unto them, Come and dine" (John 21:12). Can these post-resurrection expressions of body wounds and physical appetite be interpreted any way but literally? If Jesus' resurrection was not permanent, how can we respond to His oft-repeated invitation to "come, take up the cross [whatever it may be for each of us individually], and follow me [to a glorious resurrection]?" (Mark 10:21).
10. "But [Stephen], being full of the Holy Ghost, looked up steadfastly into heaven, and saw the

> glory of God, and Jesus standing on the right hand of God. And said, Behold, I see the heavens opened, and the Son of man standing on the right hand of God" (Acts 7:55-56). Stephen, a disciple of Christ, confirms the distinct identity of the Father, the resurrected Son, and the Holy Ghost.

Nowhere in the Bible is the word "trinity" used, nor is there any description of a triune god. Furthermore, there is no reference, scriptural or non-scriptural, that Jesus ever gave up His resurrected body. What would be the purpose of His resurrection if it were to be only temporary? Inasmuch as Jesus is in the express image of His Father, why wouldn't the Father also have a literal body? Trying to understand biblical verses from a trinitarian perspective is nonsensical. Much of the confusion over Jesus' identity centers around three verses: "I am the Lord, and there is none else, there is no God beside me" (Isaiah 45:5); "I and my Father are one" (John 10:30); "He that hath seen me hath seen the Father; and I am in the Father and the Father in me" (John 14:9-11). Do these declarations sound literal or figurative?

Imagine that you are a detective assigned to your first big case, a highly publicized crime in Smalltown, U.S.A. You go to Smalltown to look for evidence as close as possible to the time and place of the crime. You are cautious about interviewing bystanders who are eager to give testimony based only on what they read in the news.

This situation is similar to learning from contemporary sources who Jesus is. For three centuries after Jesus' mortality, the distinct personage of each member of the Godhead was declared by apostles and post-apostolic disciples. Eventually, a recognizable pattern of doctrinal drift occurred from a belief in three distinct material personages toward a trinity of three non-material personages in one. Here is a dissection of that drift, beginning with what Jesus said about Himself, followed by some of the notable Ante-Nicene Fathers:

1. **Jesus Christ** (A.D. 1-34) has been recorded to have made a number of post-resurrection appearances. A few are described here:

    - He appeared to His apostles "but they were terrified and affrighted, and supposed that they had seen a spirit. And he said unto them, Why are ye troubled? and why do thoughts arise in your hearts? Behold my hands and feet, that it is I myself; handle me, and see; for a spirit hath not flesh and bones, as ye see me have" (Luke 24:37-39).
    - Next, He showed them His hands and feet, but they still couldn't believe their eyes out of joy and wonder. So, He asked them, "Have ye here any meat? And they gave him a piece of broiled fish, and of an honeycomb. And he took it, and did eat before them" (Luke 24:41-43). Could this description of

Jesus, His body, and appetite be rendered any clearer?

- Finally, Jesus reminded them that what they were seeing was what He taught would happen when He had been with them during His mortality that "all things must be fulfilled, which were written in the law of Moses, and in the prophets, and in the psalms, concerning me" (Luke 24:44). Christianity had not just begun. It always existed—in every dispensation of history—as long as people permitted prophets to live among them to teach and testify of Christ (Amos 3:7, Jacob 7:9-11).
- After ministering among them for forty days, Jesus "was taken up; and a cloud received him out of their sight. And while they looked steadfastly toward heaven as he went up, behold, two men stood by them in white apparel; Which also said, Ye men of Galilee, why stand ye gazing up into heaven? this same Jesus, which is taken up from you into heaven, shall so come in like manner as ye have seen him go into heaven" (Acts 1:9-11). How was Jesus "taken up into heaven?" As a resurrected being! How will He return "in like manner?" As a resurrected being!
- The Apostle Paul testified that after Jesus was buried, he rose again on the third day. "And that he was seen of Cephas [Peter],

then of the twelve; After that, he was seen of above five hundred brethren at once; of whom the greater part remain unto the present, but some are fallen asleep. After that, he was seen of James; then of all the apostles. And last of all he was seen of me also, as of one born out of due time" (1 Corinthians 15:5-8).

- Paul was not the only one born out of due time to whom Jesus appeared nor the only one born out of due place. When Jesus appeared to the Nephites in America, they "went forth, and thrust their hands into his side, and did feel the prints of the nails in his hands and in his feet; and this they did do, going forth one by one until they had all gone forth, and did see with their eyes and did feel with their hands, and did know of a surety and did bear record, that it was he, of whom it was written by the prophets, that should come" (3 Nephi 11:15). Later, about two thousand and five hundred more men, women, and children saw, heard, and bore record of Him (3 Nephi 17:25). Their witness serves as *Another Testament of Jesus Christ* (*Book of Mormon—Another Testament of Jesus Christ*, title page) in confirming the Biblical account that Jesus died, was resurrected, and is an individual member of the unified Godhead.

2. **Ignatius** (A.D. 30-107), a disciple of the Apostle John, wrote, "The Lord...commanded [His apostles] to 'baptize in the name of the Father, and of the Son, and of the Holy Ghost,' not unto one [person] having three names... For there is but One that became incarnate [embodied], and that neither the Father nor the Paraclete [Holy Ghost], but the Son only, [who became so] not in appearance or imagination, but in reality."[100]

3. **Justin Martyr** (A.D. 110-165), the first Christian martyr after the apostolic era, wrote, "Jesus...said, 'No one knows the Father, but the Son; nor the Son but the Father, and those to whom the Son will reveal Him' (Matthew 11:27). The Jews being of the opinion that it was the Father of the universe who spake to Moses, though He who spake to him was indeed the Son of God. For they who affirm that the Son is the Father, are proved neither to have become acquainted with the Father, nor to know that the Father of the universe has a Son."[101]

4. **Theophilus of Antioch** (A.D. 115-181) was the first to have used the word "Trinity," but not in the context of a triune god. He spoke of the first three days of creation as "types of the Trinity of God, and His Word, and His wisdom."[102] Theophilus also taught the doctrine of deification: "... if [man] should incline to the things of immortality, keeping the

commandment of God, he should receive as reward from Him immortality, and should become God."[103] Deification was also taught by Irenaeus, Athanasius, Barnabas, Justin Martyr, Hippolytus, Cyprian, Clement of Alexandria, Arnobius, Heraclitus, and others,[104] showing that Jesus' invitation to follow Him was literal. A latter-day prophet has said of the doctrine of deification: "This lofty concept in no way diminishes God the Eternal Father. He is the Almighty. He is the Creator and Governor of the universe. He is the greatest of all and will always be so."[105]

5. **Irenaeus** (A.D. 120-202) was a pupil of Polycarp, who was the Apostle John's disciple. Irenaeus confirmed Justin Martyr's declaration that Jesus was known to ancient Israel. Irenaeus asked, "Who is meant by God? ...the Son, who came manifested to men... When the Son speaks to Moses, He says 'I am come down to deliver this people.' For it is He who descended and ascended for the salvation of men. Therefore God has been declared through the Son."[106]

6. **Tertullian** (A.D. 145-220), an ardent defender of the faith, taught:

- "The Father is one, and the Son one, and the Spirit one. They are distinct from Each Other."[107]
- "Sometimes [the devil's] aim has been to destroy the truth by defending it...reproaching the Gospels with a lie, saying in fact: 'I declare that it was God himself that I approached; it was the Almighty Himself that I tempted face to face; and it was for no other purpose than to tempt Him that I approached Him. If, on the contrary, it had been only the Son of God, most likely I should never have condescended to deal with Him."[108] Does anyone really believe that Satan tempted God the Father of the universe with appetite, power and wealth?
- "[Critics] are constantly throwing out against us that we are preachers of two gods and three gods, while they take to themselves pre-eminently the credit of being worshippers of the One God; just as if the Unity itself with irrational deductions did not produce heresy... Latins take pains to pronounce the homoousios [of the same substance], while Greeks actually refuse to understand [it]...how comes it to pass that God should be thought to suffer division and severance in the Son and in the Holy Ghost, who have the second and third places

assigned to them, and who are so closely joined with the Father in His substance?"[109]

- "He who delivered up the kingdom, and He to whom it is delivered up [1 Corinthians 15:24]—and in like manner, He who subjected (all things), and He to whom they were subjected—must necessarily be two different Beings."[110]
- "A father must needs have a son, in order to be a father; so likewise a son, to be a son, must have a father. It is, however, one thing to have, and another thing to be."[111]
- "I ask you how it is possible for a Being who is merely and absolutely One and Singular, to speak in plural phrase, saying, 'Let us make man in our own image, and after our own likeness;' [Genesis 1:26] whereas He ought to have said, 'Let me make man after my own image, and after my own likeness,' as being a unique and singular being? In the following passage, however, 'Behold the man is become as one of us,' [Genesis 3:22] He is either deceiving or amusing us in speaking plurally, if He is One only and singular."[112]
- "...from that perfect knowledge which assures us that the title of God and Lord is suitable, both to the Father, and to the Son, and to the Holy Ghost,... I will therefore not speak of gods at all, nor of lords, but I shall

follow the apostle; so that if the Father and Son are alike to be invoked, I shall call the Father 'God,' and invoke Jesus Christ as 'Lord.' But when Christ alone (is mentioned) I shall be able to call Him 'God,' as the same apostle says: 'Of whom is Christ, who is over all, God blessed forever.' For I should give the name of 'sun' even to a sunbeam, considered in itself; but if I were mentioning the sun from which the ray emanates, I certainly should at once withdraw the name of sun from the mere beam. For although I make not two suns, still I shall reckon both the sun and its ray to be as much two things and two forms of one undivided substance, as...the Father and the Son."[113]

- "The apostles...testified that Jesus was the Son of God, and that being the Son, He was anointed by the Father. Christ ["anointed one" in Greek; "Messiah" in Hebrew] therefore must be the same as Jesus who was anointed by the Father, and not the Father, who anointed the Son."[114] Two distinct persons are required for an anointing...an anointer and an anointed. No one anoints himself.

- "God was pleased to renew His covenant with man in such a way as that His Unity might be believed in, after a new manner, through the Son and the Spirit, in order that God might now be known openly, in His proper Names and Persons, who in ancient times was not plainly understood, though declared through the Son and the Spirit... Antichrists...deny the Father, when they say He is the same as the Son; and they deny the Son, when they suppose Him to be the same as the Father, by assigning to Them things which are not Theirs, and taking away from Them things which are Theirs. But 'whosoever shall confess that Jesus is the Son of God [*not the Father*], God dwelleth in him, and he in God' (1 John 4:15)... And that man has not the Son, who believes Him to be any other than the Son."[115]

- After [Jesus'] resurrection,... "He commands [His disciples] to baptize into the Father and the Son and the Holy Ghost, not into a unipersonal God."[116]

7. **Hippolytus** (A.D. 170-235) was a third-generation Greek disciple of the Apostle John through Polycarp and Irenaeus.[117] Hippolytus taught the doctrine of one God alone and three persons. He said: "I shall not indeed speak of two Gods, but of one; of two Persons however, and of a third...the Holy Ghost. For the Father indeed is One, but there are two Persons, because here is also the Son; and then there is the third, the Holy Spirit. It is the Father who commands, and the Son who obeys, and the Holy Spirit who gives understanding: the Father

who is above all, and the Son who is through all, and the Holy Spirit who is in all. And we cannot otherwise think of one God. For it is through this Trinity that the Father is glorified."[118] The word "Trinity" used by Hippolytus meant three distinct Persons in one Godhead. In explanation of John 10:30, he explained: "Understand that He [Jesus] did not say 'I and the Father *am one*, but *are one*. For the word "are" is not said of one person, but it refers to two persons, and one power. He has Himself made this clear, when He spake to His Father concerning the disciples, 'The glory which Thou gavest me I have given them; that they may be one, even as we are one' (John 17:22-23). Are all one body in respect of substance, or is it that we become one in power and disposition of unity of mind?"[119]

8. **Origen of Alexandria** (A.D. 185-255) proclaimed: "We worship, therefore, the Father of truth, and the Son, who is the truth; and these, while they are two, considered as persons or subsistences, are one in unity of thought in harmony and in identity of will. So, entirely are they one, that He who has seen the Son, 'who is in the brightness of God's glory, and the express image of His person,' has seen in Him who is the image of God, God Himself."[120] As to whether God was material or immaterial, Origen acknowledged that the Church in his day did not have a doctrinal stance on the physical nature

of God. While giving his opinion that God was immaterial, he humbly continued: "If there be any one, indeed, who can discover something better, and who can establish his assertions by clearer proofs from holy Scriptures, let his opinion be received in preference to mine."[121] By this time, over a century after the death of the apostles, the physical nature of God and Christ was in doubt.

9. **Dionysius of Alexandria** (A.D. 200-265), called "the Great," proclaimed: "[Christ is not of the same substance as God]..."parents are absolutely distinguished from their children by the fact alone that they themselves are not their children."[122] Speaking of heretics, Dionysius continues: "There are three hypostases [beings]...whether they like it or no, or else let them get rid of the divine Trinity altogether."[123] In other words, either there are three persons in the Godhead (as the apostles taught) or there is one person (as Jews and Muslims teach). But don't give me any nonsense about there being three separate, distinct persons, yet somehow only one being or substance.

10. **Novatian** (A.D. 210-280) wrote his "Treatise Concerning the Trinity" in A.D. 257, the year after the bishop of Rome first claimed that his authority was passed down from the Apostle Peter. He said: "Behold, the same Moses tells

us...that 'God was seen of Abraham.' And yet the same Moses hears from God that 'no man can see God and live.' If God cannot be seen, how was He seen?... It was not the Father who was seen, seeing that He never was seen; but the Son, who has both been accustomed to descend, and to be seen because He has descended. For He is the image of the invisible [to man] God. It is asserted that...if the Father and Christ be one God, Christ will be called the Father. Wherein they are proved to be in error, not knowing Christ,... For who does not acknowledge that the person of the Son is second after the Father, [who said] to the Son, 'Let us make man in our image and our likeness.'"[124]

# How Did the State Take Over the Church?

By the end of the third century A.D., Christianity was in the midst of its tenth and worst persecution at the hands of the Roman Empire; fortunately, it would be the last. During his reign, Emperor **Diocletian** conducted a ten-year campaign so destructive that Christianity was thought to be extinct forever. Monuments were raised in his honor, notably, two pillars erected in Spain, with inscriptions extolling the mighty emperor "for having extinguished the name of Christians who brought the Republic to ruin" and "for having everywhere abolished the superstition of Christ; for having extended the worship of the gods."[125]

Rome had worshipped many gods ever since it was founded in the eighth century B.C. There was a god for every aspect of life. Some were incorporated from Greek gods, i.e., Jupiter from Zeus, Venus from Aphrodite, Neptune from Poseidon, etc. When <u>Saturn</u>

died, his three sons divided the world evenly amongst themselves. Jupiter took the heavens, Neptune took the sea, and Pluto took the underworld. Their sister, Vesta, became the goddess of hearth and home.

Other gods included Juno (wife of Jupiter—goddess of women and fertility); Mars (son of Jupiter and Juno—god of war—tall and handsome but very mean); Mercury (god of travelers and tradesmen); Venus (goddess of love and beauty); Apollo (god of music, archery, healing, poetry, and truth); Diana (goddess of hunting, archery, and animals); Minerva (goddess of wisdom, learning arts, and industry); Ceres (goddess of agriculture, harvest, and seasons); Vulcan (god of blacksmiths and volcanoes, whose anger caused volcanoes to erupt); Bacchus (god of wine, civilization, and law); Hercules (half god from his father, Jupiter, and half mortal from his mother); Cupid (son of Venus who shot people with an arrow to make them fall in love); Pegasus (winged horse who could fly); Orpheus (son of Apollo who was the most famous musician in the ancient world); Pandora (the first woman made from clay by Vulcan); and Cerberus (a three-headed dog that guarded the underworld). The list goes on.

This worship of multiple gods, *each guarding his or her own territory*, is **polytheism**. In contrast to the Godhead, these gods stake no claim for creating the universe. Hence, polytheism fails all three tests of causal adequacy to explain 1) The universe's beginning, 2) Its ongoing fine-tuning, and 3) New functional genetic information.

When emperors of Rome died, they were *deified*, which made Roman leaders more powerful. However, bad emperors, like Nero and Tiberius, were not so lucky. Beginning with Augustus (63 B.C.-A.D. 14), Roman emperors also became the ***pontifex maximus*** (chief religious priest), presiding over and conducting sacrifices and other organized rituals to the gods at religious temples. "Pontifex (ponte + facere) maximus" literally means "greatest bridge builder," as between gods and humans. The emperor would later serve as a bridge builder between paganism and Christianity.

Tertullian (A.D. 145-220) applied the emperor's title of *pontifex maximus* derisively to Bishop Victor of Rome because of his ambition for superiority over other bishops.[126] Cyprian (A.D. 200-258) used a derivative of pontifex, "pontiff," in the context of the "pontiff of Christ who excelled the pontiffs of the world."[127] This heathen title was first applicable to all bishops, although later, it was formalized as an exclusive title for the bishop of Rome.

The God of Christianity represented a threat to Roman emperors until **Constantine** (A.D. 272-337) was crowned as the emperor of Rome in A.D. 306. He not only restored peace to the Christian world but also accepted Christianity for himself, though he remained an unbaptized believer (*catechumen*) until shortly before his death. Legend has it that he had a supernatural manifestation of a luminous cross in the sky with the inscription, "By this sign, conquer."[128] Whatever his motives may have been, Constantine was hailed as a deliverer when he decreed Christianity to be the religion of the state in A.D. 313. He didn't submit himself to church authority; instead, he became the head of the church as pontifex maximus, with the cross as his royal standard.

In the late fourth century A.D., the emperor's title *pontifex maximus* was modified to *pontifex inclytus* (honorable pontiff). Almost four centuries after the fall of the Roman Empire, a derivative of pontifex, "pontiff" (papa, father), was adopted by the Roman Catholic Church in A.D. 858 as the title for the bishop of Rome. "Western churches...alone submitted to it. Thus, it was never Catholic [universal], and came into existence only by nullifying the Nicene Constitutions [which declared all bishops to be equals among brethren, nothing more] and breaking away from Catholic communion with the parent churches of the east."[129]

Two centuries later (eleventh century A.D.), Pope **Gregory VII** declared that "the title Pope should be peculiar to only one in the Christian world."[130] This declaration, referencing the bishop of Rome, was grievous to Eastern churches, which "never paid any respect to this novelty and dictation," remembering the "admonition of our Saviour's words: 'Call no man your father [in an ecclesiastical context] upon the earth'" (Matthew 23:9).

Beginning with Constantine's reign, there was a great competition for church preferment. The office of bishop became more esteemed than the rank of a general. It became unpopular and decidedly disadvantageous in a material sense to be known as a non-Christian. Pagan temples were transformed into churches, and heathen idols were demolished. Constantine moved the capital of the government from Rome to Byzantium and renamed it after himself, Constantinople (present-day Istanbul, Turkey), which also became the headquarters of the state church.[131]

However, legislating Christianity was far easier than dictating its theology. Polytheism, like Judaism and Islam, emphasized *orthopraxy* (correct action or right practice), whereas Christianity emphasized *orthodoxy* (correct belief or right opinion).[132] During the period of Roman polytheism, Christians were permitted to *believe* in Christianity as long as they practiced the rites of honor to the gods of Rome. However, to Christians, understanding the true doctrine had always been of critical importance.

The post-apostolic era church was increasingly challenged internally over its core belief in the identity of God. Early Christian writers knew that there were three separate personages—one in purpose. The church's explosive growth had been among the Gentiles (non-Jews), whose culture was dominated by Greek philosophy. The language, culture, and values of the Greeks (Hellenes) significantly impacted the world. Throughout history, non-Hellenic people adopted and assimilated the values and aesthetics of the golden-age Hellenes. A fourth century B.C. Greek rhetorician, Isocrates, said: "And if a man should partake of our culture, let him be called Hellene." Hellenism was not polytheistic; it held the position that there could exist only one god. Plato wrote: "God is the absolute idea,... the first and final cause of all being, and consequently superior and anterior to being itself."[133]

By now, generations had passed from the days of apostles, special witnesses who declared the "Invisible God" through the "Visible Son." In the words of Edwin Hatch: "The ideas of men were trooping in one vast host to proclaim with a united voice that there are not many gods, but only One, one First Cause by whom all things were made,... one Supreme Being."[134] This formed the basis of the theological battle over three beings in the Godhead as dictated by the scriptures versus one being as dictated by philosophers. How did the battle end? Hatch correctly continues: "The struggle really ended as almost all great conflicts end, in a compromise... The dominant Theistic philosophy of Greece became the dominant philosophy of Christianity. It prevailed in form as well as substance."[135]

The setting for the transformation was the School of Theology at Alexandria, Egypt, the "mother of churches, the mother of saints, maintaining always the intellectual and even the ecclesiastical primacy of Christendom."[136] The "great school [church] of Alexandria had a character all its own...a most liberal view of human knowledge...[that]...reflects the Greek influences...but...in which the Gospel of Christ as the Light of the world was always made predominant... It was the special though unconscious mission of this school to prepare the way, and to shape the thought of Christendom, for the great epoch of the (nominal) conversion of the empire."[137] Tragically, this was where the nature and character of God would be re-defined for billions of people over the next two millennia!

Early in the third century A.D., Sibelius, a disciple in North Africa, strongly advocated the doctrine of "trinity in unity." He claimed that the Son and the Holy Ghost were not distinct from the Father, but merely a portion of the divine energy emanating from the Father, with which the Son was temporarily endowed; in like manner, the Holy Ghost was a part of the divine Father.[138] **Sibellianism,** or Modalism as it came to be called, was declared to be a Trinitarian heresy that exaggerated the oneness of the Father and the Son, for which Sibelius was excommunicated from the church.

However, the controversy over the Godhead continued until it reached a crisis in the early fourth century A.D. **Alexander**, bishop **of Alexandria**, and his deacon **Athanasius** taught that Jesus was co-eternal and co-equal to the Father. One of Bishop Alexander's presbyters (elders), **Arius** (A.D. 256-336), claimed that this blurred the distinction between the personages of the Father and the Son. He argued for the "supremacy of God the Father, and that the Son had a beginning as a true Firstborn." Christ's subordination to His Father, "**subordinationism**, was almost universally accepted by Christian theologians of that era, with the notable exception of Athanasius [and Alexander] of Alexandria."[139]

Christianity had just been legalized in the Roman Empire and was undergoing formalization. Arius' timing made him a primary topic of the **First Council of**

**Nicaea** (present-day Iznik, Turkey) in A.D. 325, convened by Emperor Constantine, who sought to unify the newly recognized church and remove theological divisions.[140] "Religious partisanship led some scholars to suggest that Silvester, bishop of Rome, convoked the Council of Nicaea, but modern Roman Catholic scholars honorably dismiss this idea."[141] In fact, Bishop Sylvester didn't attend the council. Only the emperor could call a general council of the church. "Even Damasus [a later bishop of Rome]...admitted that he could not call a general council on his own authority."[142] "Everybody recognized the right of an Emperor to call a [Church] council, or even to veto or quash its being called."[143]

At the council, the Greek word "homoousios" was introduced to describe Jesus as "consubstantial," "same in being" or "same in essence" with God the Father. The same term was later applied to the Holy Spirit in order to designate Him as being "same in essence" with the Father and the Son. The Nicene Creed, drafted by Athanasius, was constructed as a deliberately anti-Arian document and Arianism was used as an epithet to describe those who disagreed with their doctrine. The creed proclaimed:

> "We believe in one God, the Father almighty, Maker of heaven and earth, and of all things visible and invisible. And in one Lord Jesus Christ, the Son of God, the only-begotten, begotten of the Father before all ages. Light of Light, true God of true God, begotten not

> made, *of one essence with the Father* by whom all things were made; who for us men and for our salvation, came down from heaven, and was incarnate of the Holy Spirit and the Virgin Mary and became man. And He was crucified for us under Pontius Pilate, and suffered, and was buried. And the third day He rose again, according to the Scriptures; and ascended into heaven, and sits at the right hand of the Father; and He shall come again with glory to judge the living and the dead; whose Kingdom shall have no end. And in the Holy Spirit. But as for those who say, There was when He was not, and, before being born He was not, and that He came into existence out of nothing, or who assert that the Son of God is from a different hypostasis or substance, or is created, or is subject to alteration or change – these the Catholic Church anathematizes [denounces]."

The term homoousios (of one essence with the Father) was the most controversial term in the Nicene Creed. Most delegates at the council had considerable reservations about the term because, before Nicaea, that term was only used by Sibellians. The term was not part of the standard Christian language at the time and was "borrowed from the pagan philosophy of the day."[144] At one time, the council was ready to yield to the request of some of the bishops in using only scriptural expressions in their definitions of God. But, after several attempts, Athanasius described them nodding and winking to each other[145] as orthodox expressions gave way to imperial decree.

Constantine's domination of the Nicene Council, under the pretense of restoring peace to the empire, was particularly revealed by the fact that he was able to force the inclusion of the word "homoousios [which was] added to the creed by Constantine himself, bearing witness to the extent of his influence at the council."[146] Constantine "pressed for its inclusion." [147] "Overawed by the emperor, the bishops, with two exceptions only, signed the creed, many of them much against their inclination."[148] Emperor Constantine's role in the early church would have been described by President Ronald Reagan as the nine most terrifying words in the Latin language: "I'm from the government and I'm here to help."

Arius was a theological conservative, which was a rarity in fourth-century Alexandria. He was influenced by the writings of Origen, who, like Arius, taught that the Son was subordinate to the Father. However, some of Arius' views on the nature of the Godhead were adulterated from early church teachings. Unlike Origen, who taught the eternal nature of the Son, Arius incorrectly taught that there was a time when the Son did not exist [not understanding the Son's pre-mortal existence as a Spirit].[149] Origen, who died the year before Arius was born, admitted that the church in his day did not have a stance on the physical nature of God and incorrectly surmised that He was immaterial. These examples of doctrinal drift were the natural result of the loss of revelation and open canon after the martyrdom of the apostles.

Arius held tenaciously to the last bastion of Christianity—the three-person Godhead—until Bishop Alexander condemned him, not only as a heretic but as a heresiarch (leader of heretics), even though he had no sect or followers. The notion that a belief system called "Arianism [existed] as a coherent system, founded by a single figure and sustained by Arian's disciples, was a fantasy...based on the polemic of Nicene writers, above all Athanasius."[150]

Following the Council of Nicaea, Arius was excommunicated from the church and exiled by Constantine, who burned Arius' writings and posted the following notice:

> "In addition, if any writing composed by Arius should be found, it should be handed over to the flames, so that not only will the wickedness of his teaching be obliterated, but nothing will be left even to remind anyone of him. And I hereby make a public order, that if someone should be discovered to have hidden a writing composed by Arius, and not to have immediately brought it forward and destroyed it by fire, his penalty shall be death. As soon as he is discovered in this offense, he shall be submitted for capital punishment."

—Edict by Emperor Constantine against the Arians[151]

Although Constantine never repudiated the council or its decrees, he later became lenient toward those of the Council of Nicaea whom he had exiled, permitting them (including Arius) to return to their homes. In a twist of Alfred Hitchcock proportions, Athanasius was later exiled and Constantine's deathbed baptism was performed by *Arian* Bishop Eusebius of Nicomedia, whose signature of support for Trinitarianism at the Council of Nicaea was among those under constraint by the emperor. Constantine's son, **Constantius II**, who succeeded his father as emperor from A.D. 337-361, was an Arian sympathizer. Under his rule, Arianism reached its high point at the Third Council of Sirmium in A.D. 357, which declared the doctrines of *homoousios* (of one substance) and *homoiousios* (of similar substance) to be non-Biblical...and that the Father is greater than the Son. But it was too late.

Constantius II's successor, **Julian the Apostate** (A.D. 361-363), made an abortive attempt to restore Hellenistic paganism to the empire. Next was **Valens** (A.D. 364-378), himself an Arian, who persecuted Trinitarian Nicene bishops. However, Valens's successor, **Theodosius I** (A.D. 379-395), ended Arianism once and for all through a combination of imperial decree, persecution, and calling of the **Second Ecumenical Council** in A.D. 381 that condemned Arius anew while reaffirming and expanding the Nicene Creed.[152] This generally ended the influence of Arianism among the non-Germanic peoples of the Roman Empire. Despite concerted opposition, Arian Christian churches persisted for centuries throughout Europe (especially in various Germanic kingdoms), the Middle East, and North Africa. They were eventually suppressed by military conquest or voluntary royal conversion between the fifth and seventh centuries A.D.[153] The see-saw dominance of Trinitarian vs. Arian emperors finally ended with the triumph of Trinitarianism, which defined orthodox Christian doctrine from that time forth.

In retrospect, Sibellianism had been condemned as heresy during the early third century A.D. for defining three gods of such unity of substance as to allow no distinction between Father, Son, and Holy Ghost—"**synoousios**." A century later, following ten campaigns of Christian persecution and bloodshed, "orthodoxy" was imposed by a vote of bishops as directed by the emperor under the term "**homoousios"**—same nature and substance but with a distinction between Father, Son, and Holy Ghost. A belief that was once optional became mandated, the violation of which led to inquisition trials within the empire and crusades outside the empire.

Imagine the leader of a country (Rome) convening a council of the nation's religious leaders (bishops) to sign a document that had been drafted by one of the country's elite universities (Alexandria). The content of the document defined god according to the scriptures of one of the nation's small, despised colonies (Judah), mingled with the philosophy of another of its colonies whose former glory was in decline (Greece). The newly formed hybrid religion (Catholicism) and its new definition of god would be enforced by law upon all citizens. Former treasured beliefs (true Christianity) would be declared illegal.

Like evolution, which cares only about survival—not truth, Emperor Constantine sought the survival of his declining empire, not the survival of Christianity. His action proved to be fatal to both. The Roman Empire became extinct a century and a half later in the west while a form of it lasted for another millennium in the east as the Byzantine Empire. Christianity had been inoculated with a fatal mutation, rendering it into what Jesus would describe as a "whited sepulchre" (Matthew 23:27), a remote resemblance from the church He had established. However, clues were left behind for the discerning mind to discover the true nature of the Godhead and the relationship of the Son to the Father.

Professor Rendsburg points out that the Jewish Book of Genesis contains two creative accounts. Chapter one (up to the first 3 1/2 verses of chapter two) describes a cosmocentric (blueprint) creation under the direction of Elohim, God the Father. The remainder of chapter two describes an anthropocentric (physical) creation under the direction of Yahweh, the Lord God.[154] The professor goes on to say, "The wording of Genesis 1:26, 'Let us make a human in our image, by our likeness,' may suggest a belief in the Trinity, but this is a later Christian theological development not to be found in the Jewish Bible."[155]

The Hebrew "Yahweh" means "Jehovah" in English, the Son and visible God. During His mortality, Jesus identified Himself to the Pharisees as Jehovah. He said to them: “Before Abraham was, I am [Yahweh]” (John 8:58). Elohim (masculine plural for “Eli” or “Eloi”) is the presiding God of Gods—the Father, the invisible [to man] God. On the cross, Jesus identified His Father, Elohim, when He called out, “Eloi, Eloi [my God, my God], why hast thou forsaken me?” (Mark 15:34).

# What are History's Greatest Claims?

Returning to the five types of claims, here is a summary of the greatest from each:

- The **greatest fact claim** is that there is a god who created the universe, fine-tunes it for ongoing functionality, and adds to it new information and life. As we have seen, there is overwhelming scientific evidence for this claim, which rules out naturalism and pantheism as worldviews with scientific causal adequacy.
- The **greatest definition claim** is that God is our Heavenly Father. He is the literal Father of our spirits and we are brothers and sisters. God is a glorified person in whose image we have been created. We have inherited divine attributes from Him. Although He reigns supreme in the universe (beside Him there is no God), His infinite capacity to love makes it impossible for

Him to find fulfillment alone. Mankind is His only *fellow* in the universe. He delegates His title, God, in a subordinate way, like the sun shares its title with its rays. God's Firstborn Son in the spirit is His only begotten Son in the flesh. In the language of Adam, "Man of Holiness" is the name of God the Father (Elohim), and "Son of Man [of Holiness]" is the name of God the Son [Jesus Christ] (Moses 6:57). Prior to His mortality, Jesus Christ was known as Jehovah which helps us to understand the prayer He made to His Father: "And now, O Father, glorify thou me with thine own self with the glory which I had with thee before the world was" (John 17:5). This definition claim rules out non-Christian religions (Judaism, Islam) as worldviews consistent with the character of God as creator, fine-tuner, and revelator. The heavens continue to communicate and scriptural canon remains open.

- The **greatest cause claim** is that the same God who fine tunes the mass of the universe to within the weight of a dime, the energy of the universe to one part in 10 to the 120th power, the ratio of the strong nuclear force to the electromagnetic force within one in 400 quadrillion, etc., finds His greatest fulfillment in "fine-tuning" His children. Jesus invited us to "consider the lilies of the field, how they grow; they toil not, neither do they spin: And yet I say unto you, That even Solomon in all his glory was not arrayed like one of these. Wherefore, if God so clothe the grass of the field, which today is, and tomorrow is cast into the oven, shall he not much more clothe you, O ye of little faith?" (Matthew 6:28-30). He also taught: "If a son shall ask bread of any of you that is a father, will he give him a stone? or if he ask a fish, will he for a fish give him a serpent? Or if he shall ask an egg, will he offer him a scorpion? If ye then, being evil, know how to give good gifts unto your children: how much more shall your heavenly Father give the Holy Spirit to them that ask him?" (Luke 11:11-13). The operative phrase is "to them that ask him." Most do not, *and then there are some* who do. God, who has fine-tuning power over the universe, also has the power to hear the most intimate prayer. His love invites everyone to come unto Him. However, He compels no one.

- The **greatest value claim** is that to those who seek wisdom over riches, the mysteries of God are unfolded to them and they become rich. Eternal life is the only real wealth (Doctrine and Covenants 6:7, 11:7). Jesus illustrated this claim most effectively by His contrasting behavior toward sinners and fools. He was compassionate and forgiving to even the vilest sinners—providing they were willing to repent. However, He consistently condemned fools who were "not rich toward God" (Luke 12:21). The word "fool" comes from the Greek word "moros," from which we get our word moron. However, a fool isn't someone with diminished intellectual capacity. It is anyone who rebels against God. If we ever wonder whether or not we are acting foolishly, we just need to ask ourselves, "Is what I'm doing bringing me closer to God? Or, is it driving me away from God?"

- The **greatest policy claim** is that the church Jesus established on Earth was destroyed but later re-established when circumstances on Earth became favorable for its survival. . . when and where it would flourish in a free society, never again to be destroyed by mankind. In the Lord's Church, eternal covenants with God can be made under proper priesthood authority. Anyone can disagree with this claim. However, no one can deny that it is a claim, a unique one. Therefore, it merits careful scrutiny as the greatest policy claim since Christ's coming to Earth.

Our journey begins by "asking, seeking, and knocking" to know God's Son who was born into mortality, lived a sinless life, taught the greatest lessons ever given, loved others without bounds, took upon Himself the sins of the world, was crucified for all who have ever lived, rose from the dead after three days, possesses a body of flesh and bone today, and offers eternal life to all who are not offended by Him. His all-encompassing love is wide enough for everyone.

Historical figures can be studied, admired, and emulated. However, only Jesus Christ can really be known. The Holy Ghost, third member of the Godhead, is a personage of spirit whose influence is ubiquitous so He can dwell within us. His role is to testify of Christ and to reveal truths about Him that enable us to follow Him. Sadly, Jesus said that many would not take advantage of His invitation. To them, He will one day say, "Ye never knew me: depart from me, ye that work iniquity" (Matthew 7:22-23, Joseph Smith Translation). If Christ's Kingdom is on the Earth today, where can we find it?

Jesus never equivocated on who He was (John 8:58). He knows His flock and His flock knows its shepherd (Ezekiel 34:12). Strangely, many people today think that "all churches claim to be the true Church of Christ." Few churches actually do and even fewer provide evidence to back up their claim. And yet, how odd it is that so many people consider it presumptuous for a church to claim to be the true Church of Christ without investigating it.

No one would pay premiums to a bogus insurance company, knowing that when a claim was filed, it would be denied. Similarly, a church that cannot claim authority from Jesus Christ cannot pay claims beyond the bounds of mortality. Investments in man-made churches are worthwhile only to the extent that their humanitarian endeavors provide enormous relief and personal satisfaction in mortality. However, only authorized covenants in the Lord's Church, our "Father's business" (Luke 2:49), promise post-mortal payment of a claim. This is the only investment with an eternal promise.

# Which Post-Apostolic Claim is the Oldest?

Throughout my life, I have known many Roman and Eastern Orthodox Catholics whom I have regarded as among the most loving, Christ-like people on Earth. I have admired their philanthropy and participated in humanitarian projects in partnership with Catholic Charities, a noble extension of the Catholic Church. I have been thrilled by their music and admired the beauty of their cathedrals. It is neither my desire nor hope to ever offend the faith of anyone who adheres to Catholic precepts.

The word "catholic" (Greek "katholicos" meaning "universal") is not found anywhere in the scriptures. When Emperor Constantine endorsed Christianity to save a dying empire, he called it "the most holy catholic (universal) church."[156] Indeed, the secularization of the Church of Christ was catholic in its reach with the emperor at its helm. As centuries passed, a serious contention developed for "supreme bishop" between the bishop of Rome and the bishop of Constantinople. In A.D. 1054, both bishops excommunicated each other and the church was split into the Roman Catholic Church and the Orthodox Catholic Church (known to the English-speaking world as the Eastern or Greek Orthodox Church).

The **Roman Catholic Church** claims to be "founded by Jesus Christ in his Great Commission, that its bishops are the successors of Christ's apostles, and that the pope is the successor to Saint Peter, upon whom primacy was conferred by Jesus Christ. It maintains that it practices the original Christian faith taught by the apostles, preserving the faith infallibly through scripture and sacred tradition as authentically interpreted through the magisterium of the church."[157] The **Orthodox Catholic Church** "operates as a communion of autocephalous [self-headed] churches, each governed by its bishops, [with] no central doctrinal or governmental authority analogous to the head of the [Roman] Catholic Church (the Pope). The Ecumenical Patriarch of Constantinople is recognized as *primus inter pares*, 'first among equals.' [The Church's] theology is based on the scriptures and holy tradition, [that] it is the one, holy, catholic, and apostolic church established by Jesus Christ in his Great Commission, and that its bishops are the successors of Christ's apostles. It maintains that it practices the original Christian faith, as passed down by holy tradition."[158] Both are bold statements originating from the single **oldest claim of the post-apostolic period:**

The Catholic Church derives its authority from the Lord's chosen apostles through apostolic succession to bishops of the present day. Does evidence support this claim?

The scriptural basis claiming unbroken ordination from Peter to today's Roman Catholic Pope or from Jesus' apostles to today's Orthodox Catholic Bishops comes from a declaration that Jesus made to Peter: "...thou art Peter, and upon this rock I will build my church" (Matthew 16:18). In order to understand this statement in context, let's look at surrounding verses which begin with a question that Jesus posed to His apostles:

"Whom do men say that I the Son of man am? And they said, Some *say that thou art* John the Baptist: some, Elias; and others, Jeremias, or one of the prophets. He saith unto them, But whom say *ye* that I am? And Simon Peter answered and said, Thou art the Christ, the Son of the living God. And Jesus answered and said unto him, Blessed art thou, Simon Bar-jona: for flesh and blood hath not revealed *it* unto thee, but my Father which is in heaven. And I say also unto thee, That thou art Peter, and upon this rock I will build my church; and the gates of hell shall not prevail against it. And I will give unto thee the keys of the kingdom of heaven: and whatsoever thou shalt bind on earth shall be bound in heaven: and whatsoever thou shalt loose on earth shall be loosed in heaven" (Matthew 16:13-19).

Jesus tested His apostles by first asking them who men said He was, and secondly who they said He was.

This is a soul-stirring question that all of us might one day be called upon to answer. Jesus' disciples responded that men speculated, in recognition of His works and teachings, He was one of the former great messengers or prophets of God. Muslims would also come to say of Jesus that He was one of the prophets. Jews would regard Him as neither prophet nor messenger of God because, to them, His tenets were a divergence from Biblical Judaism.

However, Peter correctly identified Jesus as "the Christ, the Son of the living God." How did Peter know this? No person had told him. His knowledge came from his Father in heaven. How did he learn it from Him? By revelation through the Holy Ghost (Luke 2:26). How does anyone receive revelation? By doing God's will (John 7:17), keeping His commandments as well as by asking, seeking, and knocking with a burning desire to know (Matthew 7:7-8). The verse doesn't say that Jesus was pointing to Peter when He said, "Upon this rock I will build my church." Nor does Jesus say, "Upon thee, Peter, I will build my church."

The Bible uses a subtle Greek wordplay in recording, "Thou art petros (small rock) and upon this petra (bedrock) I will build my church." Peter was petros or cephas in Aramaic, meaning a small stone (John 1:42). Peter was part of "God's building" whose "foundation [was] Jesus Christ" (1 Corinthians 3:9-11). The bedrock to which Jesus referred was none other than Christ Himself, of whom Paul said, "That Rock was Christ" (1 Corinthians 10:4). To what was Jesus referring when He said, "The gates of hell shall not prevail against it?" Not Peter, not the church, but against the bedrock foundation which Paul described to the Ephesians: "And are built upon the foundation of the apostles and prophets, Jesus Christ himself being the chief corner stone" (Ephesians 2:20). The foundation was secure from the gates of hell as long as the church safeguarded the apostles and prophets, Christ's special witnesses on Earth.

**Jean de Launoy** (A.D. 1601-1678), noted French Roman Catholic historian and canonist, compiled a list of fifty-seven fathers of the church down to the twelfth century A.D. as to their understanding of the meaning of the word "rock" in the Book of Matthew. Forty of the fathers understood the rock refer to Christ, while seventeen interpreted the scripture to have reference to Peter's name but only rhetorically, not dogmatically. In fact, "Cephas is the very word applied to all believers."[159] Peter's name was a reminder of his role as a rock in the same way that a person named Joy might be encouraged to exemplify happiness. A name carries a reminder of higher expectations. The keys the Lord gave Peter, to bind or loose on Earth and in Heaven, were wholly personal, as ante-Nicene Fathers understood it. "Of the later claims which made his [Peter's] authority hereditary and belonging to Rome, early Fathers knew nothing."[160]

As for those claiming to have received apostolic authority over local churches, Tertullian called for a two-fold test:

1. "Let them produce the original records of their churches...running down in due succession

from the beginning...his ordainer and predecessor some one of the apostles or apostolic men...who continued stedfast with the apostles. For this is the manner in which the apostolic churches transmit their registers: as the church of Smyrna, which records that Polycarp was placed therein by John; as also the church of Rome, which makes Clement to have been ordained in like manner by Peter. Let the heretics contrive something of the same kind."

2. Compare their doctrine with that of the apostles, which "will declare, by its own diversity and contrariety, that it had for its author neither an apostle nor an apostolic man; because, as the apostles would never have taught things which were self-contradictory, so the apostolic men would not have inculcated teaching different from the apostles."[161]

These time-tested criteria for recognizing apostolic authority provided great protection to the early church. Differences existed with respect to eating idol sacrifices, dress, marriage and divorce, and some even about the hope of the resurrection. However, according to Tertullian, "about God no one disputed. No doubt, after the time of the apostles, the truth respecting the belief of God suffered corruption, but it is equally certain that during the life of the apostles their teaching on this great article did not suffer at all."[162]

Indeed, the apostles were united and consistent in their teaching about the nature and character of God.

The early fathers expected the apostles to continue in perpetuity. At first, successor apostles were chosen, such as Matthias (Acts 1:22-26), James (Acts 12:7, Galatians 1:19), Barnabas (Acts 14:14), and Paul (Acts 14:14; Romans 1:1; 1 Corinthians 4:9, 1 Corinthians 9:1). However, communication and travel were slow. The apostles were spread throughout the world, preaching the gospel as the Lord had commanded them to do (Matthew 28:19-20). With the exception of John the Beloved, all met violent deaths well before the end of the first century A.D.[163]

Notwithstanding the early church's protocol for recognizing new leaders from their ordination records and apostolic-aligned teachings, the third century A.D. brought a new face with a bold, unsubstantiated claim. According to Professor Thomas F.X. Noble of Notre Dame University, in the Roman Catholic Church, **Stephen I**, Bishop of Rome from A.D. 254-257, was "the first, as far as we know, to assert vigorously the Petrine Doctrine of Roman authority. He insisted that he held the 'chair of Peter' in succession to Peter. His assertion inaugurates the idea that each pope is Peter's successor."[164] Curiously, the Catholic Church's claim that the bishop of Rome is Peter's successor was first made by Bishop Stephen I of Rome in A.D. 256, almost two centuries after Peter died. Stephen's claim came as a shock to his fellow bishops.

**Firmilian** (A.D. 200-268), bishop of Caesarea, criticized Stephen, bishop of Rome, for his claim as

Peter's successor: "I am justly indignant at this so open and manifest folly of Stephen,... who so boasts of the place of his episcopate, and contends that he holds the succession from Peter." Firmilian made it clear to Stephen that he did not have power over other bishops: "For while you think that all may be excommunicated by you, you have excommunicated yourself alone from all... For what is more lowly or meek than to have disagreed with so many bishops throughout the whole world, braking peace with each of them in various kinds of discord...as to command the entire fraternity!"[165]

In A.D. 257, Bishop Stephen attempted to assert his command over the African Council of Bishops on the issue of whether or not a heretic needed to be rebaptized. **Cyprian** (A.D. 200-258), bishop of Carthage, convened a council of eighty-seven bishops to discuss "the bitter obstinacy of our brother Stephen."[166] The council condemned Stephen's assumption that there was a successor to Peter or a supreme bishop: "For neither does any of us set himself up as a bishop of bishops, nor by tyrannical terror does any compel his colleague to the necessity of obedience; since every bishop, according to the allowance of his liberty and power, has his own proper right of judgment, and can no more be judged by another than he himself can judge another."[167]

Ironically, it was Cyprian who taught that infants inherited the sin of Adam, a false concept that became adopted into the church as the **doctrine of original sin.** This prompted a widespread change in the mode of baptism from immersion to sprinkling which Cyprian was the first to authorize.[168] If Bishop Stephen I of Rome was occupying the Apostle Peter's presiding chair at the time, as he claimed, could such a monumental policy as the discontinuance of baptism by immersion have been initiated by the bishop of Carthage?

Stephen no doubt had received his confidence in part from the fact that Rome was becoming the Imperial City to which Christians resorted from all over. However, Hippolytus (A.D. 170-235), a predecessor of Stephen as bishop of Rome, maintained that "[spiritually] primitive Rome received orthodoxy instead of prescribing it. She embosomed the Catholic testimony brought into it from all the churches and gave it forth as reflected light, not primarily her own, but what she faithfully preserved in coincidence with older and more learned churches than herself. Doubtless she had been planted and watered by St. Paul and St. Peter; but doubtless, also, she had been expressly warned by the former of her liability to error and to final severance from apostolic communion. Hippolytus lived at a critical moment, when this awful admonition seemed about to be realized."[169]

Neither Hippolytus nor his mentor, Irenaeus, a second-generation disciple of the Apostle John, conceived that the bishop of Rome possessed pre-eminent authority over other bishops and rebuked Roman bishops who behaved as if they did.[170] However, the end of the Roman Empire in A.D. 476 emboldened bishops of Rome to claim wider jurisdictions and more exalted titles. **Boniface III** (A.D.

540-607) assumed the court title of "Universal Bishop" in A.D. 606 even though it was not recognized by the church.[171]

Political division during the early ninth century A. D. presented a challenge to church unity as German archbishops and kings paid no more than lip service to bishops of Rome. In the 840s, a series of church decrees were forged by a French cleric, claiming absolute power for the bishop of Rome as far back as the first century A.D. One of the false decretals included a letter from Emperor Constantine giving the bishop of Rome religious authority over all other bishops. During the centuries in which the decretals were assumed to be authentic, **Nicholas I** (A.D. 820-867) created himself the first "Pope" in A.D. 858, nullifying the Nicene Constitutions, which declared the equality of bishops. This eventually culminated in the Great East-West Schism of A.D. 1054, splitting the Roman Catholic Church in Rome from the Orthodox Catholic Church in Constantinople.

By A.D. 1440, Lorenzo Vallo exposed the frauds in the "False Decretals" of the 840s, forcing all parties to agree that the disputed documents were forgeries.[172] Notwithstanding, the **Council of Trent** (A.D. 1545-1563) confirmed the pope as the "Universal Bishop," with all other bishops reduced to presbyters, acting as his local vicars (clergy ministers). **Pope Pius IX** (A.D. 1792-1878) introduced the doctrine of Papal Infallibility when he convened the **First Vatican Council** in 1869.[173] That is, when a pope defines a doctrine with all his authority, it becomes a truth that cannot be changed. Today, the Roman Catholic Church addresses all prior bishops of Rome down to Rome's first bishop, Clement, and the Apostle Peter as "Pope." However, "Pope" was not a title known to any leader, church, or government prior to Bishop Nicholas I in A.D. 858.

Francis A. Sullivan, a Roman Catholic theologian and professor of theology at the Gregorian University in Rome, wrote a book entitled *From Apostles to Bishops* in which he noted, "A bishop is a residential pastor who presides in a stable manner over the church in a city and its environs. The apostles were missionaries and founders of churches; there is no evidence, nor is it at all likely, that any of them ever took up permanent residence in a particular church as a bishop."[174] Bishops were never considered equal to the apostles in authority and power. Ignatius (A.D. 35-107), bishop of Antioch who became a martyr, wrote in an epistle to the Romans: "I do not, as Peter and Paul, issue commandments unto you. They were apostles of Jesus Christ, but I am the very least [of believers]."[175]

Professor Sullivan went on to acknowledge that the argument asserting a direct line of succession is historically defective: "One conclusion seems obvious: Neither the New Testament nor early Christian history offers support for a notion of apostolic succession as 'an unbroken line of episcopal ordination from Christ through the apostles down through the centuries to the bishops of today.'"[176] As to what implication this has on the Catholic Church's claim, Professor Noble said that at the **Second Vatican Council** (A.D. 1962-65), "the most important event in the modern history of the Catholic Church, the Constitution [on the Church] said that the Church of Christ 'subsisted' in the Roman Catholic Church, instead of saying that the Church of Christ *was* the Roman Catholic Church."[177] The word "subsist" means "exist at a minimal level," "barely survive." Few people are aware that the Catholic Church's claim of authority from Christ is almost the equivalent of a disclaimer.

# Which Post-Apostolic Claim is the Darkest?

Imagine Agatha Christie had written a sequel to her best-selling novel entitled *And Then There Were None 2*. This time, the plot involves the whole world. You are a participant in a game of high-stakes "ultimate telephone" in which your life depends upon a message originating with the host and being passed along from person to person until it reaches you. Unfortunately, your position is near the end of the line of Earth's inhabitants. When you hear the message, you not only suspect that it has been corrupted, you are sure of it! What do you do?

In the absence of the host, you inquire of those close to the head of the line for information that might shed light on the true message, as we have done by seeking the input of Jesus' contemporaries and disciples from the early centuries. You hear claims from others down the line closer to you who think they know the correct message, but their interpretations don't resemble earlier messages. You have a written transcript (a Bible) that was copied by hand over and over through the centuries and passed along without the benefit of copiers or cameras until recently. You compare your copy with early ones and are bewildered by the changes.

This was the setting of the church in the fifteenth century. Corruption had become so deeply embedded into the church that "the issue was not for or against reform of the Church; everybody was for it. The question was how to bring it about, where to start and how far to go."[178] In A.D. 1522, **Pope Adrian VI** had the courage to confess what had been common knowledge for centuries:

"We know well that for many years things deserving of abhorrence have gathered round the Holy See [Chair]. Sacred things have been misused, ordinances transgressed, so that in everything there has been a change for the worse. Thus it is not surprising that the malady has crept down from the head to the members, from the popes to the hierarchy. We all, prelates and clergy, have gone astray from the right way... Therefore...we shall use all diligence to reform before all else the Roman Curia [general church leadership], whence perhaps all these evils have had their origin... The whole world is longing for such reform."[179]

Pope Adrian's tragic indictment of the Catholic Church and its clergy came five years after **Martin Luther** of Germany (1483-1546) nailed to the Wittenberg chapel doors in A.D. 1517 his famous ninety-five theses in reaction to the church's sale of indulgences for sins not yet committed. Luther only wanted church reform, but **Pope Leo X** issued a "Bull" or papal decree against him, demanding a retraction. Luther burned the demand and was summoned to appear before a council or "Diet" at Worms in A.D. 1521. His inspired words of allegiance to the holy scriptures from which the church had strayed culminated in his excommunication and the formation of a church bearing Luther's name, a designation which Luther deplored.

A religious controversy spread throughout Europe, and in A.D. 1529, the Second Diet of Spires was convened, issuing an edict against all reformers who became known thereafter as **Protestants.** The Protestants, however, soon became divided among themselves and broke up into many contending sects. As each attempted to make corrections, new errors were added. For example, Luther introduced the doctrine of absolute predestination and justification by faith alone, contrary to the scriptural declaration of the God-given right of moral agency (John 8:32, Matthew 7:13-14) and individual responsibility (James 2:14-20).

The revolt against Church despotism had begun centuries earlier. In the thirteenth century, the **Albigenses** in southern France were massacred by **Pope Innocent III** for believing in dualism, the coexistence of two mutually opposed principles, one good and one evil. In the fourteenth century, **John Wickliffe** (1320-1384), a professor at Oxford, England, gave the world an English version of the Bible for which he was declared a heretic. In Czechoslovakia, **John Huss** (1373-1415) was burned at the stake for advocating scripture reading and denouncing indulgences. **Ulrich Zwingli** (1484-1531) opposed Catholic practices, including celibacy and mass in Switzerland, resulting in a battle in which Zwingli was slain and his body mutilated. **John Knox** of Scotland (1514-1572) and countless others were willing to risk their lives in pursuit of the original church and doctrine that Jesus had established and entrusted to His apostles.

Atrocities against those who questioned the form of Christianity being administered were particularly grievous when practiced under imperial authority. **Queen Isabella I** (1451-1504) and her husband **King Ferdinand II** (1452-1516) were known as the **Catholic Monarchs**, a title granted to them by Pope Alexander VI. They are remembered today for financing the expedition of Christopher Columbus to America in 1492. What is largely unknown about them is that they also founded the **Spanish Inquisition** in 1478, which lasted until 1834. Under Queen Isabella, thousands were burned at the stake in order to suppress "heresy," which she, no doubt, regarded as rendering good service to God. She said: "In the love of Christ and His Maid-Mother, I have caused great misery. I have depopulated towns and districts, provinces and kingdoms."[180] If Queen Isabella had read the Bible, she would have learned from the Lord that "the time cometh, that whosoever killeth you will think that he doeth God service" (John 16:2).

**King Henry VIII** (1491-1547) received from Pope Leo X the distinguishing title of **Defender of the Faith** in opposition to Martin Luther's call for reforms. However, within a few years, Henry desired a divorce from his wife, Queen Catherine, to give him the freedom to remarry. The pope hesitated to grant the divorce, so Henry disregarded his authority and secretly married Anne Boleyn. The pope then excommunicated the king from the church, which prompted the king to direct parliament to pass the **Act of Supremacy** in 1534. This terminated all allegiance to papal authority and proclaimed the king as supreme head of the newly formed Church of England without claim of authority or priestly succession.

As the years went by, persecutions over differences in doctrine and practice between Catholics and Protestants were sometimes extensive and violent. At other times, Protestants fought among themselves. **John Calvin** of France (1509-1564) was a Trinitarian (like Luther). He was so committed to Trinitarianism that in 1553, he collaborated in the live burning of a Spanish physician, theologian, and fellow Protestant reformer Michael Servetus for rejecting the doctrine of the Trinity. Calvin founded the Presbyterian Church in Switzerland and Knox founded the Presbyterian Church in Scotland.

Churches began to proliferate. Some were named after their place of origin, as the Church of England. Others were designated in honor of their early promoters, Lutherans, Calvinists, Wesleyans, etc. Still others were named after a salient creed or doctrine,

Methodists, Presbyterians, Baptists, etc. Ironically, there was no church as of the beginning of the nineteenth century bearing the name of Jesus Christ. The only church existing at that time venturing to assert divine authority through a lineal ecclesiastical line of succession from Christ was the Catholic Church.

**John Wesley** (1703-1791), founder of the Methodist Church, described the apostasy from Christianity that occurred after the death of the apostles:

> "It does not appear that these extraordinary gifts of the Holy Ghost were common in the Church for more than two or three centuries. We seldom hear of them after that fatal period when Emperor Constantine called himself a Christian... From this time [spiritual gifts] almost totally ceased; very few instances of the kind were found. The cause of this was not (as has been vulgarly supposed), because there was no more occasion for them, because all the world was become Christians. This is a miserable mistake; not a twentieth part of it was nominally Christian. The real cause of it was the love of many, almost all Christians, so called, was 'waxed cold.' The Christians had no more the Spirit of Christ than the other Heathens. The Son of Man, when he came to examine his Church, could hardly find 'faith upon the earth.' This was the real cause why the extraordinary gifts of the Holy Ghost

were no longer to be found in the Christian Church; because the Christians were turned Heathens again, and had only a dead form left."[181]

The challenge for post-apostolic Christians was how to overhaul the Church of Christ after it had been "totaled." Would God have ever permitted this to happen? The Bible is replete with references to God withdrawing His covenant from mankind when invitations to repent went unheeded until a point of no return had been reached. A few examples include the generations after Adam, Enoch, Noah, Abraham, and Moses. The Old Testament provides its own evidence of Israel's apostasy in the words of its last entry in the fifth century B.C.: "THE END OF THE PROPHETS."

Jesus warned the chief priests and Pharisees of His day: "Did ye never read in the scriptures, The stone which the builders rejected, the same is become the head of the corner: this is the Lord's doing, and it is marvellous in our eyes? Therefore say I unto you, The Kingdom of God shall be taken from you, and given to a nation bringing forth the fruits thereof" (Matthew 21:42-3). The stone to which Jesus referred was not Peter. It was Christ Himself who was rejected by the builders (the very chief priests and Pharisees to whom Jesus was speaking), and His kingdom was taken from them and given to another more worthy nation, *as a direct result of Israel's apostasy*.

Was that "more worthy nation" Rome? Jesus answered that question Himself. He said, "Render to

Caesar the things that are Caesar's, and to God the things that are God's" (Mark 12:17). He did not say, "Render to Caesar the things that are God's," which is what the church did in the early fourth century A.D. in submitting itself to the authority of Emperor Constantine. Renown Florentine Renaissance author and father of political science **Niccolò Machiavelli** (1469-1527) addressed the question as to whether Rome qualified as a "nation bringing forth the fruits thereof" (Matthew 21:43):

> "Had the religion of Christianity been preserved according to the ordinances of the Founder, the state and commonwealth of Christendom would have been far more united and happy than they are. Nor can there be a greater proof of its decadence than the fact that the nearer people are to the Roman Church, the head of their religion, the less religious are they. And whoever examines the principles on which that religion is founded, and sees how widely different from those principles its present practice and application are, will judge that her ruin or chastisement is near at hand."[182]

As Machiavelli described, it doesn't take a prophet to observe apostasy in action. A massive worldwide reform was imminent in Machiavelli's day to return to the Church of Christ. However, as early as the third century A.D., the *Apostolic Constitutions* addressed the impossibility of such a task: "If, therefore, Christ did not glorify Himself without the Father, how dare any man thrust himself into the priesthood who has not received that dignity from his superior, and do such things which it is lawful only for the priests to do?"[183] Paul said as much to the Hebrews: "And no man taketh this honor unto himself, but he that is called of God, as was Aaron." (Hebrews 5:4).

We tend to think of obedience as not doing what we are specifically forbidden. However, Jesus took obedience to a new level by doing only what He was commanded. Following His resurrection, He appeared to His covenant people in America, who would experience a similar apostasy to the one in Jerusalem in the fourth century A.D. To them, He said: "...this is the land of your inheritance; and the Father hath given it unto you. And not at any time hath the Father given me commandment that I should tell it unto your brethren at Jerusalem" (3 Nephi 15:13-14). Jesus never took liberties to act without His Father's approval.

Given that Jesus followed His Father's commands with exactness, is it reasonable to assume that He would authorize His name and authority to be used in unbroken succession from apostles to popes and bishops without revelatory guidance? Inasmuch as Christ's Church *is* His Kingdom on Earth to which He will one day return in triumphal glory, is it conceivable that He would accept a church bearing only a "subsisting" resemblance to the church He established? The *Apostolic Constitutions* say "No": "And to be a Christian is in our own power; but to be an apostle, or a bishop, or in any other such office, is not in our power, but at the disposal of God, who bestows the gifts."[184]

**The darkest claim of the post-apostolic period** was that *no one* could claim the legitimate authority to preside over Christ's Church on Earth. Eighteenth-century Wesleyan thought was that the Bible could be trusted while claims of miracles and revelations were to be regarded with suspicion. How did this viewpoint become so prevalent?

A contemporary of Wesley, German Lutheran Church historian **Johann Lorenz von Mosheim** (1693-1755) indicated in his *Ecclesiastical History* that as early as the fourth century, a disregard for truth gained currency in the church. It became "an act of virtue to deceive and lie, when by that means the interests of the church might be promoted." Sins other than those of falsehood and deceit were justified when committed in the supposed interests of church advancement. Even crime was condoned under the specious excuse that the end justifies the means. "Many of the fables and fictitious stories relating to the lives of Christ and the apostles, as also the spurious accounts of supernatural visitations and wonderful miracles, in which the literature of the early centuries abound, are traceable to this infamous doctrine that lies are acceptable unto God if perpetuated in a cause that man calls good."[185]

The understandable but tragic suspicion over any claim of a miracle or revelation became the unacceptably high price society paid for the dishonesty of the ages. The church Jesus founded had both miracles and revelations as long as His apostles were alive. The fact that the Bible ended is powerful evidence that revelation and the Church of Christ were gone. Ironically, people assumed that their vulnerability to oral dishonesty did not apply to the written word of God. However, as early as the third century, Tertullian (A.D. 145-220) corrected such a misassumption by warning that the corruption of scriptures was already well underway:

"One man perverts the Scriptures with his hand, another their meaning by his exposition. For although **Valentinus** seems to use the entire volume, he has none the less laid violent hands on the truth only with a more cunning mind and skill than **Marcion**. Marcion expressly and openly used the knife, not the pen, since he made such an excision of the Scriptures as suited his own subject-matter. Valentinus, however, abstained from such excision, because he did not invent Scriptures to square with his own subject-matter, but adapted his matter to the Scriptures; and yet he took away more, and added more, by removing the proper meaning of every particular word, and adding fantastic arrangements of things which have no real existence."[186]

Valentinus and Marcion were two out of a sea of heretics whose forgeries passed unnoticed by many in a world where even dedicated copyists made mistakes.

Our earliest New Testament manuscripts date to the late second/ early third century A.D. The first true mechanical copier wasn't manufactured until A.D. 1780 when James Watt, inventor of the steam engine, created the copying press. Without living apostles to facilitate the Lord's fine-tuning of His Church and the faith of His covenant people, the Bible became a deistic creation, leading to thousands of subsequent interpretations. No wonder the Apostle John warned: "If any man shall add unto these things, God shall add unto him the plagues that are written in this book. And if any man shall take away from the words of the book of this prophecy, God shall take away his part out of the book of life" (Revelation 22:18-19).

The same command not to add to the word of God nor to diminish from it was given to the ancient Israelites through Moses (Deuteronomy 4:2). This command was intended for people like Valentinus and Marcion, not for God Himself, who is certainly under no restriction from revealing more! If there is one takeaway from science, it is that the God of the universe is not just a creator; He is also a fine-tuner:

*We serve no God whose work is done*
*Who rests within His firmament*
*Our God whose work has just begun*
*Toils ever more with powers unspent.*

How many ways can the Bible be interpreted? According to the Center for the Study of Global

Christianity, today's world has over two billion Christians separated into a staggering 45,000 denominations globally.[187] Slightly over half of Protestant Churches in the United States belong to an interdenominational movement called **Evangelism**, Evangelical Christianity, or Evangelical Protestantism. Evangelicals emphasize the centrality of being "born again" through a personal conversion, the authority of the Bible as God's revelation to humanity, and spreading the Christian message.[188] This noble effort to bring people to Christ using "scripture as the sole basis for faith" includes many Protestant faiths, such as Baptists, Lutherans, Presbyterians, Pentecostals, Methodists, and others.

Evangelical Protestantism is my paternal background. My great-great-grandfather, Alvin Clark, and his brother, John Jay Clark, were ministers who founded the first Baptist Church in the state of Washington in 1860 at Brush Prairie. Their father, as well as their grandfather and four brothers, were also Baptist ministers. Curiously, my grandfather Clark was reared a Campbellite while grandmother Clark, whose mother and grandmother were Quakers, converted to the Baptist faith. The children were reared as Baptists, although one daughter, my aunt Quest, converted to Presbyterianism. When my father brought home his Latter-day Saint bride to meet the family, his mother commented, "At least she is a Christian."

Such were the values of my family—united in Christianity but divided on how to practice it. Gratefully, my ancestors were tolerant of opposing viewpoints.

Embracing a new variation of faith was not considered abandoning the family. Traditions were breakable except for one—THE BOOK. The Bible was the gold standard from which time-tested principles had come to define civilization. People of the ages were blessed as long as they followed Biblical principles, even when they didn't realize that their lives were patterned after principles of Biblical origin.

During Queen Victoria's sixty-four-year reign in the nineteenth century, the British empire grew to over a fourth of the entire globe. Britain also became the world leader in science, trade, colonization, commerce, and culture. She ruled the waves and the Sun never set on the British Empire. It is small wonder that her nation came to be called Great Britain. When Queen Victoria was asked to explain her unparalleled success, she would always place her hand upon the Bible and say, "Britain is the land of the book."[189] In other words, her people as a whole honored the teachings of the Bible to which she attributed her country's greatness and prosperity.

But conditions changed and the nation released its hold on important Christian ideals. As Great Britain declined as the land of the book, she also declined in her influence, culture, prosperity, and power. Providence passed the Bible over to America. There is powerful evidence that God superintended the discovery of America and raised up its Founding Fathers to establish a great nation to be the citadel of liberty and to serve as the world's chief advocate of Christianity. Indeed, America's Founding Fathers were inspired to establish a "nation bringing forth fruits thereof" (Matthew 21:42-43) worthy of hosting the return of the covenant people.

**Thomas Jefferson**, Founding Father, third president of the United States, and primary author of the Declaration of Independence, recognized the disparity between the churches of his day and Christian doctrine, which he believed would one day be restored if freedom of religion were allowed to flourish. He wrote:

"I hold the precepts of Jesus, as delivered by himself, to be the most pure, benevolent, and sublime which have ever been preached to man. I adhere to the principles of the first age; and consider all subsequent innovations as corruptions of this religion, having no foundation in what came from him... If the freedom of religion, guaranteed to us by law in theory, can ever rise in practice under the overbearing inquisition of public opinion, truth will prevail over fanaticism, and the genuine doctrines of Jesus, so long perverted by his pseudo-priests, will again be restored to their original purity. This reformation will advance with the other improvements of the human mind, but too late for me to witness it."[190]

True to his prediction, Jefferson (along with John Adams) died on Independence Day in 1826, just four years shy of the restoration of the original Christian doctrine for which he longed. Thanks to Jefferson and his loyal contemporaries, the foundation of a free government produced an environment that, unlike Rome, provided fertile soil where the Church of Christ could survive.

# Which Post-Apostolic Claim is the Boldest?

In the 1963 movie *Charade*, Cary Grant enlists Audrey Hepburn's help in recovering a quarter of a million dollars in stolen money. He and others try to convince her that she has the money somewhere in her possession even though she doesn't know it and that it is imperative for her own safety to turn it over to them. Confused by everyone's dishonesty, she asks Grant, "Why do people have to tell lies?" His answer to her is straightforward: "Usually it's because they want something. They're afraid the truth won't get it for them."

Hepburn trusts Grant until she discovers he has also been deceiving her with assumed names and false identities. At a critical moment when she is running away from him, Grant warns her to stop and that she is running toward her real assailant. Bewildered, Hepburn stops and exclaims, "Oh, I don't know who anybody is!" Grant pleads to her, "I beg you... Just trust me once more!" Wanting to believe him in spite of his lies, she cries, "Why should I?" Exasperated, he responds, "I can't think of a reason in the world why you should!" Sensing his sincerity and concern for her, she begins to move toward him, forcing her assailant to reveal himself, and Grant saves her life.

This thrilling scene illustrates how frustrating it can be to distinguish truth in a crisis, particularly when the environment is dishonest. If a person's true motive can be discerned, the objective can usually be determined. In the absence of knowing the motive, sensing one's sincerity might be all there is to go on. This is what saved Audrey Hepburn's character in *Charade*, as well as Phillip and Vera in *And Then There Were None*.

For earnest seekers after Christ's true spokespersons, early nineteenth-century America was such an environment of confusion. The **Second Great Awakening** of Protestant revivalism swept the country, beginning in Kentucky and Tennessee with the Presbyterians, Methodists, and Baptists. The Methodist Church used circuit riders to reach out to people in frontier locations. At one of these meetings in western New York, the Reverend George Lane (1784-1859) of the Methodist Church preached a sermon entitled, "Which Church Should I Join?" In it, he quoted James 1:5: "If any of you lack wisdom, let him ask of God, that giveth to all men liberally, and upbraideth not; and it shall be given him." He encouraged his audience to ask of God as the scripture directs.

William Smith (1811-1893), a nine-year-old boy at the time, said that he, along with his whole family, attended that meeting and heard Reverend Lane's sermon.[191] Some of the family had been proselyted to Presbyterianism, while William's fourteen-year-old brother **Joseph Smith Jr.** (1805-1844) was partial to Reverend Lane's Methodist faith. However, the strife among churches, each trying to prove with reason and sophistry the errors of others, made it, in Joseph's words: "impossible for a person young as I was...to come to any certain conclusion who was right and who was wrong... In the midst of this war of words and tumult of opinions, I often said to myself: What is to be done? Who of all these parties are right; or, are they all wrong together? If any one of them be right, which is it, and how shall I know it?" (Joseph Smith—History 1:8, 10).

In his history, Joseph makes no mention of Reverend Lane's sermon. He simply describes his response to the verse from the Epistle of James:

> "Never did any passage of scripture come with more power to the heart of man than this did at this time to mine. It seemed to enter with great force into every feeling of my heart. I reflected on it again and again, knowing that if any person needed wisdom from God, I did; for how to act I did not know, and unless I could get more wisdom than I then had, I would never know; for the teachers of religion of the different sects understood the same passages

> of scripture so differently as to destroy all confidence in settling the question by an appeal to the Bible. At length I came to the conclusion that I must either remain in darkness and confusion, or else I must do as James directs, that is, ask of God. I at length came to the determination to 'ask of God,' concluding that if he gave wisdom to them that lacked wisdom, and would give liberally, and not upbraid [chastise], I might venture. So, in accordance with this, my determination to ask of God, I retired to the woods to make the attempt. It was on the morning of a beautiful, clear day, early in the spring of eighteen hundred and twenty. It was the first time in my life that I had made such an attempt, for amidst all my anxieties I had never as yet made the attempt to pray vocally" (Joseph Smith—History 1:12-14).)

In a grove near his home in Palmyra, New York, young Joseph offered his first prayer. As he began to offer up the desires of his heart to God, he was overcome by an overwhelming power of darkness that bound his tongue and seized him with such power as to cause Joseph to feel he had been abandoned to destruction. Exerting all his power to call upon God for delivery from this being from the unseen world with such power he had never before felt. Just at this moment of great alarm, Joseph states:

"I saw a pillar of light exactly over my head, above the brightness of the sun, which descended gradually until it fell upon me. It no sooner appeared than I found myself delivered from the enemy which held me bound. When the light rested upon me I saw two Personages, whose brightness and glory defy all description, standing above me in the air. One of them spake unto me, calling me by name and said, pointing to the other—*This is My Beloved Son. Hear Him!* My object in going to inquire of the Lord was to know which of all the sects was right, that I might know which to join. No sooner, therefore, did I get possession of myself, so as to be able to speak, than I asked the Personages who stood above me in the light, which of all the sects was right (for at this time it had never entered into my heart that all were wrong)—and which I should join. I was answered that I must join none of them, for they were all wrong; and the Personage who addressed me said that all their creeds were an abomination in his sight; that those professors were all corrupt; that: 'they draw near to me with their lips, but their hearts are far from me, they teach for doctrines the commandments of men, having a form of godliness [Isaiah 29:13], but they deny the power thereof' [2 Timothy 3:5]. He again forbade me to join with any of them; and many

> other things did he say unto me, . . ." (Joseph Smith—History 1:16-20).

On that brilliant spring morning in 1820, Joseph Smith learned what Christianity had once known but lost: the Father and the Son are two separate personages. Joseph said that God the Father introduced His Son, Jesus Christ, the personage who addressed Joseph. Had Joseph said that the Father was the one who instructed Joseph, we would have known that Joseph was not telling the truth.[192] But he did not. He said the Son did the talking, which is consistent with holy writ. Ever since the Fall of Adam, the Father has spoken to man only to introduce and bear witness of His Son, the mediator between God and man (Matthew 3:17, Mark 9:7, 3 Nephi 11:7).

A few days later, Joseph was in the company of a Methodist preacher to whom he took occasion to give an account of his vision. Joseph expressed surprise at the reaction he saw in the Reverend: "...he treated my communication not only lightly, but with great contempt, saying it was all of the devil, that there were no such things as visions or revelations in these days; that all such things had ceased with the apostles, and that there would never be any more of them" (Joseph Smith—History 1:21).

Why do you suppose that Joseph's communication wasn't just treated lightly or dismissed altogether? It would have been logical for him to have wanted to share his intimate experience with someone who had encouraged him to ask God in the first place. Joseph does not identify the reverend by name. It wasn't in Joseph's nature to rail on others and, in fact, he readily forgave those who injured him. Joseph's brother, William, and his scribe, Oliver Cowdery were the ones who identified the reverend, George Lane, whom Joseph told about his vision.[193] It would have made sense in young Joseph's mind to think that Reverend Lane would have welcomed feedback on his own sermon.

Unexpectedly, "the seemingly good feelings of both the priests and the converts were more pretended than real; for a scene of great confusion and bad feeling ensued—priest contending against priest, and convert against convert; so that all their good feelings one for another, if they ever had any, were entirely lost in a strife of words and a contest about opinions" (Joseph Smith—History 1:6). The belief that "there were no such things as visions or revelations in [those] days...that all such things had ceased with the apostles" was the prevailing attitude during the Second Great Awakening two hundred years ago. It was the natural result of distrust that had accumulated over the centuries and has persisted to this day.

And so, we see the terrible price of dishonesty. It was responsible for the great apostasy of the church Jesus established in Jerusalem during His mortal ministry. It contributed to a simultaneous apostasy of His church on the American continent. It was a cause of failure for the people in Joseph Smith's day to recognize the voice of truth. And today it keeps many honorable people from taking a closer look at the

Lord's Church. Sir Winston Churchill quipped: "Men occasionally stumble over the truth, but most of them pick themselves up and hurry off as if nothing ever happened." And yet, truth is the most priceless commodity in the universe. Notwithstanding, all scientific evidence points to a god who creates and fine-tunes, not to one who creates and walks away. Joseph learned that God does answer prayers, offered in faith, to those seeking to make sense of His nature and character.

Following the visit of the Father and the Son to Joseph, heavenly messengers were sent to assist Joseph in re-establishing God's covenant church upon Earth on April 6, 1830—never to be destroyed again by government takeover or apostolic martyrdom. Some of the messengers of the great restorative period of the nineteenth century who came in preparation for the Lord's Second Coming include the following:

- Several visits from **Moroni**, an American prophet of pre-Columbian times who delivered to the world the Book of Mormon, another witness of Jesus Christ (Joseph Smith—History 1:30-60).
- The Aaronic Priesthood—from **John the Baptist** (Doctrine and Covenants 13).
- The Melchizedek Priesthood—from **Peter, James and John** (Doctrine and Covenants 27:12).

- The keys of the gathering of Israel from the four corners of the earth—from **Moses** (Doctrine and Covenants 110:11).
- The dispensation of the gospel of Abraham, blessing all of our future generations—from **Elias** (Doctrine and Covenants 110:12). This event was prophesied by the Lord during His mortal ministry (Matthew 17:11).
- The keys of sealing families together eternally...turning the hearts of the fathers to the children and the children to the fathers—from **Elijah** (Doctrine and Covenants 110:13-16). This event was prophesied by the Lord during His mortal ministry (Matthew 17:11) and also by Malachi, the last prophet of the Old Testament (Malachi 4:5-6). Elijah's appearance at the temple in Kirkland, Ohio, in 1836 gave birth to the great family history research that has flourished ever since.

These events led to **the boldest claim of the post-apostolic period:** 1) Jesus established His Church on Earth during His mortality, 2) Men destroyed it, and 3) Jesus re-established it on Earth. Its name is **the Church of Jesus Christ of Latter-day Saints** (Doctrine and Covenants 1:30, 115:4). One can argue that the claim is false. However, no one can argue that the claim does not exist. Moreover, criticizing the claim leaves one with the enormous task of trying to give an alternative explanation for countless Biblical references and fulfillment of prophecies.

Claims exist to address missing facts. The process of researching facts to evaluate claims is our responsibility. It is what makes faith so necessary to lead us to truth and growth. Everyone needs to be aware of significant claims, particularly this one, in order to respond appropriately for his or her own personal benefit. Through Joseph Smith Jr., three great volumes of scripture (Book of Mormon, Doctrine and Covenants, Pearl of Great Price) have been added to the Bible to clarify the gospel in its simplicity as Jesus Himself described:

> "Behold I have given unto you my gospel, and this is the gospel which I have given unto you—that I came into the world to do the will of my Father, because my Father sent me. And my Father sent me that I might be lifted up upon the cross; and after that I had been lifted up upon the cross, that I might draw all men unto me, that as I have been lifted up by men even so should men be lifted up by the Father, to stand before me, to be judged of their works, whether they be good or whether they be evil" (3 Nephi 27:13-14).

These words of Jesus are consistent with His personality as well as His perfect alignment with the will of His Father. Jesus goes on to define the principles and ordinances of His gospel as follows:

> "And no unclean thing can enter into his [God's] kingdom; therefore nothing entereth into his rest save it be those who have washed their garments in my blood, because of their **faith**, and the repentance of all their sins, and their faithfulness unto the end. Now this is the commandment: **Repent**, all ye ends of the earth, and come unto me and **be baptized** in my name, that ye may be sanctified by the **reception of the Holy Ghost**, that ye may stand spotless before me at the last day. . . And whoso taketh upon him my name, and **endureth to the end**, the same shall be saved at the last day" (3 Nephi 27: 6, 19-20).

This is the **doctrine of Christ,** which is also taught in the Bible. It consists of: 1) Faith in Jesus Christ and His Atonement, 2) Repentance, 3) Baptism by someone who holds the priesthood authority of God, 4) Receiving the gift of the Holy Ghost, and 5) Enduring to the end. "This is the doctrine of Christ and the only and true doctrine of the Father, and the Son, and the Holy Ghost which is one god [in purpose] without end" (2 Nephi 31:21). When scriptures refer to the doctrine of God or the doctrine of Christ, the word "doctrine" is used in its singular form. In contrast, when scripture uses the word in Its plural form—"doctrines"—it has a negative connotation, such as "doctrines of men," the "doctrines of devils," or "divers and strange doctrines"

(Colossians 2:22, 1 Timothy 4:1, Doctrine and Covenants 46:7, Hebrews 13:9).[194]

Because of the singular nature of the doctrine of Christ, one might be prone to "looking beyond the mark" (Jacob 4:14). Instead of accepting Ockham's razor of gospel simplicity, some seek to encumber themselves with the complex doctrines of Satan, the author of confusion. I have never known anyone who quit gospel covenants because of the doctrine of Christ. There was always a stumbling block along the way.

# What is a Major Stumbling Block in Coming to Christ?

In the 1951 movie *The Great Caruso*, famed tenor Enrico Caruso (played by my favorite singer Mario Lanza) arrives late for his first rehearsal at Covent Garden in London. This infuriates his leading lady, Maria Selka, who insults his English, his clothes, and his manners. Caruso storms off the stage and the opening of *Rigoletto* is in jeopardy. Hutchins, the stage manager, speaks to Caruso and his associates off-stage to persuade him to return. The following dialogue ensues:

Caruso: "I do not sing with Maria Selka!"

Hutchins: "I don't blame you. I spent my life being insulted by prima donnas. I wonder how I stand it...or why? ... She behaves badly but she sings beautifully."

Caruso: "She makes me so mad I cannot sing!"

Hutchins: "You're not mad at me, are you, Signor Caruso?"

Caruso: "Not at you, signor."

Hutchins: "And you're not mad at the music. So, why make her too important? She'd be delighted if she drove you out. After the performance you have my permission to kill her!" (Everyone laughs in relief at the thought of having Maria Selka behind them).

Caruso: "For you and for the music I go back!"

Caruso performs beautifully and his fame spreads from Europe to America, where his performances establish him as the world's first renowned lyric tenor.

Had Caruso allowed his pride to cause him to walk off the London stage because of a soprano's behavior, you and I might have never connected the name "Caruso" with one of the greatest tenors of all time. His feelings were hurt, a condition everyone experiences in life. When running into opposition, it is important to identify all possible alternative reactions so that the worst of them, *resentment* ("re"= again + "sentire" = to feel), can be avoided. In resentment, we "feel again" a single hurt over and over. It's bad enough to be injured once. But when we carry resentment, we compound the injury a thousand times. We "gather evidence" to justify our hurt and magnify every little thing to support our injured pride.

The dictionary defines resentment as "ill will," which is a very good description, inasmuch as our will gets ill. Just one soreness can be allowed to go deep enough to condition all of our future responses. And the injury doesn't have to be in the past. Real snakes are not nearly as dangerous as imaginary ones. **Resentment is a major stumbling block in coming to Christ.** The important thing to remember is not to chase and try to kill snakes that bite us but to get the poison out of our system.

If allowed to grow, resentment can overpower the finest logic, ruin our judgment, and destroy our success. It can become especially devastating in our path toward God. We become upset when a church leader tries to give us constructive criticism. We quit church because we don't like what a leader does. We poison ourselves because we feel someone was given preferential treatment over us. We even withdraw ourselves because we don't like someone else who attends church. The list goes on.

If someone were to throw sand in your eyes, you wouldn't repeat throwing sand in your own eyes to compound the problem. And yet, that is precisely how we sabotage ourselves by voluntarily subjecting ourselves to re-feeling our injuries. Brigham Young said: "He who takes offense when offense was not intended is a fool, yet he who takes offense when offense is intended is an even greater fool for he has succumbed to the will of his adversary."

Jesus said, "Blessed is *he,* whosoever shall not be offended in me" (Matthew 11:6, Luke 7:23). He also said, "Inasmuch as ye have done *it* unto one of the least of these my brethren, ye have done *it* unto me" (Matthew 25:40). In other words: "Blessed is *he,* whosoever shall not be offended, period." What a hard lesson that is to learn!

On the evening of Wednesday, July 6, 2022, actor James Caan passed away at the age of 82. Upon hearing the news, I thought of his Oscar-nominating role as Sonny Corleone in *The Godfather*. As the oldest son, he was being groomed to take over the family business. However, he had an emotional "Achilles Heel." The moment he received a call that his sister's husband had given her a beating, Sonny became enraged and headed out in his car to his sister's house to get even with his brother-in-law. At the tollbooths, his enemies who had set him up were waiting for him and filled him with bullet holes. Sonny's temper not only cost him his position in the family business...but cost him his life as well.

Earlier on the afternoon of the same day as Caan's death, I had had my own "Sonny experience." At a social gathering, a comment was made, which I perceived to be a calculated jab at my religious beliefs. Like Sonny in the movie, I fell for the trap and responded unadvisedly. The subject was an abductive criticism against the Book of Mormon, which needed no defense, but I responded anyway. It was my own reaction that filled me with emotional bullet holes that I later came to regret. At age 75, I had had sufficient experience to recognize when facts supporting faith were unwelcome.

Double coincidentally, that very morning, before this incident and Caan's death, I had read about Moses' "Sonny experience" when he was taunted by the children of Israel over thirst: "Because they provoked his spirit, so that he spake unadvisedly with his lips" (Psalm 106:33). Weary over the children of Israel's complaints of thirst, Moses cried out to them,

"Hear now, ye rebels; must we fetch you water out of this rock?" (Numbers 20:10). Moses' weariness had overcome his patience to the point of taking credit to himself, instead of giving it to the Lord, for striking the rock that provided water for the Israelites. I experienced three variations of lessons on resentment in one day!

Resentment is one of the most self-destructive mysteries in the world. It reflects how little we know about ourselves and our purpose on Earth. Agatha Christie's island guests judged everything around them, from the comfort of their accommodations to the quality of their dinner, until they heard their host's after-dinner message. When they realized that they were the ones on trial, their perspective changed completely along with their behavior. This is a plot that is analogous to life.

The word ***test*** is not found in the scriptures. Rather, ***prove, examine,*** and ***try*** are used to describe the role that tests have in our lives. If you haven't been tested for a while, be patient. When it comes, it won't seem fair to you. If it had seemed fair, it wouldn't have been a test. Each of us has trials uniquely tailored to our individual mortal curriculum. If trials seem random to you, remember that the same God who fine-tunes the universe, fine-tunes each of us. Jesus' trials were uniquely tailored for a curriculum of one person only—Himself! In the words of the Apostle Peter, "Beloved, think it not strange concerning the fiery trial which is to try you, as though some strange thing happened unto you" (1 Peter 4:12). The important thing to never forget is that life is a test.

One of the great art treasures of the world, da Vinci's "Mona Lisa," is displayed in the Louvre in Paris. Because of its great value, it is constantly protected by an armed guard. It is reported that on one occasion, some tourists made their way through the gallery. As they stopped before this famous painting that they had heard so much about, one of them was heard saying, "I don't see anything very exciting about that." The guard stepped up to him and said, "But don't you wish you could?"[195] Many of us are like that tourist. We go through life, missing the greatest experiences, sights, and ideas. By resisting spiritual nudges, we train ourselves so that we can't respond to anything but evil. The picture in the Louvre was not placed there to be judged by tourists; it is the spectator who is on trial.

Thomas Jefferson once pointed out that while life is trying to educate us, it is also sorting us. Jesus expressed this idea in parables: the goats being separated from the sheep and the tares from the wheat so that the tares could be tied in bundles and burned. Elder Sterling W. Sill related this principle to his experience in sorting apples. Apples were graded according to their size, color, and freedom from defects. Sorters would put the Grade-A apples into one box. Grade-B apples would go into a second box. And the culls would be put into a third box. If an apple was smaller than a certain size or if it lacked color, it was considered to be Grade-B. Wormy apples and those with other defects that made them unfit for commercial use were carried away and fed to the pigs. Of course, the Grade-As fetched the highest price and were the most pleasant to work with. It was pretty hard to get buyers interested in less-developed apples, and no one wanted the culls at any price.[196]

The similarities between growing apples and living life are striking. To get the best results, a certain amount of cultivating, fertilizing, irrigating, and spraying must be done. And through the growing operations, one must always keep his mind on the harvest and the substantial premium paid for every Grade-A product. There is never a great demand for cull apples, scrubby potatoes, runt pigs, diseased beef, knotty lumber, or inferior human beings. No intelligent farmer would put his cull onions, rotten apples, wormy gooseberries, and knotty potatoes in the same package with those that are Grade-A. At a state fair, all of the choicest fruits are beautifully displayed. Culls are conspicuous by their absence. We know what happens when even one rotten apple gets into a Grade-A barrel.

Just as one integrated carrier of a contagious disease can cause an epidemic, so can the integration of evil destroy us individually and collectively. Sometimes, a tree is shaken in order to improve its health. Wormy apples have the weakest hold upon the tree. They are the most likely to fall when the tree is shaken to conserve the tree's strength in order to mature the Grade-A apples. This also prevents contamination of a barrel of Grade-A apples from a rotten apple.

Like a postal clerk who sorts mail according to its destination, we sort ourselves. Reaching out to others to cultivate their faith and strengthen them facilitates the sorting process. When a storm comes, the first structures to get blown away are those that aren't firm. Similarly, those with weak faith are the first to get blown away in a crisis. That's why we sometimes shake each other to rid ourselves of rotten attitudes and a wormy commitment. The Lord described this process through the Apostle Paul: "Yet once more I shake not the earth only, but also heaven . . . that those things which cannot be shaken may remain" (Hebrews 12:26-27).

After sorting ourselves in mortality, we are sorted in the spirit world, and at the judgment, we are sorted further, not like apples (according to our size, color, or freedom from defects) but according to our *desire, perseverance, and meekness*. When we rid ourselves of resentment, we have taken the first step toward turning our stumbling blocks into stepping stones.

# What Personal Attributes are Required in Coming to Christ?

What is it that enables some people to draw so much information from a piece of evidence that eludes others completely? When I was a medical student rotating through the pediatric service in El Paso, I can remember getting ready for rounds one morning when a pipe-smoking pediatrician walked into the newborn nursery, greeted all of us, and said, "I smell Shigella! Which baby has Shigellosis?" Dumbfounded, we looked at each other for a few seconds. Then, one of the residents said, "It's this baby over here." The pediatrician had made a claim that sounded absurd to all of us...except for the one who knew the facts.

Similarly, some detectives are able to recognize a dozen or more clues at a crime scene before others begin to sort through the mess. Although crime scenes rarely reveal the identity of their criminals, at least initially, claims begin to cry out immediately to astute observers who can distinguish claims that are facts from those that are traps.

In coming to Christ, one needs to avoid the missed opportunities of those who lived with Him, saw Him pass along the street, heard Him speak, and knew of His miracles. Lacking sufficient investigation, they pronounced sentence upon themselves by rejecting their Redeemer. Three essential attributes can enable us to avoid pitfalls and take advantage of the claims of Christianity: **1) Desire, 2) Perseverance, and 3) Meekness.**

## Desire

A fundamental law of life states that an inch of brain with a foot of desire is a far greater asset than a foot of brain with an inch of desire. The most valuable ingredient for success in the most important arena of life isn't talent. It's what Jesus taught in His fourth beatitude: "Blessed are they which do hunger and thirst after righteousness: for they shall be filled" (Matthew 5:6).

A young man once said to Mozart, "Will you teach me how to write symphonies?" Mozart said, "You are too young to write symphonies." The young man said, "But you were fifteen years younger than me when you began writing symphonies." Mozart replied, "But I didn't have to ask anyone to teach me."[197] Mozart's hunger for symphonies put symphonies in his soul.

When Michelangelo was placed before a piece of marble, he could see a beautiful image within it. This drove him to hew away the rough walls that imprisoned the figure so he could free the beautiful statue for everyone to see. Michelangelo thought of God as the first sculptor, having molded man out of the dust of the earth. This thought led him to a hunger for sculpturing, which was stronger than his hunger for food or sleep. Wanting to be the best sculptor he could be, Michelangelo was prepared to pay a higher price for success than anyone had ever paid before. When he was asked if such long hours and furious effort exhausted him, Michelangelo responded, "Cutting stone doesn't take strength out of me, it puts strength into me." His chief source of strength came from his great hunger for carving. Upon seeing how vigorously he was driving himself, someone pointed out that his furious ambition would cost him his life. Michelangelo said, "What else is life for?" He not only lived until he was eighty-nine years old, but he filled each of those years with interest, uplifting himself and others.[198]

Nineteen-year-old Joan of Arc chose to be burned at the stake rather than deny the divinity of her mission. She said, "I know this now—every man gives his life for what he believes; every woman gives her life for what she believes... One life is all we have, and we live it as we believe in living it and then it's gone. But to surrender what you are, and live without belief, is more terrible than dying, even more terrible than dying young."[199]

Today, people tend to live on one of three levels of performance. The first level is the "must" level. That is the lowest. Above the "must" level is the "ought" level. But, the highest level of performance is the "want" level. This is the level at which we stop measuring out teaspoonfuls of desire to avoid the risk of an overpayment.

A physician judges physical health by appetite. The same principle applies to spiritual health, which is invariably lost if the appetite for it is lost. Desire must be a relentless battle to be waged by those wanting to become true Christian soldiers instead of weekend warriors. It is the father of initiative, resourcefulness, ambition, and all other virtues.

## Perseverance

In Jesus' day, Jews were subjected to a military regulation, giving a Roman soldier the right to command a civilian to carry his burden for one mile. This was very unpleasant for those who hated their Roman masters. It must have been a double shock for them to hear Jesus say, "Whosoever shall compel thee to go a mile, go with him twain" (Matthew 5:41). To accompany a Roman soldier was a defiling business. To carry his burdens for any distance was disagreeable, but to voluntarily go even beyond the demands of Imperial Rome was unthinkable. Try to imagine how you'd feel if you were forced to carry the burdens of an oppressive foreign conqueror. It could not have been easy for the Jews.

In 1908, Harry Emerson Fosdick wrote a book entitled *The Second Mile,* in which he asserts that the best way to solve our problems and confidently face the things we hate and dread in life is to cheerfully do more than is required of us. In the story of Ben Hur, a fictional contemporary of Jesus, the protagonist became a Roman slave who was consigned to work the oars of a Roman galley. His companions accepted their assignments with bitterness and hate. While their backs were being lashed by their Roman masters, Ben Hur adopted the philosophy of the second mile. He rowed as if he were on a pleasure cruise on the way to some worthwhile objective. He worked twice as hard as he was required to work, asking nothing in return except that he be permitted to work on both sides of the galley so his muscles could develop symmetrically. Then came a shipwreck, and Ben Hur earned his freedom by rescuing a Roman Tribune.[200]

History is filled with examples of those who were able to overcome the hate and drudgery of life by living the spirit of the second mile. Marie Curie lived in an attic and worked tirelessly in a cold, leaky shed to discover radium. With tremendous patience, she did the work of four scientists. After the 487$^{th}$ failed experiment, her husband Pierre threw up his hands in despair and said, "It will never be done. Maybe in a hundred years but never in our day." Marie confronted him with a resolute face and said, "If it takes a hundred years it will be a pity, but I will not cease to work for it as long as I live."[201] And, of course, she was successful.

The teachings of the Master only make sense in the second mile. Think of these admonitions: forgive seventy times seven, turn the left cheek to those who smite you on the right cheek, give your cloak to those who sue you for your coat, and go two miles for those who ask you to go one mile. If we only perform our duties, we're no better than slaves. It is when we reach the second mile that we become liberated from mediocrity and abound in life's privileges. Often, we are only vaguely aware of the value at the time of our ministering. When Jesus was carrying His cross toward Golgotha near the point of total exhaustion, He stumbled and fell under His heavy burden. From this fall, He seemed unable to rise. Roman soldiers turned to a little group of interested onlookers, looking for a strong man to carry the cross for Jesus.

Among the crowd was a Jew from Cyrene, a settlement in the North African province of Libya, by the name of Simon. He had probably come to Jerusalem for the Passover, and on this Friday morning, as he was going into the city, he met this strange procession. Probably piqued by his own curiosity, Simon was drawn to the site of Jesus' struggle. The Roman officer in charge, impatient to get his job done, selected Simon from the crowd. Each of the three Bible accounts mentions the fact that Simon was compelled to carry the cross. In planning this journey, Simon had probably wondered what interesting events would be encountered along the way. Many of our blessings come unexpected and in disguise, and it was Simon's unexpected privilege to walk by the side of the Savior of the world and carry the cross on which the atoning sacrifice would be made for everyone.

There are many people who live in history because their lives touched that of Jesus of Nazareth. One woman is remembered because she gave him a drink of water. One because she prepared a dinner in His honor. One poured oil on his feet. Another woman is remembered because she asked forgiveness at His hands. One man doubted Jesus, one denied him, and one betrayed him. Another man sentenced Jesus to death and another loaned him his sepulcher. By the merest of circumstances, all these people are known to us because they crossed Jesus' path, often unexpectedly. It was Simon's good fortune to be forced into what would forever be the most outstanding experience of his life. As the passing of time enhanced the crucifixion's importance, Simon must have felt unusual gratitude for his significant role in the central scene in the history of the world. But he held the focus of history's stage only briefly while his strong, vigorous body carried the heavy cross of Christ to the top of Calvary. The moment he laid down the cross, he disappeared from sight, never to be heard of again.

Years later, we learn that two of his sons, Alexander and Rufus, were staunch, loyal followers of the Lord. The Apostle Paul refers to them as "chosen in the Lord" (Romans 16:13). Even if Simon had been upset at the time of his enforced service, he undoubtedly would have talked about the experience for the rest of his life. It would have been only natural for him to make an effort to learn something about the man whose cross he had carried. Then, as the world began to buzz with the fame of Jesus and it became known that He had risen from the dead, Simon's interest must have greatly increased in Jesus and His mission.[202]

Sometimes, our chance opportunities and experiences turn out to be of tremendous importance. We may wish to have realized their real significance at the time they were happening. Any reluctance Simon might have had in carrying the Savior's cross certainly would have vanished as he learned whose cross he was carrying. The good record of Simon's sons indicates that he might have set a good example by being baptized and becoming a faithful follower of Him who said, "If any man will come after me, let him deny himself, and take up his cross and follow me" (Matthew 16:24).

The term "cross," as it was used by Jesus, was intended to indicate a test of devotion and loyalty to the cause by those who followed him. It might also represent the two great commandments. Like the cross, the gospel has a vertical as well as a horizontal direction. The vertical bar points us upward to God, reminding us to love and serve Him with all our heart, might, mind, and strength. The horizontal bar points us to our fellow men, reminding us that when we are in the service of our fellow men, we are only in the service of our God. Next only to His love for His Father, the life of Jesus is characterized by His love for those around him. When Jesus stumbled on the road to Calvary, no one volunteered, so the great privilege of bearing his cross was forced upon Simon. What a miserable experience it would have been—crowding around Jesus to witness his suffering and doing nothing! If you and I had been standing there only to realize later the opportunity we had missed, don't you think that we would spend the rest of our lives trying to compensate for our reluctance and lack of understanding?

Every chance to serve the Lord is a "Simon opportunity." Once a second-mile philosophy is adopted, there is no stopping. One wants to go thirty, sixty, or even one hundred miles because mediocrity can never be settled for. In the religion of Jesus, we see the greatest characterization of the spirit of the second mile. This principle is what distinguishes Christianity from all other worldviews and elevates mankind from goodness to godliness. It can only flourish in a world in which God does not micromanage all tragedies confined to the short space of mortality. Tragedies turn to triumphs as God's children rise up to their second-mile potential and meekly turn to Him for help.

President Calvin Coolidge once said, "Nothing in the world can take the place of persistence. Talent will not. Nothing is more common than unsuccessful men with talent. Genius will not. Unrewarded genius is almost a proverb. Education will not. The world is full of educated derelicts. Persistence and determination alone are omnipotent." There are numerous examples in history of people who gave up on the cusp of victory.

The great Roman patriot Cato committed suicide on the very eve of his triumph. If he had only hung on to his courage and industry until morning, he would have been victorious.

One of the best ways to avoid bitterness and slavery caused by life's necessities is to enthusiastically give more service than is asked for. When we go further than is required, when we do more than we're paid for, only then do we get paid for more than we do. The second-mile philosophy translates duty into privilege. The first mile is usually drudgery. But discoveries come in the second mile. The Lord tried to teach the Israelites that Roman soldiers could only force them to do unwilling service. They could not force them to go the extra mile, nor could they deprive Jews of their joy of going willingly.

## Meekness

Jesus is the master of converting the complexity of life into the simplicity of meekness. His arms are ever open as He beckons, "Come unto me, all *ye* that labour and are heavy laden, and I will give you rest. Take my yoke upon you, and learn of me; for I am meek and lowly in heart: and ye shall find rest unto your souls. For my yoke *is* easy, and my burden is light" (Matthew 11:28-30). No greater comfort can enter one's heart than to know that the God of the universe is meek and lowly of heart...an essential attribute to acquire in our quest to find Him.

Throughout my life, I have known people whom I had observed to be pillars of strength under unimaginably difficult circumstances, only to crumble over small stumbling blocks or even over success. Others performed well as long as things went smoothly but were unprepared when tragedy struck, as though they had never given the remotest consideration that catastrophe could ever happen to them. They became quitters in life—particularly in their faith. Happily, some came back later...but tragically alone, unaccompanied by those they once led astray. *And then there were some* under-the-radar souls who exceeded my wildest expectations as they stepped up to their trials and revealed the staying power of their characters.

From Mongolia to Mozambique, the attribute that I have observed to be common to all truly successful, happy people was **meekness**. In their countenances and daily actions, they taught me that meekness was strong, not weak; active, not passive; courageous, not timid; restrained, not excessive; modest, not self-aggrandizing; and gracious, not brash. Although they were not proud, they exhibited healthy self-esteem and were not easily provoked, pretentious, or overbearing. They readily acknowledged the accomplishments of others, were aware of their own shortcomings, and taught me that it is better to walk by faith and receive its quiet evidence of things not seen than to see extraordinary things and then stumble over ordinary challenges.

Professional athletes say that as they begin to experience physical fatigue, the first thing to go is their legs. When disciples of Christ begin to experience spiritual fatigue, the first thing to go is their meekness. Unlike physical fatigue, from which recovery comes from rest, recovery from spiritual fatigue comes from exertion...moving forward. Unless the spirit is reignited by the self-renewing ingredient of meekness, spiritual fatigue becomes chronic and recovery is difficult. Joseph Smith taught that unless we have an assurance that the course of life we are pursuing is according to the will of the Lord, we grow weary in our minds and become faint[203] (Hebrews 12:3). To maintain that assurance, we need to keep ourselves nourished by gospel feasting, else we become vulnerable instead of durable.

Throughout his ministry, latter-day Apostle Neal A. Maxwell described, better than anyone I ever read, the attribute of meekness that Jesus personified better than anyone who ever lived. After reading all of Elder Maxwell's collected works, I concluded that meekness should be at the top of anyone's list who has an interest in coming to Christ. Sadly, "meekness ranks low on the mortal scale of things, yet high on God's: 'For none is acceptable before God, save the meek and lowly in heart'" (Moroni 7:44).[204] Here are twenty thoughts about meekness, in no particular order, inspired by Elder Maxwell's teachings:

1. **Meekness helps us to better understand life's ironies and seeming unfairness.** At least as much divine attention and forethought were given to the nature of the human experience our Father's children would undergo here as to creating our

earth and universe. Our Heavenly Father customizes the curriculum for each of us. There is a divine design in which He sets the thermostat on the furnace of affliction for each of us individually. Irony, the hard crust on the bread of adversity can try both our faith and our patience. Meekness comforts us when our outcomes seem to violate our expectations. Like blips on the graphs of individual stocks, unexpected and undeserved suffering, as registered in our limited database, are simply the smooth flow of events and decisions that are part of a much larger plan.[205]

2. **Meekness teaches us to think before we speak.** An interesting anecdote illustrating the problem of unmeekness is told about a man who survived the deadly 1889 Johnstown Flood and insisted on sharing the story with everyone. He finally became a perfect bore and people avoided him. Upon his death, he was ushered into the midst of heavenly hosts and told that each new arrival was to be given one wish. His immediate response was to ask for an audience to whom he might tell the story of how he had survived the Johnstown Flood. The audience of heavenly hosts, including the greats of yesteryear, were assembled. As the congregation was delivered to the man who had survived the Johnstown Flood, he was told: "Now you may tell your story of how you survived the Johnstown flood. Of course, you need to understand that Noah is in the audience." One of

the late realizations of life is that in almost every situation, there will be some Noahs in the audience, people whose mortal and spiritual experiences exceed our own. In time, meekness helps us to understand this reality.[206]

3. **Meekness is a companion to love.** Where there is meekness, love is close by. "Our capacity to love determines the extent to which we can be patient, meek, forgiving, and kind."[207] Coupled with meekness, love achieves fulfillment through trusting others. Meekness isn't an attribute that can be acquired quickly. Speaking with solicitors has taught me that it is a lifetime pursuit. The combination of a finite number of intelligences in the universe (Doctrine and Covenants 93:29) with an infinite amount of time together (Doctrine and Covenants 93:33) suggests to me that we either need to learn how to love each other or figure out how to avoid each other for a long time. Eternal evasion seems like a difficult task, even in an expanding universe.

4. **Meekness lightens our load**—particularly of self-pity. "A constructive critic truly cares for that which he criticizes, including himself, whereas self-pity is the most condescending form of pity; it soon cannibalizes all other concerns."[208] As a forerunner to murmuring, self-pity tends to disappear when we meekly expect more from ourselves than we do from others. It is naive to expect, and certainly

unfair to demand, perfection in our peers. Meekness is a cure for murmuring. It helps us become less preoccupied with being defrauded.

5. **Meekness is courageous**. The first thing the prodigal son said when he came to himself was, "Living like this is ridiculous!" He realized how much better off he would be if he returned to his father. He didn't worry about, "What will they say? Will anyone come out to meet me?" Instead, he just got up and went home. Meekness prompted the prodigal son to act which in the end saved his soul (Luke 15:11-32).[209] Meekness also enables the rest of us to "reclassify" former prodigals so we can delete their labels of prodigality from our hearts, empowering them and us to press forward unencumbered.

6. **Meekness perseveres while everything around it is quitting.** Few people in history could have endured the trials of Valley Forge without giving up. George Washington's meek steadfastness qualified him for such unassailable power that he was offered a crown. However, he refused to be king, preferring instead the freedom and welfare of his fellow countrymen. While riding through a small town one day, a girl of seven was brought out to see the hero. Upon seeing him, she exclaimed, "Why, he is only a man!" Hearing her,

General Washington swept off his hat, bowed, and said, “Yes, miss, that’s all I am.”[210]

7. **Meekness helps us prioritize our agenda.** What the proud, having “not submitted themselves unto the righteousness of God” (Romans 10:3), are determined to do is sometimes not actually inappropriate and may even involve doing good. The problem lies in their excluding that which God or His leaders counsel them to do. Pressing one’s own agenda to the exclusion of divine counsel (whether given by the Spirit, the scriptures, or those in authority over us) puts us in spiritual jeopardy. If we are submissive, we will demonstrate “unfeigned love of the brethren” (1 Peter 1:22). After all, as Alma said, discipleship means “being led by the Holy Spirit, becoming humble, meek, submissive, patient, full of love, and all long suffering” (Alma 13:28). Being easy to be entreated requires intellectual humility which is at obvious odds with the styles of the world.[211]

8. **Meekness helps us manage our time.** It’s delusory to think that we own ourselves, our time, our talents, and our possessions. If we think we own twenty-four hours a day, we come to resent unexpected interruptions of our time, feeling that the hour or the evening is being stolen from us. Unwilling to put everything we have on the altar without demanding a receipt from Him who gives us

our lives, our time, our family, and our future, we ultimately forfeit our ability to govern ourselves unless we learn to trust the Lord.[212]

9. **Meekness leads us to the Lord early.** Life ultimately commits us to religion, the religion of God or the religion of self. Either way, it's still religion. In the religion of God, worshippers kneel early and are empowered upward. In the religion of self, stiff knees unable to bend are compelled downward when "every knee shall bow...and every tongue shall confess...[and] give account...to God" (Romans 14:11-12). Converts to the religion of self-worship typically find pleasure in hobbies for a few seasons. They find welcome fellowship among the ranks of other former faithfuls until they are no longer useful. The more devoted they become to their new religion, the fewer proselytes they acquire along the way since self-worship isn't conducive to growth, neither personal nor congregational. Unmeekness blinks at first, closes its eyes, and then turns away...choosing to cultivate doubts in order to release itself from its covenants. It defers a temporary debt to the soul for a bankrupting one later.[213]

10. **Meekness helps us to identify the Lord's disciples.** Angelic emissaries from the Lord have meekly bidden overwhelmed mortals to arise because they are fellow servants. John the

Revelator said, “I fell at his feet to worship him. And he said unto me, See thou do it not: I am thy fellow servant, and of thy brethren that have the testimony of Jesus: worship God: for the testimony of Jesus is the spirit of prophecy” (Revelation 19:10). Moses, described as the meekest man on Earth (Numbers 12:3), was chosen because he preferred the reproach of Christ to the riches and honors of the courts of Pharaoh (Hebrews 11:24-26).[214]

11. **Meekness empowers forgiveness.** W. W. Phelps, whose betrayal had helped put the Prophet Joseph Smith in the Liberty Jail, wrote to the prophet just over a year later, seeking to regain the fellowship and membership he once had. Joseph's reply was classic: “It is true that we have suffered much in consequence of your behavior—the cup of gall, already full enough for mortals to drink, was indeed filled to overflowing when you turned against us... Believing your confession to be real, and your repentance genuine, I shall be happy once again to give you the right hand of fellowship, and rejoice over the returning prodigal. Come on, dear brother, since the war is past. For friends at first are friends again at last.” Following the prophet's martyrdom, it was this talented prodigal who composed “Praise to the Man” (Hymn #27). Joseph's letter to W.W. Phelps should ring deeply within the soul of everyone who has ever turned against the Church

and is now looking for a way back. The way back is meekness.[215]

12. **Unmeekness is why many are not chosen.** In promising that not one soul should be lost, Lucifer desired to impress. Interested in counting numbers instead of saving souls, he wanted to be worshipped in act one of our premortal life—but didn't want the responsibilities of godhood…nor the task of shepherding and loving a disobedient mortal flock whose misused agency would result in many being lost. Of course, there is no way in which misery caused by misused agency could be removed without removing agency itself. Meekness doesn't take its bows when the curtain opens![216]

13. **Meekness opens communication while unmeekness closes it.** When Brigham Young confronted Sidney Rigdon in the latter's bid for power after the martyrdom of Joseph Smith, President Young took hold of Sidney's hand, looked him in the face, and asked him a series of questions. To evade the questions, President Rigdon said, "Don't crowd my feelings too much." Yet President Young did so out of duty—not malice—on behalf of the salvation of the saints. Brigham loved Sidney. He stood in defense of his life and laid on the floor night after night to defend him, but he drew the line when Sidney turned down frequent invitations to meet with the Twelve, who

intended to show him every mark of esteem, deference, and respect.[217]

14. **<u>Meekness is soul-stretching</u>.** "God, as a loving Father, will stretch our souls at times. The soul is like a violin string: it makes music only when it is stretched. God will tutor us by trying us because He loves us!" Some of us run from the implications and responsibilities of the doctrines in which we believe—not because we're bad—but because of the impending demands that goodness makes on us. We allow ourselves to become offended by the gospel's theological simplicity, reasoning that if it should turn out that there is a God, He will be harmlessly indulgent. Such foolish thinking is a reflection of not knowing the will of God. If we can prove ourselves by stepping up and saying, "Here am I," the Lord has promised, "my grace is sufficient for the meek, that [others] shall take no advantage of your weakness" (Ether 12:26).[218]

15. **<u>Meekness replaces doubt as a cover for unfaithful behavior.</u>** Unlike the satisfactions of the world that come for a season, meekness leads to eternal truth that makes spiritual weariness disappear. It is what prepares us to learn (in the words of Moses) things "[we] never had supposed" (Moses 1:10). The meek willingly submit to the rod of iron. However, that rod of iron is the liberating word of God. The meek search—not just read or

quote from—all scriptures (John 5:39). They discover "new" verses in their very next reading, being now ready for that which has been there, unnoticed, all along.[219]

16. **Meekness teaches us about the employer-employee relationship.** When a difficult employer-employee relationship exists, the employee might feel inclined to take counsel from other employees rather than from the employer. This imposes a strain upon both of them since the employer offers hope for job advancement, raises, and improved working conditions. A mutual understanding is critical for an employer to maintain loyalty in the workforce and for the employee to know his or her role in a growing business whose employer's productivity is a key element in everyone's success. The analogy to life is a striking one. In the words of King Benjamin: "For how knoweth a man the master whom he has not served, and who is a stranger unto him, and is far from the thoughts and intents of his heart?"(Mosiah 5:13). If our master is a stranger to us, we merely end up serving other masters whose power over us is just as real, even if it is subtle. We are all enlisted if only in the ranks of the indifferent.[220]

17. **Meekness enlightens our understanding of history.** Why did the Lord authorize plural marriage to be practiced in His Church for fifty years during

the nineteenth century? Nobel prize-winning Irish author George Bernard Shaw said: "There was a time when the Mormons were so few in number that they were in very great danger of being killed by their pious neighbors because their views were unpopular. But they were themselves a very pious people. They were brought up with the strictest old-fashioned ideas with regard to the relations of the sexes and the sanctity of marriage: marriage, of course, being the established monogamous marriage of the Christian west... I do not know any more moving passage in literature than that in which Brigham Young describes how, after receiving the appalling order [of plural marriage], he met a funeral on his way home and found himself committing the mortal sin of envying the dead... [Joseph Smith] said, 'Unless we multiply our numbers, we are lost; and we can multiply our numbers rapidly only by polygamy. And, therefore, whatever our prejudices, whatever our feelings may be, if we are to save the Church...from annihilation by the superior numbers of its enemies in this State, we must take to polygamy. 'And they did it. That was the wonderful American thing."[221]

I am a beneficiary of plural marriage through my wife, a great-great-granddaughter of Apostle Charles C. Rich, who had six wives. His posterity down to our grandchildren's generation is calculated to approach 400,000 descendants in contrast to what might have been closer to 65,000 if he had only one wife. At Rich Family reunions, I have been deeply impressed by the strength and integrity of Apostle Rich's descendants. Plural marriage was an extraordinary measure commanded by the Lord in the early part of this final dispensation of the fulness of times. It was an exception to the rule that "there shall not any man...have save it be one wife; and concubines he shall have none" (Jacob 2:27), which helped to safeguard God's Kingdom on Earth from being destroyed as it had been in earlier dispensations.[222]

18. **Meekness helps us overcome our impulse to criticize hastily.** Why were persons of African lineage not granted all blessings of the priesthood for over a century? The Church of Jesus Christ of Latter-day Saints was restored in the midst of a highly contentious nineteenth-century racial culture. In contrast to other churches, it remained an integrated faith, never having a policy of segregated congregations. The Church's practice of plural marriage introduced interracial marriages at a time when it was illegal in many states and frowned upon virtually everywhere else. Reverend Thomas DeWitt Talmage of the Central Presbyterian Church in New York City was representative of many voices during the mid-1800s in calling attention to the threat of Mormonism's introduction of racial blending. Described by the *New York Times* as enjoying "a more widespread reputation than any other American preacher of the gospel," with the possible

exception of Henry Ward Beecher, Reverend Talmage said, "Unless we destroy Mormonism, Mormonism will destroy us. Mormonism will never be destroyed until it is destroyed by the guns of the United States government... The Chinese may stay, but the Mormons must go."[223]

It was during this period of self-preservation that the Church restricted priesthood blessings from baptized saints of African heritage. Their patience in deferring the blessings of temple ordinances is comparable to that of those in the Spirit World who were born outside of a gospel dispensation that required them to await the vicarious performance of ordinances on their behalf. An **election of grace** (Romans 11:1-5; Doctrine and Covenants 84:98-102), enabling some people to be "born at a time, at a place, and in circumstances where [they] come in favorable contact with the gospel" (Latter-day Saint Bible dictionary, p. 634) is not an unconditional election to eternal life. Elder Maxwell taught, "Ordinances...serve to acknowledge submittal to God's timetable, since all things must come to pass in their time." Each of us on both sides of the veil must patiently wait our turn by doing our own waiting upon the Lord. "Furthermore, meekly submitting to ordinances also constitutes an open submittal to authority as held by those God has called to administer His ordinances."[224]

Whatever the reasons were for the delay of temple blessings for our brothers and sisters of

African lineage, we can be grateful that the Lord is mindful of them by providing needful revelation to His Church leaders "in their weakness, after the manner of their language, that they might come to understanding. And inasmuch as they erred it might be made known; And inasmuch as they sought wisdom they might be instructed; And inasmuch as they sinned they might be chastened, that they might repent; And inasmuch as they were humble they might be made strong, and blessed from on high, and receive knowledge from time to time" (Doctrine and Covenants 1:24-28).

19. **Meekness facilitates promptings from the Holy Ghost.** That which is of God is recognizable by its edification. The Lord has said: "And that which doth not edify is not of God and is darkness" (Doctrine and Covenants 50:23). My experience in reading the Quran, Zhuan Falun, and other good non-Christian religious works was the absence of the meek and lowly still, small voice (1 Kings 19:12, 1 Nephi 17:45, Doctrine and Covenants 85:6). A lifetime of experience with this recognizable voice teaches one that the perishable promptings of the Holy Ghost invite time-sensitive responses to act. If they are responded to, the promptings come more frequently. If not, they come less frequently until they eventually disappear. In the modern world, there are those who see no reason to obey anyone or anything—including God. Stubbornly holding out like an unbroken colt, they forfeit the discipline of

discipleship that would have led them to royalty and perpetual paternity. In his great high priestly prayer, Jesus said, "This is life eternal, that they might know thee the only true God, and Jesus Christ, whom thou hast sent" (John 17:3). Knowing the Lord is more than simply acknowledging that He is there. Knowing Him requires intellectual meekness that opens our minds to things we "never had supposed" (Moses 1:10).[225]

20. **The meek shall inherit the earth…when the earth will be really worth inheriting.** This promise is repeated in the Old Testament (Psalms 37:11), New Testament (Matthew 5:5), Book of Mormon (3 Nephi 12:15), and Doctrine and Covenants (88:17). Inasmuch as "none is acceptable before God, save the meek and lowly" (Moroni 7:44), unmeek defiance of God is really an expression of ignorance, not individuality. Even a deep belief in a distant, undemanding God neither stirs the soul nor changes wrong behavior. Belief in a vague life force somewhere in space does not open the windows of the mind to the "truth…of things as they really are, and of things as they really will be" (Jacob 4:13). Remarkably, our Heavenly Father is giving away the secrets of the universe to those who are willing to be patiently meek…if only we can avoid being offended by His generosity![226]

If I could collect to my heart's content one attribute above all others, it would be meekness. If I could bequeath without measure a single virtue to my posterity, it would not be status, power, or wealth but meekness—the facilitator of all other Christ-like virtues. It is one of the few things that can be taken into the resurrection when so much else will be left behind. Meek behavior facilitates celestial thinking. In any given situation, a good question to ask oneself is, "What would the meekest response be?"

In college, I took an American History course in which the professor announced on the first day of class that anyone wanting an "A" or "B" would need to write a term paper. Without it, even a perfect performance on homework, exams, and quizzes could qualify a student for a grade of no higher than a "C+." Meekness can be thought of as that "term paper" that must be submitted if we are to rise above mediocrity in eternity. It cannot be developed in an instant or in a vacuum but requires taking Jesus' yoke upon us in order to learn of Him through a blend of intellect and experience.

If we can rid ourselves of **resentment**, deepen our **desire**, prime ourselves with **perseverance,** and become magnified by **meekness**, we can accelerate our approach to Christ. Those whom the Lord "would have gathered...as a hen gathereth her chickens under her wings and...would not" (Matthew 23:37) are not necessarily "bad" folks...they are just unwilling to take upon themselves the demands of goodness. One can progress only so far abductively—questioning everything even after abundant evidence has already been presented. By introspectively addressing these four big elements in ourselves...resentment, desire, perseverance, and meekness...we enter the realm of deductive learning through the Holy Ghost, priming us for questions that matter.

# Why Does Joseph Smith Matter?

We don't get to choose our evidence or how it is presented to us; we can only look for evidence and evaluate it as we find it. Imagine a crime scene in which there is a body but no weapon. Is it logical to conclude that no crime was committed because our preferred mode of evidence was unavailable? Similarly, we can't conclude that the Book of Mormon is not an authentic ancient record because we don't have the plates from which it was translated. We also don't get to choose our own translator.

On the eve of the American Revolutionary War, Paul Revere made a night ride to give colonists notice of the British Army's advance. His warning played a crucial role in the colonists' victory in subsequent battles. Imagine that you were there and heard someone accuse Revere of an indiscretion or of having a disagreeable personality, suggesting that his warning be ignored. Paul Revere's credentials as a credible witness would have been a distraction from the warning that you needed to heed.

Joseph Smith Jr. has been a stumbling block to many people for the past two centuries. He was only fourteen when he received a visit from the Father and the Son (Joseph Smith—History 1:23-25). This should come as no surprise to anyone familiar with the Bible. The Apostle Paul said: "God hath chosen the foolish things of the world to confound the wise; and God hath chosen the weak things of the world to confound the things which are mighty; And base things of the world, and things which are despised, hath God chosen, *yea,* and things which are not, to bring to nought things that are: That no flesh should glory in his presence. But of him are ye in Christ Jesus, who of God is made unto us wisdom, and righteousness, and sanctification, and redemption: That, according as it is written, He that glorieth, let him glory in the Lord" (1 Corinthians 1:27-31).

Noah was ordained at age ten (Doctrine and Covenants 107:52). Samuel had a personal visit from the Lord in the Temple at Shiloh when he was just a child, probably age twelve (1 Samuel 3:10, 21). He lived at a time not unlike Joseph's when "the word of the Lord was precious in those days; there was no open vision" (1 Samuel 3:1). David was anointed king of ancient Israel when he was just a shepherd boy (1 Samuel 6:12). Joseph, son of Israel, was sent to Egypt on an errand for the Lord when he was seventeen (Genesis 37:2). Jesus taught wise men in the temple at age twelve (Luke 2:42). Jeremiah was called when he was a mere child, probably thirteen (Jeremiah 1:6).[227] Mormon, one of the great prophets of pre-Columbus America, was called at age ten (Mormon 1:10).

God has an interesting advantage in selecting those to perform His work on Earth. He knew every one of us as His spirit children in the pre-mortal world. Jeremiah said, "Then the word of the Lord came unto me, saying, Before I formed thee in the belly I knew thee; and before thou camest forth out of the womb I sanctified thee, *and* I ordained thee a prophet unto the nations. Then said I, Ah, Lord God! behold, I cannot speak: for I *am* a child. But the Lord said unto me, Say not, I *am* a child: for thou shalt go to all that I shall send thee, and whatsoever I command thee thou shalt speak. Be not afraid of their faces: for I *am* with thee to deliver thee, saith the Lord. Then the Lord put forth his hand, and touched my mouth. And the Lord said unto me, Behold, I have put my words in thy mouth" (Jeremiah 1:4-9).

Jeremiah's intimidation over such an assignment was by no means unique. When Methuselah's father, Enoch, was called, "He bowed himself to the earth, before the Lord, and spake before the Lord, saying: Why is it that I have found favor in thy sight, and am but a lad, and all the people hate me; for I am slow of speech; wherefore am I thy servant? And the Lord said unto Enoch: Go forth and do as I have commanded thee... Open thy mouth, and it shall be filled, and I will give thee utterance" (Moses 6:31-32). Moses was also overwhelmed and said: "O my Lord, I *am* not eloquent...but I *am* slow of speech, and of a slow tongue. And the Lord said unto him, Who hath made man's mouth?... Now therefore go, and I will be with thy mouth, and teach thee what thou shalt say" (Exodus 4:10-12).

Ironically, there is at least one prophecy about Joseph Smith on which both Latter-day Saints and critics can agree, at least in substance. On September 23, 1823, "a messenger sent from the presence of God...[whose] name was Moroni...[told Joseph] that God had a work for [him] to do; and that [his] name should be had for good and evil among all nations, kindreds, and tongues, or that it should be both good and evil spoken of among all people" (Joseph Smith 1:33—Pearl of Great Price). Certainly, no one would disagree that Joseph Smith is a well-known controversial figure. That prophecy alone is remarkable about an obscure young man from early nineteenth-century frontier America! What would you think if someone made that claim today about an unknown person from your home town?

Joseph's brother, William, said: "We all had the most implicit confidence in what [Joseph] said. He was a truthful boy. Father and Mother believed him, why should not the children?... We never knew we were bad folks until Joseph told his vision. We were considered respectable till then, but at once people began to circulate falsehoods and stories in a wonderful way."[228] Joseph was a victim of "lies getting halfway around the world before the truth had a chance to get its pants on," as Winston Churchill would later famously quip. Alexander Pope expressed in verse our natural reaction to accounts that exceed our understanding. It is also a phenomenon in the game of "telephone."

> *"The flying rumor gathered as it rolled,*
> *And all who told it added something new,*
> *And all who heard it made enlargement too;*
> *In every ear it spread, on every tongue it grew."*

Those who knew Joseph personally spoke of him highly. Even those who thought he had been carried away by superstition described his motives as pure and noble.[229] People of Joseph's day who accused him projected onto him their own sense of human nature—the same way people do today.[230] In 1852 (eight years after his death), a non-Latter-day Saint, independent federal judge decreed that there was no fraud or other moral impropriety by the Prophet Joseph Smith.[231] Notwithstanding, in the words of Elder Neal A. Maxwell: "Some insist upon studying the Church [and Joseph Smith] only through the eyes of its defectors—like interviewing Judas to understand Jesus. Defectors always tell us more about themselves than about those from whom they have departed."[232]

Some accused Joseph of being motivated by greed. However, as early as July 1830—three months after the restoration of the Church of Christ—Joseph was told by revelation, "And in temporal labors thou shalt not have strength, for this is not thy calling" (Doctrine and Covenants 24:9). Had Joseph become wealthy, it would have contradicted his own revelation. Two years earlier, he recorded a revelation containing a strong personal rebuke from the Lord (Doctrine and Covenants 3:6-11). Another revelatory rebuke was published three years later (Doctrine and Covenants 93:47). Is this the type of behavior expected from an imposter?

On September 11, 1831, the Lord made the following noteworthy declaration about Joseph Smith...and about those who were critical of him:

> "And the keys of the mysteries of the kingdom shall not be taken from my servant Joseph Smith, Jun., through the means I have appointed, while he liveth, inasmuch as he obeyeth mine ordinances. There are those who have sought occasion against him without cause; Nevertheless, he has sinned; but verily I say unto you, I, the Lord, forgive sins unto those who confess their sins before me and ask forgiveness, who have not sinned unto death. My disciples, in days of old, sought occasion against one another and forgave not one another in their hearts; and for this evil they were afflicted and sorely chastened. Wherefore, I say unto you, that ye ought to forgive one another; for he that forgiveth not his brother his trespasses standeth

> condemned before the Lord; for there remaineth in him the greater sin. I, the Lord, will forgive whom I will forgive, but of you it is required to forgive all men. And ye ought to say in your hearts—let God judge between me and thee, and reward thee according to thy deeds" (Doctrine and Covenants 64: 5-11).

Joseph's authority to act on behalf of the Lord was not of his own choosing. It was a calling conditioned upon his willingness to repent and obey. According to the Lord, Joseph had been accused without cause. He had sinned, not in a malignant manner, but was forgiven. The greater sin is not to forgive...which includes any misgivings we might harbor toward him or anyone else. Our focus should be on our own worthiness as we carry our cross and follow Christ as Joseph Smith did. He was able to go further in obeying the Lord's commands because he went further in trusting Him. Joseph's commitment wasn't an intellectual one. He didn't ask for an explanation before he obeyed. He learned that understanding follows obedience rather than precedes it.

Joseph was so concentrated on laying the foundation of the great latter-day work that his empathy for others superseded his desire to defend himself against false allegations. His preoccupation with rolling off the kingdom onto the backs of the Twelve Apostles overrode other concerns. Just before his martyrdom at the age of thirty-eight, he blessed and instructed the

Twelve and said, "I feel as light as a cork. I feel that I'm free."[233] He then paced the room almost in exhilaration and said to the Twelve, "The hosts of Satan will not be able to tear down the kingdom, as fast as you will be able to build it up."[234] The foundation for the **dispensation of the fulness of times** (Ephesians 1:10, Doctrine and Covenants 128:20) had been laid. The Church of Christ would never again be taken from the Earth.

In 2005, a significant event was held at one of our country's centers of learning: the Library of Congress in Washington, D.C. It was a national conference commemorating the bicentennial celebration of the birth of Joseph Smith. Some of the world's greatest scholars who study world religions, the history of American religion, and Joseph Smith, were in attendance. It was an unusual collection of people who knew Joseph Smith inside out. The organizers of the conference didn't realize the kind of celebration and recognition of the greatness of Joseph Smith that would be expressed.

Robert V. Remini, a great American biographer, was one of the speakers at the conference. As a non-Latter-day Saint, he said that Mormons have tended to mute the importance of Joseph Smith in American history. They were more interested in what he did for Latter-day Saints. "We haven't spent enough time appreciating what he actually did for our country."[235] Other speakers made similarly positive observations.[236]

The same year, another bicentennial celebration was held in the parliament house in New South Wales, Australia. A historian of religion and scholar of world renown, Professor Wayne Hudson, said: "I argue that there are grounds for construing Joseph Smith as a genuine prophet of world historical importance. A case can be made that the world church has much to learn from the astonishing achievements of Joseph Smith. Indeed, taking respectful account of this one human being may make possible major advances in multi-faith dialogue, including dialogue with Islam. Joseph Smith was an outstanding American religious leader and visionary who has still not received the universal recognition he deserves, partly because sectarian and secular prejudices have prevented many scholars from grasping the astounding religious reality manifested in Joseph Smith and his revelations, above all the Book of Mormon."[237]

More graduate students pursuing master's degrees and PhDs are spending all or part of their professional or free time studying Joseph Smith and/or the history of the Church of Jesus Christ of Latter-day Saints. An increasing number of works that meet the highest standards of academic discourse have been written by people who have devoted their lifetime to the study of these subjects."[238]

Elder Neal A. Maxwell taught: "To make up one's mind about Joseph Smith or the Church as a bystander is a fatal mistake. One cannot appreciate holy things without being inside them. Those who recognized Peter on the night of Christ's arraignment did not see

Peter in his finest hour; for them to have made a decision about the validity of Christianity on the basis of that one encounter would have been a fatal mistake. The Peter they saw was a Peter in process. His stage of growth had very little to do, however, with the validity of the sermon on the Mount or the reality of the resurrection that was impending."[239]

Josiah Quincy, noted writer and mayor of Boston, interviewed Joseph Smith shortly before his martyrdom. In the book he later authored, entitled *Figures from the Past*, Mr. Quincy wrote, "It is by no means improbable that some future textbook for the use of generations yet unborn will contain a question something like this: 'What historical American of the nineteenth century has exerted the most powerful influence upon the destinies of his countrymen?' And it is by no means impossible that the answer to that interrogatory may be thus written: 'Joseph Smith, the Mormon prophet.' And that reply, absurd as it doubtless seems to most men now living, maybe an obvious commonplace to their descendants. History deals in surprises and paradoxes quite as startling as this. The man who establishes a great religion in this age of free debate, and who was and is today accepted by hundreds of thousands as a direct emissary from the most high, is not to be disposed of merely by pelting his memory with unsavory epitaphs."[240]

Elder John Taylor, who was wounded during the assault that murdered the prophet on June 27, 1844, wrote: "Joseph Smith, the Prophet and Seer of the Lord, has done more, save Jesus only, for the salvation of men in this world, than any other man that ever lived in it. In the short space of twenty years, he has brought forth the Book of Mormon, which he translated by the gift and power of God, and has been the means of publishing it on two continents; has sent the fulness of the everlasting gospel, which it contained, to the four quarters of the earth; has brought forth the revelations and commandments which compose this book of Doctrine and Covenants, and many other wise documents and instructions for the benefit of the children of men; gathered many thousands of the Latter-day Saints, founded a great city [Nauvoo], and left a fame and name that cannot be slain. He lived great, and he died great in the eyes of God and his people; and like most of the Lord's anointed in ancient times, has sealed his mission and his works with his own blood" (Doctrine and Covenants 135:3).

Moses left a great heritage, including the Ten Commandments. Isaiah, Ezekiel, Jeremiah, and other Old Testament prophets left books that bear their names. Matthew, Mark, Luke, Peter, James, John, Paul, and others left wonderful writings and letters that have been informative and inspirational to the world. But **Joseph Smith matters** because he restored to the latter-day world an understanding of the individual nature of the Godhead. God, the Almighty Father of our spirits, is a personal god of flesh who presides over the universe. His only begotten son in the flesh, Jesus Christ, is our Savior, Redeemer, and Mediator. The third member of the Godhead is the Holy Ghost, a spirit who reveals the Son to all who inquire of the Father. In contrast to the Christian world that says, "I believe in God," Joseph Smith was able to essentially say, "I know there is a God, for I have seen Him."

Joseph gave to the world three great volumes of new scripture, outlining in detail the simple principles of the gospel. He was the prophet who was commissioned to re-establish the original Church of Christ on Earth in 1830 with its authority, organization, ordinances, and doctrine. He also re-established, under direct command from God, the ancient custom of building temples where covenantal sealing ordinances take place that cannot be performed anywhere else. On March 27, 1836, the first temple of this dispensation was dedicated at Kirtland, Ohio. A few days later, on April 3, 1836, Joseph Smith and Oliver Cowdery retired to the temple pulpit around which veils were dropped. After silent and solemn prayer, they received the following visions and personal manifestations:

> "The veil was taken from our minds, and the eyes of our understanding were opened. We saw the Lord standing upon the breastwork of the pulpit, before us; and under his feet was a paved work of pure gold, in color like amber. His eyes were as a flame of fire; the hair of his head was white like the pure snow; his countenance shone above the brightness of the sun; and his voice was as the sound of the rushing of great waters... After this vision closed, the heavens were again opened unto

us; and Moses appeared before us, and committed unto us the keys of the gathering of Israel from the four parts of the earth, and the leading of the ten tribes from the land of the north. After this, Elias appeared, and committed the dispensation of the gospel of Abraham, saying that in us and our seed all generations after us should be blessed. After this vision had closed, another great and glorious vision burst upon us; for Elijah the prophet, who was taken to heaven without tasting death, stood before us, and said: Behold, the time has fully come, which was spoken of by the mouth of Malachi—testifying that he [Elijah] should be sent, before the great and dreadful day of the Lord come—To turn the hearts of the fathers to the children, and the children to the fathers, lest the whole earth be smitten with a curse [Malachi 4:5-6]—Therefore, the keys of this dispensation are committed into your hands" (Doctrine and Covenants 110:1-3, 11-16).

These are bold declarations that require study, thought, research, and prayer to understand. They also require personal worthiness as the Lord has explained the pattern for learning from the Holy Ghost: "If any man will do his [God's] will, he shall know of the doctrine, whether it be of God, or *whether* I speak of myself" (John 7:17). People in our day who are unwilling to investigate bold declarations are modern equivalents of those in Jesus' day who, when faced with the responsibility of performing their due diligence, threw up their arms and asked, "Can there any good thing come out of Nazareth?" (John 1:46). Like Abraham Lincoln, Joseph Smith came from a log home in rural 19$^{th}$-century America. To find out if Joseph spoke for God, Jesus made the following declaration: "For every one that asketh receiveth; and he that seeketh findeth; and to him that knocketh it shall be opened" (Matthew 7:8). In other words, "Only those who fail to ask, fail to receive; those who fail to seek, fail to find; and those who fail to knock, fail to have it opened unto them."

The important thing to remember is to face your claims squarely and fairly. Avoid the pitfalls of the Four "I's:" indifference, ignorance, indecision, and inflexibility. Care to become accurately informed and act expeditiously on the evidence, even if you don't like it. Don't let yourself get tripped up over criticizing anyone who is in a position to help you. You wouldn't refuse information from the second person in line of "ultimate telephone" no matter what rumor you had heard about that person, would you?

The more you learn about the Prophet Joseph Smith, the more your admiration and love for him will grow.

# Why Does the Book of Mormon Matter?

The purpose of the Book of Mormon may be described in at least three ways:

1) First and foremost, it is a witness of Jesus Christ...along with the Bible.
2) Secondly, it is the vehicle for the latter-day gathering of Israel throughout the earth that has been prophesied for millennia (Isaiah 56:8, Hosea 1:11, Matthew 24:14).
3) Finally, it is the story of a family's experiences in following the Lord's command to flee Jerusalem, travel across the Arabian peninsula, build a ship, sail to America, and develop a civilization lasting a thousand years. Two other civilizations they encountered along the way are also described.

The Book of Mormon was translated from reformed Egyptian in sixty-three days during the spring of 1829 by Joseph Smith, a 23-year-old plowboy with the equivalent of a 3rd-grade formal education. He translated 531 pages with the aid of scribes. No one saw him use a manuscript or ever found one. Some critics claimed that the book is fiction, plagiarized or authored by Sidney Rigdon, Solomon Spaulding, or someone else. However, no nineteenth-century person knew enough to clarify obscure Biblical passages on the Doctrine of Christ (2 Nephi 31-32, 3 Nephi 11); describe the plan of salvation in detail (2 Nephi 9-11, Jacob 6, Jarom 1, Alma 24, 34); bring to light the Atonement of Jesus Christ (2 Nephi 2, 9, Mosiah 3-4, 13-16, 27, Alma 11-12, 33-34, 36, 41-42); employ chiasmus—a Hebrew form of parallel reverse poetic expression (Alma 36, 41, 1 Nephi 15, 17, 2 Nephi 27, 29, Mosiah 3, 5); or describe geographic features unknown in his day that would become recognizable two centuries later.

Models have been developed to explain possible geographic locations for Book of Mormon settlements in North, Central, and South America. Each model has pros and cons based on evidence collected so far. No model can be confirmed or ruled out conclusively per se. However, the following prophecy by Nephi gives us a clue as to the possible locations of Lehi's descendants today:

> "...in the latter days, when our seed shall have dwindled in unbelief, yea, for the space of

> many years, and many generations after the Messiah shall be manifested in body unto the children of men, then shall the fulness of the gospel of the Messiah come unto the Gentiles, and from the Gentiles unto the remnant of our seed—And at that day shall the remnant of our seed know that they are of the house of Israel, and that they are the covenant people of the Lord; and then shall they know and come to the knowledge of their forefathers, and also to the knowledge of the gospel of their Redeemer, which was ministered unto their fathers by him; wherefore, they shall come to the knowledge of their Redeemer and the very points of his doctrine, that they may know how to come unto him and be saved. And then at that day will they not rejoice and give praise unto their everlasting God, their rock and their salvation? Yea, at that day, will they not receive the strength and nourishment from the true vine? Yea, will they not come unto the true fold of God? Behold, I say unto you, Yea; they shall be remembered again among the house of Israel; they shall be grafted in, being a natural branch of the olive tree, into the true olive tree" (1 Nephi 15: 13-16).

Church growth among the native populations of the Western Hemisphere is far greater in Mesoamerica and South America than it is in the U.S. and Canada. If demographics are any indication of the location of

Book of Mormon descendants today, then Nephi's prophecy would favor remnants of people living in Latin America who "know they are of the house of Israel, and that they are the covenant people of the Lord." Notwithstanding, regardless of lineage, all who accept the covenant are "Christ's,... Abraham's seed, and heirs according to the promise" (Galatians 3:29).

A few critics have concluded that the absence of Near Eastern DNA among Native American groups is evidence against a family moving from Jerusalem to America two and a half millennia ago. However, as we discussed about abduction, absence of evidence is not evidence. Nothing is known about the DNA that Lehi's family brought to the Americas...or of any DNA typical of the Near East (**founder effect**). The loss of genetic variation from natural disaster, epidemic disease, massive war, or other calamity, resulting in the death of a substantial part of a population over the millennia, is unknown (**population bottleneck).** The gradual loss of genetic markers over time (**genetic drift)** makes it virtually impossible to make a case for or against the Book of Mormon from DNA analysis.[241]

For example, a study in Iceland combining both genetic and genealogical data demonstrates that the majority of people living in that country today inherited mitochondrial DNA from just a small percentage of the people who lived there only 300 years ago. The mitochondrial DNA of the majority of Icelanders living at that time simply did not survive the random effects of drift. As Elder Dallin H. Oaks of the Quorum of the Twelve Apostles observed, "It is our position that secular evidence can neither prove nor disprove the authenticity of the Book of Mormon."[242]

Nonetheless, secular evidence in support of the Book of Mormon is unequivocally powerful. Archeologist John Clark prepared a list of sixty anachronisms (elements not matching time and place) compiled by nineteenth-century critics of *the Book of Mormon*. In 1842, only 13.3% of the criticisms had been disproven. By 2005, the percentage of disproven claims had risen to 58%. By 2019, the number of publicly available claims of anachronisms in the Book of Mormon had risen to two hundred and five...of which 69% had been disproven and 13% were trending.[243] In the words of Dr. Clark, "critics...have done more to establish the authenticity of *The Book of Mormon* than have their Mormon brethren. In recognition of their past efforts, Dr. Clark dedicated his 2005 FAIR Conference remarks to two critics who "helped establish the truth of *The Book of Mormon* more than they know. In 1830 the book was a 23-pound weakling. Now, thanks to 175 years of criticism, it is a 900-pound colossus."

My own research has convinced me that even the label "900-pound colossus" is a gross understatement. There is enough physical evidence for any unbiased twelve-person jury to acquit the Book of Mormon of all charges of fraud. Twelve persons did, in fact, attest to the book's authenticity...as eyewitnesses of the plates (See *Book of Mormon—Testimony Three Witnesses, Testimony of Eight Witnesses,* and *Testimony of the Prophet Joseph Smith*). Although some became disaffected later, none ever denied his witness of the plates or testimony of the Book of Mormon. For more comprehensive treatises on physical evidence, I recommend Anderson's *Investigating the Book of Mormon Witnesses,*[244] Callister's *A Case for the Book of Mormon,*[245] and Potter and Wellington's *Lehi in the Wilderness—81 New, Documented Evidences that the Book of Mormon is a True History.*[246]

In 2023, I had the opportunity of exploring much of the trail that Lehi took through the Arabian peninsula. In May, my wife and I joined explorer George Potter in a Land Cruiser down the Saudi Arabian portion of the Frankincense Trail. In November, two of our daughters joined us on another exploration of the same trail as well as at its conclusion in Oman, where Lehi's family built a ship and sailed to America. As we traveled, we studied the first Book of Nephi as a guide to our journey.

The Book of Mormon begins with Lehi being warned by the Lord in a dream to flee Jerusalem with his family in 600 B.C. before the Babylonian captivity of Judah in 586 B.C. Traveling south from Jerusalem, Lehi's family had four possible escape routes. Only one led "into the wilderness" (1 Nephi 4:34-36) east through Wadi El Kharrar to "the Way of the Wilderness" (2 Samuel 15:23), outside the jurisdiction of Judean authorities. The other three routes, controlled by King Zedekiah, would have invariably culminated in the family's apprehension. The record says that Lehi "came down by the **borders near** the shore of the Red Sea; and he traveled in the **wilderness** in the **borders** which are **nearer** the Red Sea" (1 Nephi 2:5). In

Semitic languages and to the Arabs of northwest Arabia, "borders" mean "mountains" or "mountain barriers" and "wilderness" means "desert."[247]

Our drive south from the Gulf of Aqaba (mountain road) in northwest Arabia (Midian) was through desert with a mountain range on our left—*near* the Red Sea—and on our right—*nearer* the Red Sea. The landmarks precisely fit the physical description in the Book of Mormon. Down the shoreline was a small cleft in the mountain, hardly noticeable in the distance, which marked the opening of an impressive canyon. Known locally as Wadi Tayyib al-Ism, the valley exhibited the following features:

1. "Firm, steadfast, and immovable" (1 Nephi 2:10), its enormous granite walls extend over two thousand feet into the air.
2. It was located seventy-two miles from the northeast tip of the Red Sea...the distance of a three day's walk or camel ride (1 Nephi 2:5-6).
3. It was not an interior valley but one that reached the Red Sea (1 Nephi 2:8).
4. It had a "river of water" (1 Nephi 2:6) "continually running" (1 Nephi 2:9). The expression "river of water" strikes a Westerner as odd since the word "river" implies the existence of water...but not in Arabia where river beds are dry.

Little was known about Arabia's interior until the discovery of oil in 1938, which opened the land to explorers. Prior to that time, D.G. Hogarth (1862-1927), a specialist in the science of archeology, said that Arabia "probably never had a true river in all its immense area." Even long after the discovery of oil, the Saudi Arabian Ministry of Agriculture and Water, with the assistance of the U.S. Geological Service, spent forty-four years surveying Saudi water resources. Their study consisted of seismic readings, surface and aerial surveys, and land satellite photo analysis. They concluded that "Saudi Arabia may be the world's largest country without any perennial rivers or streams."[248] Professor Hugh Nibley noted that the river of water, which Lehi named the River Laman, would have been a small but life-sustaining local stream,[249] which was what we found at Wadi Tayyib al-Ism.

Author and wife at Wadi Tayyib al-Ism

The claim that Lehi's Valley of Lemuel contained a river of running water in Arabia had long been a criticism of the Book of Mormon. In 1984, the United States and Saudi Arabian Joint Commission of Economic Development completed for the Saudi Arabian Ministry of Agriculture and Water a mapping of the soils of Saudi Arabia. The soil at Wadi Tayyib al-Ism was classified as poor, with 0% arable. Of the entire twenty-four-mile length of Wadi Tayyib al-Ism, only the last four miles show perennial water with edible vegetation. Near the mouth of the canyon, George discovered on an earlier expedition a buried stone box designed to be covered by a large stone. Such boxes for keeping valuables safe are a custom among bedouins in Midian...reminiscent of the box Joseph Smith described in Palmyra, New York (Joseph Smith History: 51-52).[250]

Nephi wrote of this valley: "We had gathered together all manner of seeds of every kind, both of grain of every kind, and also of the seeds of fruit of every kind" (1 Nephi 8:1). With a government permit, we were able to enter the valley and hike its last four miles (eight miles round trip) from the Red Sea. There, we found an abundance of date palms, the traditional food source for travel in that part of the world. It was so impressive that we returned to hike it again six months later, just two and a half weeks before it was closed to the public in order to accommodate the massive NEOM building project that would include skyscraper resorts.

When Joseph Smith translated the Book of Mormon in 1829, only twenty-five percent of the seventeen-hundred-mile course that Lehi took through Arabia had been seen and described in writing by Westerners (Verthema, Wild, and Pitt).[251] In 1878, explorer Sir Richard Francis Burton referred to this area as still unexplored. However, our search, using the Book of Mormon's geographical description, not only helped us to identify stops along the journey out of Jerusalem but also enlightened our understanding of the stunning imagery of Lehi's dream in the context of the Valley of Lemuel where Lehi's family camped.

Professor Nibley pointed out that it is "natural enough for men to dream by night of the things they see by day—that is what makes Lehi's dream so convincing as authentic testimony."[252] Nibley goes on to explain, "Long ago Sigmund Freud showed that dreams are symbolic, that they take their familiar materials from everyday life and use them to express the dreamer's real thoughts and desires...the peculiar materials of which Lehi's dreams are made, the images, situations, and dream-scenery which though typical come from the desert world in which Lehi was wandering."[253] A description follows of some of the dream imagery we found at Wadi Tayyib al-Ism[254]:

1. **A Dark and Dreary Wilderness** (1 Nephi 8:4)—The beginning of Lehi's dream depicted his travel through a "dark and dreary waste" (1 Nephi 8:7). Lehi's concern was real since the family had just traveled through the land of Midian in the northwest corner of Saudi Arabia in a wilderness second only in barrenness to the

Empty Quarter (Rub' al Khali) in central Arabia. With a limited supply of water, the burning sun would have forced the family to travel at night through uncharted territory. In desperation, Lehi prayed that the Lord "would have mercy on [him]" (1 Nephi 8:8).

2. **A Large and Spacious Field** (1 Nephi 8:9)—The wadi ends where the canyon begins, a fertile area. Surrounding high mountain walls give the impression of a self-contained, walled garden, which Lehi alludes to in his dream as a "large and spacious field, as if it had been a world" (1 Nephi 1:20).

3. **Tree of Life** (1 Nephi 8:10-11)—The date palm tree has been known by many cultures as the tree of life because of its medicinal and life-sustaining properties. The wadi is filled with date palms whose branches represent the Son of God (John 12:13, 1 Nephi 11:7). Along the canyon, one tree seemed to stand out to us because of its visibility from a distance. To Westerners, dates are brown. However, Arabia, has varieties that approach a very light color as they mature to their sweetest taste in summer, when temperatures do not drop below 90 degrees F. In the Near East, the date palm was a mainstay of survival. It was a literal life-saving tree to Lehi's family and symbol of the love of God, which is "the greatest of all gifts of God" (1 Nephi 15:36).

4. **A River of Water Near the Tree** (1 Nephi 8:13)—About two hundred yards into the canyon, a spring emerges, which feeds a small river that flows underground into the Red Sea. The word "river" could have meant a large stream, a small, continuously flowing one, or a seasonal flood. It could not have been an important one or Lehi would have known it by name. Like the date palms, this river would be easily recognized as a tender mercy or love of God to Lehi's family in the middle of a barren wilderness. Nephi described the spring where the river rises as "the fountain of living waters" (1 Nephi 11:25), the same terminology the Lord uses to describe Himself (Jeremiah 2:13, John 4:10).

However, in a later scene, Nephi described the water as filthiness...an awful gulf...representing that awful hell to divide the wicked from the righteous (1 Nephi 15:27-30). Wadi Tayyib al-Ism is the only water outlet from the watershed of 105 square miles of surrounding mountains. Early rains have been known to produce deadly flash floods of muddy water through the canyon with no means of escape.

5. **Strait and Narrow Path** (1 Nephi 8:20)—A strait (narrow, not directionally straight) path extends along the river. It leads to the tree, the head of the fountain, and to the large field at one end of the canyon, and to a great and spacious

building at the other. The wadi path is confined by towering canyon walls that are seldom more than forty feet apart at the base...without side canyons. Other wadis in northwest Arabia are wide and open with side paths. But the narrow and confining nature of Wadi Tayyib al-Ism is unique, a representation of the "narrow...way, which leadeth unto life, and few there be that find it" (Matthew 7:14).

6. **Rod of Iron** (1 Nephi 11:25)—The rod of iron would be seen as figurative since no rod of iron could occur naturally. However, the vertical canyon walls could easily represent the word of God. The hard granite walls of Wadi Tayyib al-Ism were a stark contrast to the sandstone walls elsewhere. Firm, immovable, and secure, like the word of God, the canyon wall was a rod to anyone wanting to "press forward through a mist of darkness, clinging to the rod [wall] of iron, even until they did come forth and partake of the fruit of the tree" (1 Nephi 8:24). Multitudes not clinging to the wall/rod could be visualized losing their way, getting lost, or "feeling their way towards [a] great and spacious building" (1 Nephi 8:23, 31).

7. **Mist of Darkness** (1 Nephi 8:23)—A thick fog has sometimes been observed to fill the canyon, caused by cool air descending from the surrounding mountains and mixing with moist, warm air circulating from the Red Sea. Since the lower end of the canyon opens onto the shore

of the sea, Lehi and Sariah would have naturally been concerned about "an exceedingly great mist of darkness, insomuch that they who had commenced in the path did lose their way, that they wandered off and were lost," especially into the sea.

8. **Great and Spacious Building** (1 Nephi 8:26-27)—The walls of Wadi Tayyib al-Ism reach over 2,000 feet high. As I looked up from the canyon floor, I had the feeling of being very small and imagined I was standing next to "a great and spacious building; and it stood as it were in the air, high above the earth. And it [the top of the wall] was filled with people, both old and young, both male and female; and their manner of dress was exceedingly fine; and they were in the attitude of mocking and pointing their fingers towards those who had come at and were partaking of the fruit" (1 Nephi 8:26-27). The forthcoming construction of resorts at Wadi Tayyib al-Ism adds another interesting dimension to the imagery.

9. **An Awful Gulf** (1 Nephi 15:28)—"An awful gulf...separated the wicked from the tree of life, and also from the saints of God." The high vertical walls of the canyon are an appropriate type for the awful gulf since anyone falling off the wall could not survive. There would be no way back up because of the "justice of God [which] did divide the wicked from the righteous" (1 Nephi 15:30).

Proposed Resort at the Red Sea Entrance of Wadi Tayyib al-Ism[255]

10. **Depths of the Fountain** (1 Nephi 8:32)—Lehi's vision included the fate of those who "were lost from his view, wandering in strange roads," and who "were drowned in the depths of the fountain." The fountain of the Red Sea is the Gulf of Aqaba (1 Nephi 2:9 note a), which has a depth of six thousand feet. The drop is precipitous. One can walk out on the coral reef and stand in shallow water while, only a few feet away, there is a submerged underwater wall with a drop-off of hundreds of feet.

Wadi Tayyib al-Ism is the only geographic candidate for the Valley of Lemuel. It not only meets the physical description of the valley found in 1 Nephi but provides striking imagery for Lehi's vision of the tree of life, as well. Its recent discovery as a candidate for the Valley of Lemuel post-dates the Book of Mormon's publication by almost two centuries. Ockham's razor would be compelled to conclude that the Book of Mormon is an ancient record.

In the Valley of Lemuel, Lehi's mind was enlightened so he could recognize the Lord at every turn. The Quran teaches: "Whithersoever ye turn, there is the presence of Allah." Then it adds, "They say: 'Allah hath begotten a son. Glory be to Him.' Nay, all that is in the heavens and on earth, everything renders worship to Him [Allah alone]."[256] However, the Valley of Lemuel is a powerful witness of the majesty of God through the compassionate redemption of His beloved Son "who is the image of the invisible God, the firstborn of every creature" (Colossians 1:15).

From the Valley of Lemuel, Lehi's family journeyed through halts [stops] corresponding to landmarks described in the Book of Mormon that were unknown in Joseph Smith's day. Traveling four days (about 100 miles) in a south-southeast direction, they came to Shazer, an area abounding with trees and shrubs. Wadi Agharr is a site that perfectly matches the definition of an oasis in a desert, and the description of Shazer, where they went to "slay food for [their] families" (1 Nephi 16:14). The police general in nearby al-Bada said that the best hunting in the entire area was in the mountain of Agharr.[257]

Nephi wrote that after leaving Shazer, they "did go forth again in the wilderness, following the same direction, keeping in the *most fertile parts* of the wilderness, which were in the borders near [not nearer] the Red Sea" (1 Nephi 16:14). Several days of travel down the Frankincense Trail, he says, "The directions of the ball [Liahona]...led us in the *more fertile parts* of the wilderness" (1 Nephi 16:16). In other words, the family traveled from the "most" fertile to the "more" fertile parts. Three geographical observations attest to the authenticity of his statements:

1. The Hijaz Mountains "near" the Red Sea are most fertile at their northern end and become less fertile traveling south. Hence, the family began the journey in the "most fertile parts," which later became "more fertile parts," and finally, the most inhospitable terrain where the trail passed along the edge of the empty quarter.
2. Had Nephi said they traveled in the borders "nearer" the Red Sea, they would have encountered areas of least fertility at the northern end with increasing fertility southward (more fertile) at Mecca and finally into the most fertile Tihama plain.
3. Although the Frankincense Trail had been well established long before Lehi's day, the "trail" is not well marked and changes as sands shift in the wind. Direction, location of water, provisions, supplies, and payment of local tributes for protection from plunder, enslavement, or death made the Liahona an absolute necessity as a survival guide...and a powerful motif of the covenant path to eternal life.

The journey from Jerusalem to Bountiful took Lehi's family eight years. Nowadays, well-equipped professional caravaners can cover the seventeen-hundred-mile Frankincense Trail in about three months. However, Lehi had "left his house, and the land of his inheritance, and his gold, and his silver, and his precious things, and took nothing with him, save it were his family, and provisions, and tents, and departed into the wilderness" (1 Nephi 2:4). His family had not only been blessed with wealth but also with education, including the ability to read and write in Hebrew and Egyptian (Mormon 9:32-33). This would have made them sought-after tutors in exchange for provisions and services they needed along the trail to supplement their hunting and gathering efforts.

In a revelation through Joseph Smith in 1830, the Lord said to two prospective missionaries: "Open your mouths and they shall be filled, and you shall become even as Nephi of old, who journeyed from Jerusalem in the wilderness" (Doctrine and Covenants 33:8). The beautiful oasis of Dedan (now Al-Ula where we stayed at the lovely Shaden Resort) would have been an ideal place for the family to wait out the hot summer and teach the gospel before resuming their journey in the desert.

The Dedanites, named after their ancestor Dedan, a grandson of Abraham (Genesis 25:3), changed their name to Lihyanites (sometimes spelled Lehianites) shortly after the time Lehi would have passed that way. We visited the Lihyanite museum as well as petroglyphs in the surrounding area, which contain thousands of Lihyanite inscriptions. Many inscriptions are about their temple worship. Interestingly, the name "Lehi" appears twenty-five times and "Nephi" appears fourteen times.

Traveling many days, the family "followed the directions of the ball [Liahona]...in the more fertile parts" (1 Nephi 16:16) to a place where Nephi broke his bow (1 Nephi 16:18). This would have occurred along the southern part of the trail (1 Nephi 16:33). Nephi needed to quickly find a quality hardwood with the unusual property of remaining flexible when it was dead. However, most trees in Saudi Arabia are short, brittle, and warped. We saw acacia trees throughout our trip with missing nettle-laden branches that camels would eat up to the height of their reach. Nephi could not have made a decent bow from acacia wood.

"According to the directions which were given upon the [Liahona]" (1 Nephi 16:30), Nephi went to the top of a nearby mountain. Near modern-day Bishah stands Mount Jasmin, where atim (olive) trees are found. Wood from these trees is ideal for making a good bow...grain that is "close, straight and even; the line dividing the sap and wood...clear, even and well defined,... free from knots and pins."[258] If Nephi broke his bow here, it couldn't have happened in a better place! After making a new bow and arrow, and taking along his sling and some stones, Nephi had a bounteous hunt, no doubt a surprise and delight to his family. It made them happy to the point of humility in giving thanks to the Lord (1 Nephi 16:32).

After fourteen hundred miles of travel in a south-southeast direction along the Hijaz mountains, they arrived at a place which "was called Nahom" (1 Nephi 16:34). Wadi Naham, located in present-day Yemen (which we did not enter), existed at the time of Lehi. Somewhere in that vicinity, Ishmael died, precipitating a rebellion against Nephi, whose older brothers accused him of seeking authority over them so "that he may lead us away into some *strange wilderness*" (1 Nephi 16:34).

The term "strange wilderness" is an interesting geographic statement. Eastward from this point lies the most arduous part of the journey. Skirting an arm of the empty quarter (Rub 'al Khali) where sand dunes can reach 700 to 800 feet in height, their caravan would next take them through a region known for its sandstorms, oppressive heat, flies, camel spiders, and scarcity of water...not an ordinary wilderness but a strange one indeed! Nephi uses the word "wade" (1 Nephi 17:7) to describe the nature of this section of deep sand travel. The threat of being raided by unfriendly Bedu tribes would have prevented them from having fires, so they had to eat raw meat (1 Nephi 17:2, 12). And yet, "they began to bear their journeyings without murmurings" (1 Nephi 17:2).

When they stopped complaining, they were able to endure this most challenging part of their journey, including childbearing. Nephi describes this seeming anomaly in the next verse: "And if it so be that the children of men keep the commandments of God he doth nourish them, and strengthen them, and provide means whereby they can accomplish the thing which he has commanded them; wherefore, he did provide means for us while we did sojourn in the wilderness" (1 Nephi 17:3).

This last leg of the trail, "nearly eastward," is in harmony with the route of the Frankincense Trail. Its specific geographical direction stands as one of the strongest evidences of the authenticity of the Book of Mormon. No contemporary source in Joseph Smith's day knew about the location of the turn to the east, which was the most unknown part of the Frankincense Trail. In 1936, Freya Stark wrote, "No European has been along this way...practically nothing is known about the country through which this...route travels."[259]

At long last, Lehi's family arrived at the tiny segment of the southern coast of the Arabian Peninsula, which they called "Bountiful because of its much fruit and also wild honey" (1 Nephi 17:5). The Frankincense Trail ends at the lush, green Dhofar area in Oman which meets all criteria for Bountiful as well as Nephi's harbor. In 1830, the whole of Arabia was known in Europe and America only as a desert wasteland. Even Oman remained a *terra incognita* to the rest of the world until a general survey was undertaken between 1989-1995 as part of the Trans Arabia Expedition and later between 2005-2011 for the Office of the Advisor to His Majesty the Sultan for Cultural Affairs.[260] A few of our surprising discoveries in this area included:

1. **An Accessible Seashore** (1 Nephi 17:6)—The mountains of Dhofar form an almost impenetrable barrier to the seashore, except for the Thammarit

Pass on the Frankincense Trail. This route has been in use for thousands of years and leads to the Salalah Plain, which is characterized by numerous springs, five freshwater lakes, and a seashore on the Indian Ocean: "Irreantum" or "many waters."

2. **Fruit in Abundance** (1 Nephi 17:5, 6, 18:6)—Bountiful was populated in Lehi's time. Although modern irrigation has expanded the variety of fruits available today, there is evidence that in Nephi's time, the 'Adites, who were highly adept at agriculture, occupied the Salalah Plain, with rich soil capable of producing three crops in a year. This was the end of the Frankincense Trail, so named because it was the Frankincense capital of the world and a center of trade.

3. **Wild Honey** (1 Nephi 17:5)—Bees are rare in Saudi Arabia. Salalah of the Dhofar coast (Bountiful) is one of the few places where bees are found. Salalah is still famous for its wild honey, which we found to be delicious.

4. **Ore and Flint** (1 Nephi 17:9-11)—The Dhofar region is one of the few places throughout the Arabian Peninsula where ore deposits are found. Bronze tools have been found in the region dating back to 1100 B.C.[261] We found flint in several places.

5. **Wild Game** (1 Nephi 17:11, 18:6)—Dhofar is the only place in Arabia where cattle can be found. Wild beasts are also plentiful from which skin could be obtained to make bellows for fire to produce tools.

6. **Large Timber** (1 Nephi 18:1)—Wadi Dharbat has been designated a national park and nature reserve. Receiving a greater rainfall than surrounding areas, this is the only area where large trees grow with hardwood capable of building a ship. Locals call it "the valley of the big trees."[262] Nearby India was also a trading partner and source of teak wood used for shipbuilding.

7. **Metal Plates** (1 Nephi 19:1)—The National Museum of Oman displays metal plates with ancient writings found at the port of Khor Rori in the Dhofar area dating back to Lehi's time. Metal plates have also been found at camps on the Khor Rori cliffs, overlooking the seashore. Nephi could have learned metal writing here during the family's sojourn in Bountiful.

8. **Cliffs Overlying Deep Water** (1 Nephi 17:48)—At one point, Nephi's brothers became so angry at him that they threatened to "throw [him] into the depths of the sea." This wouldn't have been a threat at almost any other seashore. However, the cliffs at Khor Rori are around 100 feet high and extend 400-450 yards into the Indian Ocean. Looking down from the edge of the cliffs at the breaking waves against the rocks below caused a chill in all of us (good swimmers) as we imagined being thrown into the ocean and trying to swim around the cliffs to the shore.

A highlight of our trip was our visit to the home of Omani historian and author **Ali Ahmed Al-Shahri.** Ali presented to me a copy of one of his eleven published books entitled *The Language of Aad,* which traces his lineage back to his ancestor, Jerah, son of Joktan.[263] He showed me in the Bible that Joktan had thirteen sons. Jerah was the fourth son and his younger sibling, the eleventh son, was named Ophir (Genesis 10:26-29). Depending on the language, the name "Jerah" is spelled differently. One of them is "*Jared*," meaning "ruling" but also "coming down," as in leading his family from Babel down through the empty quarter "where there never had man been" (Ether 2:5) to the southern coast of the Arabian Peninsula.

The name "Ophir" means "fruitful" or "bountiful" and was the name of the famous port, mentioned ten times in the Bible where King Solomon's ships were sent for gold and other riches. The Latter-day Saint Bible Dictionary, as well as many historians, identify Ophir as a port in southern Arabia. It was the ancient capital of frankincense and myrrh, which still abound there today.

Ali, a Muslim who has made presentations at Brigham Young University, said that the mountain where Nephi and the brother of Jared went to pray was descriptive of a sacred mountain just east of Khor Rori. In Shahri (language of Jerah), it is called the "mountain of prayer,"[264] the tallest mountain in southern Oman at 6,000 feet. Jaredites called it "Mount Shelem because of its exceeding height" (Ether 3:1). It is the same mountain as Mount Sephar (Genesis 10:30), where the children of Joktan (Jared's father) settled.

When Jared's family first arrived, "they called the name of the place Moriancumur" (Ether 2:13). The two mountain ranges just west of Khor Rori are called the Marah and Qamar (also spelled Camar or Comar) Mountains. In Arabic, vowels are not written, rendering these mountains as "Mrcmr" from which the name "Moriancumer" can be derived...the harbor where the Jaredites built their barges (Ether 2:16).

The brother of Jared is not mentioned by name in the Book of Mormon. At the "mountain of prayer," he was privileged to see the Lord God, who declared to him: "Behold, I am he who was prepared from the foundation of the world to redeem my people. Behold, I am Jesus Christ... In me shall all mankind have life, and that eternally, even they who shall believe on my name; and they shall become my sons and my daughters...never has man believed in me as thou hast. Seest thou that ye are created after mine own image? Yea, even all men were created in the beginning after mine own image. Behold, this body, which ye now behold, is the body of my spirit; and man have I created after the body of my spirit; and even as I appear unto thee to be in the spirit will I appear unto my people in the flesh" (Ether 3:14-16).

Because of his faith, "There never were greater things made manifest than those which were made manifest unto the brother of Jared" (Ether 4:4) while he was in the "mount [in] the presence of the Lord." It is little wonder that the tallest mountain in southern Oman holds such sacred significance to its people. The brother of Jared was commanded to "write the things which he had seen" but not show them "unto the world until after Christ should show himself unto his people"

(Ether 4:1). True to the Lord's command, the brother of Jared's experience on the "mountain of prayer" was unknown until after Christ's mortal ministry. Even his identity was not known to the world until 1834, when it was revealed to the Prophet Joseph Smith that his name was Mahonri Moriancumur.[265] Moriancumr was the name by which the Jaredite settlement at Ophir was known.

There is so much evidence in Oman of the remnants of the sons of Joktan who migrated there when the Lord confounded the languages that **Reverend Charles Forster** (1848-1894), a preacher of the Cathedral of Christ, Canterbury, believed he could trace the names of all thirteen sons of Joktan to southern Arabia.[266] The entire colony was known as Jaredites. However, "Jerah was in fact no less than, the father, or chief source throughout southern Arabia, of its Joktanite colonizations." A small number of the Jaredites built eight barges and sailed to the promised land (Ether 2:16, 6:12)...but not before the brother of Jared had been chastened for three hours by the Lord for not calling upon Him for four years (Ether 2:14). Visiting this paradise enables one to understand how difficult it would have been for them to leave it behind and venture out toward an unknown destination.

Friends of Jared and his brother who joined them on their voyage to America numbered twenty-two (Ether 6:16). The vast majority of the families of Joktan's thirteen sons (including quite possibly some of Jared's and his brother's own families) stayed behind, settling in one of three divisions that were named after

Joktan's sons. From west to east, these regions were: Uz or Uzal, where Job was from (Job 1:1), Ophir, and Jerah.[267] They leave an interesting trail of evidence of scriptural significance.

For example, "Dhofar" (the region where Khor Rori is located) is derived from the name "Zophar," one of Job's friends (Job 2:11, 11:1, 20:1, 42:9). Eliphaz, another of Job's friends, said to him: "If thou return to the Almighty [repent], thou shalt...lay up gold as dust, and the gold of Ophir as the stones of the brooks" (Job 22:23-24). This reference to "the gold of Ophir as the stones of the brooks" would have been significant to Job, who lived and died just forty miles from Ophir.

A compelling case can be made for Khor Rori as the ancient Port Ophir, as well as the Jaredites' Moriancumur (Ether 2:13) and the Nephites' Bountiful (1 Nephi 17: 5). A renowned shipbuilding industry existed in Khor Rori, quite possibly by those Jaredites who did not sail to America, but who might have preserved the lives of Lehi and his family. The monumental task of Nephi's building a ship became apparent to us as we visited the Maritime Museum and harbor at nearby Muscat, Oman. While the Lord gave Nephi the instructions on how to build the ship, He did not give him the lifetime of experience that shipwrights needed for crossing the ocean. Shipbuilding was a specialized profession. Nephi needed a competent crew and the seamanship skills to train them. It takes years to learn and practice the skills needed to control a sailing ship across two oceans.

The largest Arab freighters in Nephi's day were probably over fifty feet long, pointed at both ends, quarter rudder, square sails sewn together with coconut ropes (instead of fastened by nails), and small decks or none at all.[268] However, Nephi said, "I...did not work the timbers after the manner which was learned by men, neither did I build the ship after the manner of men; but I did build it after the manner which the Lord had shown unto me; wherefore, it was not after the manner of men" (1 Nephi 18:2).

Some scholars have calculated that Nephi's ship carried seventy people or more, including experienced crew members, plus tons of supplies, even though they would have had opportunities to make some stops along the way. The ship would have had a hull with a covered deck because Nephi wrote, "We did go down into the ship, with all our loading and our seeds, and whatsoever thing we had brought with us" (1 Nephi 18:6). Nephi guided and "sailed" his ship, implying that it was a sailing ship with a rudder (1 Nephi 18:13, 22). It had to be strong enough to withstand the powerful forces of the pounding seas, including at least one "great and terrible tempest" (1 Nephi 18:13). According to ship expert Frank Lineman, the ship would have been from 80 to 120 feet long and most likely a split rig with a "main mast forward and a mizzenmast aft."[269] This rules out a launch from the beach.

Some of the other requirements for Nephi's ship to have been ocean-worthy included:

- Preshaping planks to form a hull...knowing exactly where to place the ship's ribs so the hull could withstand the forces of the sea.
- Woodworking for tapering a mast, shaping perfectly fitted joints, and preventing leaks by carving planks to within 1/64 of an inch in exactness.
- Rope working and sewing timber.
- Caulking the ship and knowing how to mix the caulking compounds to prevent leaks.
- Oiling the ropes so they didn't fail.
- Antifouling the ship by mixing a coating compound to protect against shipworms.
- Outfitting the ship by knowing how and where to anchor the mast and how to install a complicated set of riggings and sails.
- Access to long, straight hardwoods.
- Fabric for sails.
- Iron ore and metal workers.
- Expert shipwrights.
- Seamanship skills.

We spent a full day each at two candidates for Nephi's harbor: Khor Kharfot westward and Khor Rori eastward. Our visit to **Khor Kharfot** was from the seaside with the help of Yemenese boatmen who took us in an outboard motor boat. Slightly off of the

Frankincense Trail, access for a camel caravan to Khor Kharfot would have been steep and difficult for Lehi's party, even if they had mountain camels. The site was likely unpopulated in Nephi's day and, therefore, unable to provide services and supplies Nephi would have needed for a shipbuilding project. It has an open beach with no protected harbor. We hiked the site, and when we were ready to leave, launching our small boat took three tries, with each of us having to wade in the water to get on board.

**Khor Rori**, on the other hand, met all the criteria for Nephi's harbor. It was the premier harbor and port in the known world during Lehi's time, with access to all kinds of supplies and experts in all trades related to shipbuilding and sailing. The world's best shipbuilders worked here and the best sea captains and crews sailed to and from here, where most waited out the winter. Nephi could have gained needful experience from these people to supplement what he received by revelation.

Khor Rori had dry docks for shipbuilding and logs to safely move large, ocean-sailing ships into the harbor. The remains are still there today. The harbor was protected by high granite cliffs that jut into the Indian Ocean, creating a large, calm harbor carved by powerful waterfalls from five freshwater lakes above that overfill during monsoon season. Large ocean-worthy ships were able to dock here.

The calm, protected harbor allowed crews to conduct sea trials to test and adjust ships, allowing the crew significant sailing practice. There is currently a sandbar that formed between 1646 and 1690 AD, blocking the passage to the Indian Ocean. However, it is known to have been open anciently. Arabs were the first to be able to consistently sail in open seas safely (as opposed to sailing along the coast) because they were the masters of stellar navigation. They knew how to find their way based on the stars so they wouldn't get lost in their sandy landscape, which was often void of landmarks.

The Lord asked Nephi to "construct a ship, after the manner which I shall show thee." (1 Nephi 17:8). The Lord clearly helped, or it would not have been possible. One of the ways He helps us is to place certain people and resources near us. What resources and services they lacked locally could be traded. Oman enjoyed a rich trading network with nearby Africa and India as early as the fourth millennium B.C.[270] Speaking of the many resources in Bountiful, Nephi was grateful that "all these things were prepared of the Lord that we might not perish" (1 Nephi 17:5)

What are the chances that Joseph Smith guessed the geographic details and the resources of the Arabian Peninsula so accurately? The odds approach those of Steven Weinberg's cosmological constant. One cannot travel Lehi's trail from Jerusalem to Bountiful without being overwhelmed by Nephi's superbly accurate physical description, unknown to anyone in Joseph Smith's day. Nonetheless, all of the evidence is abductive. The only sure-fire way to get deductive evidence of the authenticity and soul-stirring ability of the Book of Mormon in leading one to Christ begins with a prayerful perusal of its pages..."seek[ing] learning, even by study and also by faith" (Doctrine and Covenants 88:118).

**The Book of Mormon is a book with a claim** to everyone wanting to know its truth and power. Prior to burying the thousand-year history of his extinct Nephite people, Moroni, the last prophet of the Book of Mormon, signed out with the following "10-4" (Moroni 10:4): "And when ye shall receive these things, I would exhort you that ye would ask God, the Eternal Father, in the name of Christ, if these things are not true; and if ye shall ask with a sincere heart, with real intent, having faith in Christ, he will manifest the truth of it unto you, by the power of the Holy Ghost."

# Why Does the Church of Jesus Christ of Latter-day Saints Matter?

In 1892, forty-eight years after Joseph Smith's martyrdom, Dr. Andrew D. White, U.S. Ambassador to Russia, told of an experience he had while discussing the topic of religion with Count Leo Tolstoy:

"Dr. White," said Count Tolstoy, "I wish you would tell me about your American religion."

"We have no state church in America," replied Dr. White.

"I know that, but what about your American religion?"

Patiently then, Dr. White explained to the count that in America, there are many religions and that each person is free to belong to the particular church in which he is interested. To this, Tolstoy impatiently replied: "I know all of this, but I want to know about the

American religion. Catholicism originated in Rome; the Episcopal Church originated in England; the Lutheran Church in Germany, but the Church to which I refer originated in America, and is commonly known as the Mormon Church. What can you tell me of the teachings of the Mormons?"

"Well," said Dr. White, "I know very little concerning them. They have an unsavory reputation, they practice polygamy, and are very superstitious."

Then Count Leo Tolstoy, in his honest and stern but lovable manner, rebuked the ambassador. "Dr. White, I am greatly surprised and disappointed that a man of your great learning and position should be so ignorant on this important subject. The Mormon [Latter-day Saint] people teach the American religion; their principles teach the people not only of Heaven and its attendant glories, but how to live so that their social and economic relations with each other are placed on a sound basis. If the people follow the teaching of this Church, nothing can stop their progress—it will be limitless. There have been great movements started in the past but they have died or been modified before they reached maturity. If Mormonism is able to endure, unmodified, until it reaches the third and fourth generation, it is destined to become the greatest power the world has ever known."[271]

Tolstoy had identified America as the nation that merited the birthplace of the Latter-day Kingdom of God (Matthew 21:43). It would be the same kingdom that Daniel of Old told King Nebuchadnezzar "which shall never be destroyed...but...shall break in pieces and consume all...kingdoms, and it shall stand for ever (Daniel 2:44). From America, the covenant of God would spread throughout the earth.

The power to which Tolstoy referred would not be in membership statistics. When Tolstoy made his prediction, church membership numbered close to 200,000. Today, it has grown to over seventeen million members in 160 countries with 90,000+ missionaries worldwide. Nevertheless, this small fraction of the world's 8.1 billion people is typical of the minority that the Lord's covenant people have represented historically. In a vision of the latter days, the Prophet Nephi said in the sixth century B.C: "I beheld the church of the Lamb of God, and its numbers were few...the church of the Lamb, who were the saints of God, were...upon all the face of the earth; and their dominions upon the face of the earth were small, because of...wickedness" (1 Nephi 14:12). In the words of Elder Maxwell: "The Church does not become more true when more people join it (only more glorious in scope)—nor does it become less true when some choose to leave it. Validity has nothing to do with numbers, as the eight on [Noah's] ark and the three who successfully fled Sodom will testify."[272]

What Tolstoy predicted as "destined to become the greatest power the world has ever known" is a phenomenon I have observed in the hearts and lives of countless people I have met throughout my life. It invariably followed those who accepted the Lord's invitation to deny themselves, take up their cross, and follow Him (Matthew 16:24), whether by His own voice or by the voice of His servants; it is the same (Doctrine and Covenants 1:38).

From 2010 to 2013, I had the opportunity of presiding over missionary work in Mongolia, where I was able to meet many of the Church's 11,000 members in the country. In 2011, I met a man in the city of Darkhan who became so disgruntled with one of his church leaders one day that he resolved to never come back. Three months later, the branch president and I visited the man at his home. When we arrived, he was dressed in Sunday clothes and waiting for us outside. He told us that when he had left the Church, he determined that there were twenty-seven other Christian faiths in Darkhan. I was surprised to hear him quote that statistic in an overwhelmingly Buddhist country. This man decided to attend a different church each week until he found the "true Church of Christ."

By the time of our visit with him, he had attended over half of the churches and said, "There was no Plan of Salvation, no doctrine of Christ, no priesthood authority, no Holy Ghost, etc." He went on to describe a blueprint of more than a dozen qualifications of what he expected the Church of Christ to have from his study of the scriptures. This amazed me since it was coming from a man who had grown up a Buddhist in northern Mongolia! He went on to explain how pointless it would be for him to attend the remaining churches on his list. He was visibly touched by our visit and said that it was he who should be asking us to allow him to return to the church rather than us coming to him to invite him back. The branch president and I were moved by this man's sincerity. He had overcome personal pride and humbly expressed gratitude for our visit. The next day, his reunion with the saints at church was delightful.

As a postscript, this man commented that at each of the churches he had visited, he recognized at least one other member of the Church whom he had known. To each one, he asked, "What are you doing here?"

"Just visiting," they answered. Then they asked him in return, "What are you doing here?"

"Just visiting," he responded.

Though temporarily lost, most came back as they recognized the Church as not only a social organization but as the Kingdom of God on earth preparing for the Kingdom of Heaven to come (Doctrine and Covenants 65:6).

Like an architect who is able to distinguish the unique blueprint of the White House from all other buildings on Earth, a disciple of Christ recognizes the unique blueprint of the Lord's Church, as our friend in northern Mongolia had done. The following organizational outline is an adaptation from Tad R. Callister's *Blueprint of Christ's Church*:[273]

1. **Organization**
   - The Church of Christ is "built upon the **foundation of the apostles and prophets**,

Jesus Christ himself being the chief corner stone" (Ephesians 2:20).

- Other offices include the **Seventy** (Luke 10:1), **bishops** (1 Timothy 3:1-7; Titus 1:7; Philippians 1:1), **elders** (Acts 14:23; Titus 1:5), **deacons** (1 Timothy 3:8-13; Philippians 1:1), **evangelists**—also known as patriarchs (Ephesians 4:11), **pastors**—including bishops and stake presidents who preside over a flock of saints (Ephesians 4:11)
- A **lay ministry**, not a professional ministry, is another recognizable feature of the Lord's Church. Peter was a fisherman who fed "the flock...willingly; not for filthy lucre, but of a ready mind" (1 Peter 1:5). Matthew was a tax collector, Paul was a tentmaker, etc. Each was **chosen by God** and given priesthood authority (John 15:16; Hebrews 5:4).
- **The Church of Christ bears the name of Christ** (3 Nephi 27:8), not Apollos, Cephas, Paul, or someone else (1 Corinthians 1:12-13). In the sixteenth century, Martin Luther derided his followers for calling themselves Lutherans:

  "I pray you leave my name alone and call yourselves not 'Lutherans' but 'Christians.' Who is Luther? My teaching is not mine. I have not been crucified for anyone... How then does it befit me, a miserable bag of dust and ashes, to give my name to the children of Christ? Cease, my dear friends, to cling to these party names and distinctions; away with them all; let us call ourselves only 'Christians' after Him from whom our teaching comes!"[274]

Until the early nineteenth century, "there was no church even claiming name or title as the Church of Christ."[275]

## 2. Teachings

- **God and Jesus are two separate persons** (Mark 15:34; Luke 22:42; Acts 7:55-56; Joseph Smith—History 1:17).
- **God and Jesus have glorified bodies of flesh and bone** (Luke 24:37; Acts 1:9; Hebrews 1:3; Doctrine and Covenants 130:22).
- **The gospel is preached to the dead.** The Apostle Peter taught: "For this cause was the gospel preached also to them that are dead, that they might be judged according to men in the flesh, but live according to God in the spirit" (1 Peter 4:6). The Lord's blueprint does not discriminate against anyone who died without an opportunity to make an informed decision whether to accept the gospel. On October 3, 1918, the Prophet

Joseph Smith's nephew, Joseph F. Smith, a prophet himself, taught:

> "Thus was the gospel preached to those who had died in their sins, without a knowledge of the truth, or in transgression, having rejected the prophets. These were taught faith in God, repentance from sin, vicarious baptism for the remission of sins, the gift of the Holy Ghost by the laying on of hands, And all other principles of the gospel that were necessary for them to know in order to qualify themselves that they might be judged according to men in the flesh, but live according to God in the spirit" (Doctrine and Covenants 138:32-34).

- **There are multiple heavens (three degrees of glory).** The Apostle Paul taught: "There is one glory of the sun, and another glory of the moon, and another glory of the stars: for one star differeth from another star in glory. So also *is* the resurrection of the dead" (1 Corinthians 15:41-42). He later confirmed this three-tiered heaven when he recounted the vision of a man "caught up to the third heaven" (2 Corinthians 12:2). This doctrine was lost during the great apostasy from the Lord's Church. However, it was restored to the Prophet Joseph Smith on

February 16, 1832, in a revelation on the three heavens (Doctrine and Covenants 76).

- **Marriage continues for eternity.** Jesus conferred binding authority to His twelve apostles...not only to teach...but to seal for eternity. He said: "Whatsoever ye shall bind on earth shall be bound in heaven: and whatsoever ye shall loose on earth shall be loosed in heaven" (Matthew 18:18). What were they to bind? Families—beginning with parents. Paul declared that "neither is the man without the woman, neither the woman without the man, in the Lord" (1 Corinthians 11:11). The Apostle Peter confirmed that husbands and wives are "heirs together of the grace of life" (1 Peter 3:7).

### 3. Ordinances

- **Infants are blessed, not baptized.** Mark recorded that Jesus "took [children] up in his arms, put *his* hands upon them, and blessed them" (Mark 10:16). Matthew confirmed that the Savior "laid his hands upon them" (Matthew 19:15). There is not one account of an infant baptism occurring anywhere in the New Testament. It was not an ordinance in Christ's Church because children do not need baptism unto repentance until they become accountable (Doctrine and Covenants 68:25). In 1830, it was revealed that "every member of the church of Christ having children is to bring them unto the elders before the church, who are to lay their hands upon them in the name of Jesus Christ, and bless them in his name" (Doctrine and Covenants 20:70).

- **Baptism is essential for salvation.** After Christ set the example for us by being baptized, He declared unequivocally: "Except a man be born of water and *of* the Spirit, he cannot enter into the kingdom of God" (John 3:5). Peter emphasized this same point (Acts 2:38). In 1829, the Lord reiterated it by way of revelation to Joseph Smith (Doctrine and Covenants 18:22).
- **Baptism is done by immersion.** Paul explained that baptism is symbolic of the death, burial, and Resurrection of Jesus Christ (Romans 6:3-5). This can be accomplished only by immersion in water, as Jesus was in the River Jordan, after which He "went up straightway out of the water" (Matthew 3:16).
- **Baptisms are performed for the dead.** In Paul's day, members of the Church at Corinth doubted the reality of the Resurrection but were nevertheless practicing baptism for the dead. To them, Paul asked: "Else what shall they do which are baptized for the dead, if the dead rise not

at all? why are they then baptized for the dead?" (1 Corinthians 15:29). Knowing the need for the living to perform proxy baptisms for the dead, Paul wrote "...that they without us should not be made perfect" (Hebrews 11:40). In other words, the dead who accept the gospel in the post-mortal spirit world are still heirs of the Kingdom of God even if they did not have the opportunity of baptism in mortality since baptism could be performed for them vicariously by the living. Along with other exalting ordinances, baptism for the dead has been restored to Earth and authorized when performed in a temple dedicated to the Lord (Doctrine and Covenants 124, 128).

- **The Gift of the Holy Ghost is received by the laying on of hands.** After Stephen had baptized men and women in Samaria, "the Holy Ghost...as yet...was fallen upon none of them: only they were baptized in the name of the Lord Jesus. Then [Peter and John] laid they *their* hands on them, and they received the Holy Ghost" (Acts 8:15-17). In Ephesus, Paul "baptized in the name of the Lord Jesus. And when Paul had laid *his* hands upon them, the Holy Ghost came on them" (Acts 19:5-6). This ordinance was also restored to the Prophet Joseph Smith by revelation: "But now I give unto thee a commandment, that thou shalt baptize by water, and they shall receive the Holy Ghost by the laying on of the hands, even as the apostles of old" (Doctrine and Covenants 35:6).

**4. Fruits— Jesus gave this test for truth:** "Wherefore by their fruits ye shall know them" (Matthew 7:20). People of the Covenant are associated with:

- **...a healthy lifestyle...** The Apostle Paul taught: "Know ye not that ye are the temple of God, and *that* the Spirit of God dwelleth in you? If any man defile the temple of God, him shall God destroy; for the temple of God is holy, which *temple* ye are" (1 Corinthians 3:16-17). Accordingly, he discouraged wine (Ephesians 5; 1 Timothy 3) while giving general counsel conducive to a healthy body as the repository of the spirit. On February 27, 1833, Joseph Smith received a revelation known as the *Word of Wisdom*, which indicated that alcohol, tobacco, coffee, and tea were not good for the body (Doctrine and Covenants 89). Today, multiple independent studies have shown that Latter-day Saints who practice the *Word of Wisdom* are healthier... They live longer, have a higher fertility rate, and lower incidence of cancer and cardiovascular morbidity.

- ...**high moral standards...** The blueprint of Christ's Church requires high moral standards. Paul condemned immodesty (1 Timothy 2:9), adultery, fornication (Galatians 5:19), and homosexuality (Romans 1:26-27). Jesus included pornography: "whosoever looketh on a woman to lust after her hath committed adultery with her already in his heart" (Matthew 5:28). In an 1831 revelation to Joseph Smith, the Lord added: "And he that looketh upon a woman to lust after her shall deny the faith, and shall not have the Spirit; and if he repents not he shall be cast out" (Doctrine and Covenants 42:23). The blessing of a life of high moral standards was revealed to Joseph eight years later: "let virtue garnish thy thoughts unceasingly; then shall thy confidence wax strong in the presence of God; and the doctrine of the priesthood shall distill upon thy soul as the dews from heaven" (Doctrine and Covenants 121:45).
- **...happy families...** The Lord's people have always been family-oriented. From the beginning, God has declared that "a man leave his father and his mother, and shall cleave unto his wife: and they shall be one flesh" (Genesis 2:24; Mark 6:7-8). Even a bishop is not celibate but is "a husband to one wife" (1 Timothy 3:2). Fathers are to "bring [their children] up in the nurture and

admonition of the Lord" (Ephesians 6:4). Children are to "obey [their] parents in the Lord" and to "honor [their] father and mother, which is the first commandment with a promise" (Ephesians 6:1-2). The very purpose of the Church is to conduct activities that are home-centered and Church supported.

- **...miracles and gifts of the Spirit...** In principle and in practice, members of Christ's Church are blessed with "God also bearing them witness, both with signs and wonders, and with divers miracles, and gifts of the Holy Ghost, according to his own will" (Hebrews 2:4). From the gift of tongues to the gift of healing, gifts of the Spirit are diverse, numerous, and usually quiet, anonymous, without fanfare or drama so they do not become the primary basis for one's faith. They are the product, not the predecessor, of faith. Miracles are often so profoundly personal and sacred that they are not shared.

- **...angels and visions...** At the very heart of Christ's Church are accounts of angels and visions. Here are a few from the early Church:

  a. The Angel Gabriel announcing the birth of Christ to Mary (Luke 1:26-38). This is the same Gabriel honored by Muslims as the angel who revealed the Quran to Mohammed...including the denial that God had a Son. Joseph Smith identified Gabriel as the Patriarch Noah.[276]

b. The Angel Gabriel announcing six months earlier to Zacharias the forthcoming birth of his son, despite the fact that his wife was barren and they "both were now well stricken in years." Their son was to be John the Baptist who would turn many to the Lord their God, going "before him in the spirit and power of Elias" (Luke 1:7, 11-19).
c. Elias and Moses coming to Jesus in the presence of Peter, James, and John on the Mount of Transfiguration, followed by the voice of God bearing witness of His Son (Matthew 17:1-5).
d. The angel releasing Peter from prison (Acts 12:5-11).
e. The angel sent by the Lord to His Apostle John (Revelation 1:1, 22:8).
f. The angel speaking to Cornelius (Acts 10:1-8).
g. The vision of Peter directing the gospel to go to the Gentiles (Acts 10:9-48).
h. Stephen's vision of the Father and the Son (Acts 7:55-56).
i. John's vision of the last days (Revelation).

No scripture anywhere states that angels and visions have ceased to exist. In fact, they teach the opposite, those who "deny the revelations of God, and say that they are done away, that there are no revelations, nor prophecies, nor gifts, nor healing, nor speaking with tongues, and the interpretation of tongues...knoweth not the gospel of Christ... has not read the scriptures...or does not understand them.... God is the same yesterday, today, and forever, and in him there is no variableness neither shadow of changing...a God of miracles" (Mormon 9:7-10). The universe itself bears witness!

- **...missionary work...** Christ's Church is a missionary church. The Lord commanded his apostles: "Go ye therefore, and teach all nations, baptizing them in the name of the Father, and of the Son, and of the Holy Ghost: Teaching them to observe all things whatsoever I have commanded you: and, lo, I am with you alway, even unto the end of the world" (Matthew 28:19-20). Notwithstanding, Jesus knew that after His departure the temple would be destroyed, false prophets would deceive many and "because iniquity shall abound, the love of many shall wax cold." However, He went on to say that "this gospel of the kingdom shall be preached in all the world for a witness unto all nations; and then shall the end come" (Matthew

> 24:11-12, 14). Paul made it clear that "that day shall not come, except there come a falling away first..." (2 Thessalonians 2:3), which he described as "grievous wolves" that would not spare the [Lord's] flock after Paul departed.

Missionary work is necessary in order to fine-tune the faith of the flock while inviting all others to come unto eternal life as Jesus described in His parable of the marriage of the king's son:

> "The kingdom of heaven is like unto a certain king, which made a marriage for his son, And sent forth his servants to call them that were bidden to the wedding: and they would not come. Again, he sent forth other servants, saying, Tell them which are bidden, Behold, I have prepared my dinner: my oxen and *my* fatlings *are* killed, and all things *are* ready: come unto the marriage. But they made light of *it,* and went their ways, one to his farm, another to his merchandise: And the remnant took his servants, and entreated *them* spitefully, and slew *them.* But when the king heard *thereof,* he was wroth: and he sent forth his armies, and destroyed those murderers, and burned up their city.

> Then saith he to his servants, The wedding is ready, but they which were bidden were not worthy. Go ye therefore into the highways, and as many as ye shall find, bid to the marriage. So those servants went out into the highways, and gathered together all as many as they found, both bad and good: and the wedding was furnished with guests" (Matthew 22:2-10).

5. **Ongoing revelation is the Church of Christ's link to heaven.** Paul confirmed that ongoing revelation was an integral part of the Church of Christ. Of his own role as an apostle (special witness) of Christ, he said: "I will come to visions and revelations of the Lord" (2 Corinthians 12:1). Paul was not a contemporary of Jesus, but he knew Him through personal experience. Similarly, modern apostles have varied personal experiences that enable them to know Him as His special witnesses...qualifying them to bear that certain witness, beyond faith, that Jesus is the Christ.

The Apostle John proclaimed a future day in which "The kingdoms of this world are become the kingdoms of our Lord, and of his Christ; and he shall reign for ever and ever" (Revelation 11:15). It should be apparent that the infrastructure to which the Lord will return and through which He will reign is neither political nor "subsisting," albeit ecclesiastical, in nature. The blueprint of His Kingdom on Earth has been revealed by Him and His apostles in holy writ.

**The Church of Jesus Christ of Latter-day Saints is the only church on earth that matches the Lord's blueprint in every material aspect.** It is not only where Ockham's razor leads, but also in the Lord's words, "The only true and living church upon the face of the whole earth, with which I, the Lord, am well pleased, speaking unto the church collectively and not individually" (Doctrine and Covenants 1:30).

Jesus said: "Be ye therefore perfect, even as your Father which is in heaven is perfect" (Matthew 5:48). Such eventual perfection to qualify for the Lord's Kingdom is attainable only through His perfect doctrine that is encompassed in His covenant path as it is administered in His Church. Elder Maxwell taught: "While it is possible to have an imperfect people possessed of perfect doctrines (indeed, such is necessary to change their imperfections), you will never, never see the reverse: a perfect people with imperfect doctrines."[277]

# Why Do You Matter?

The Lord wants us to "remember, the worth of souls is great in the sight of God" (Doctrine and Covenants 18:10). Is this just a cliché? Why did "God so love the world, that he gave his only begotten Son, that whosoever believeth in him should not perish, but have everlasting life?" (John 3:16). At least one reason is because we are irreplaceable. As discussed earlier, we were not created out of nothing, *ex nihilo*. In what way, then, are we children of God? What was it exactly that He created?

From Moses (Numbers 16:22) to the Apostle Paul (Hebrews 12:9), it has been revealed to men and women that God is the Father of our spirits. Jesus was God's firstborn Son in the spirit and His only begotten son in the flesh. In essence, God is saying to each of us individually: "Thou art my son [or daughter]; this day have I begotten thee [spiritually]" (Psalms 2:7). Jesus reaffirmed this relationship after His resurrection when

He said, "I ascend unto my Father, and your Father; and to my God, and your God" (John 20:17).

Before we were begotten spiritually, we were "also in the beginning with God. *Intelligence* (italics mine)...was not created or made, neither indeed can be" (Doctrine and Covenants 93:29). To Abraham of old, God showed that intelligences "have no beginning; they existed before, they shall have no end, they shall exist after, for they are...eternal" (Abraham 3:18). God goes on to say, that for every two intelligences, one is more intelligent than the other. As strangers in time and space, we are prone to misinterpreting this statement as a vertical ranking of superiority. However, the multidimensional nature of the universe's unique intelligences (personalities) is far too complex for a simple comparative grading system.

The Apostle Paul taught: "And the eye cannot say unto the hand, I have no need of thee: nor again the head to the feet, I have no need of you... And whether one member suffer, all the members suffer with it; or one member be honoured, all the members rejoice with it" (1 Corinthians 12:21, 26). To use an orchestra analogy, no matter which section we are in—string, woodwind, brass, percussion, etc.—our performance is paramount to the harmony of the symphony. We need to be happy with who we are, learn well our individual parts, and follow the conductor.

In a face-to-face meeting with the Lord "as one man talketh with another" (Abraham 3:11), Abraham learned the following about a pre-mortal council God conducted with us prior to His creative activity:

> "We will go down, for there is space there, and we will take of these materials, and we will make an earth whereon these may dwell; And we will prove them herewith, to see if they will do all things whatsoever the Lord their God shall command them; And they who keep their first [pre-mortal] estate shall be added upon; and they who keep not their first estate shall not have glory in the same kingdom with those who keep their first estate; and they who keep their second [mortal] estate shall have glory added upon their heads for ever and ever. And the Lord said: Whom shall I send? And one answered like unto the Son of Man [Jesus]: Here am I, send me. And another [Lucifer] answered and said: Here am I, send me. And the Lord said: I will send the first. And the second was angry, and kept not his first estate; and, at that day, many followed after him" (Abraham 3:24-28).

One-third of the intelligences opted to follow Lucifer (Satan) in not keeping their first (pre-mortal) estate (Doctrine and Covenants 29:36). These were denied birth into mortality. Their willingness to forfeit the gift of a physical body also constituted a forfeiture of future immortality via the resurrection. As spirit devils, they are bent on our destruction. One statistic in their favor as reported in nationwide polls is that fewer people today believe in Satan, devils, and hell than in God, angels, and heaven. The most effective way to destroy an enemy is to convince him that he doesn't have one...or at least divert his attention away from the real enemy (2 Nephi 28:22).

The fact that we have physical bodies shows that we were part of the two-thirds who chose to follow God's plan by accepting the risks along with the growth of this probationary second estate. We incorrectly blame God for our problems and the injustices of the world when we falsely assume that He created us out of nothing. In reality, **we brought to God our own raw materials (intelligence/personality) and asked Him to "add upon" us so we could become more glorious like Him.** The fact that there is a finite number of intelligences in the universe is worth thinking about. Eternity is a long time. The law of supply and demand should make it evident that we are of infinite worth with unlimited potential. God Himself said that among His [intelligences], "there were many of the noble and great ones" (Abraham 3:22). We are God's most valuable asset in the universe, and our training on Earth is of tremendous importance to Him as well as to us.

Imagine yourself as a veteran detective, and your son expresses a desire to become a sleuth like you. You are thrilled at the prospect of working with him and go to great lengths to train him personally. Sometime later, a crime is reported which gives you an opportunity to take your budding detective to conduct an investigation under your supervision. You are impressed by his survey of the scene. His inquiry into the details and timing of events is superb, and his questioning of witnesses about all relevant clues is flawless.

As the investigation proceeds, you notice that your initial enthusiasm was premature. Your protégé has a blind spot to the most important part of the investigation...the criminal. None of his investigative efforts lead to the perpetrator of the crime. You discover that he doesn't read the training manual, which, you learned long ago, was paramount to getting inside the mind, motive, and character of the criminal. In the best of faith, you offer suggestions from your experience, but they make him sore at you and so you back off. Predictably, his investigation fails. He loses interest in the business and drops out.

Like becoming a detective, joining our Heavenly Father's business requires rigorous training (living gospel covenants) and includes the study of a training manual (scriptures) in order to get inside the mind, motive, and character of God. Because we ourselves are a vital part of the evidence, our search is incomplete unless we investigate the most important "persons of interest," God and us together. Failure to do so results in a blind spot which makes our worldview investigation incomplete.

One of the more common conditions I treated as an ophthalmic surgeon was **glaucoma**, a silent, potentially blinding condition. When patients are first diagnosed with glaucoma, it isn't unusual for them to say, "But I feel fine. I see fine. Doctor, are you sure you're not mistaken?" In the early stages of the most common variety of glaucoma, patients are asymptomatic, which can make it difficult to convince some of them of their need for eyedrops, pills, lasers, or surgery. Initially, blind spots are small and unnoticeable. However, if the condition is left untreated, blind spots grow until the risk of permanent, irreversible blindness becomes serious. As debilitating as physical glaucoma is, there is a far more devastating spiritual analog. Most physical glaucoma patients want to know about their blind spots. Spiritual glaucoma patients often don't like to be shown theirs.

Worldviews are harder to replace than careers. One lesson that a study of worldviews teaches us is that there is nothing worldly that is really worth holding onto. The Lord taught: "For whosoever will save his life shall lose it: and whosoever will lose his life for my sake shall find it. For what is a man profited, if he shall gain the whole world, and lose his own soul? or what shall a man give in exchange for his soul?" (Matthew 16:25-26). Elder Maxwell added: "When we speak of letting go of the world, this does not mean forgetting its sunsets, its beautiful music, nor, best of all, its people. The 'world' is a way of life that takes us away from, not toward God. Away from, not toward, happiness. Away from sense to nonsense."[278] Away from God in any direction is toward Satan, who tries to persuade us that what he offered Jesus and was turned down is still a bargain. We need to have the sense and courage to refuse his offer by letting go of the world and gaining the grasp of the outstretched hand of Him, who was once offered the world.

The truly great discoveries in life come to those who think about the evidence and act on it. Sir Isaac Newton was once asked how he discovered the law of gravity. His answer was, "by thinking about it all the time."[279] If you'll ponder, pray, study, and covenant with God, your worldview will make sense to you and your future will be exciting. One of your discoveries will be an understanding of how much God wants you to petition Him for help.

Jesus illustrated this principle effectively through a parable of a man who importunes his friend for three loaves of bread at midnight. Although the friend doesn't want to get out of bed over the friendship, he gets up because of the importunity and gives the man as many loaves as he wants [to get rid of him]. Jesus invites us to prove our Father's love by importuning Him. He says, "If a son shall ask bread of any of you that is a father, will he give him a stone? or if he ask a fish, will he for a fish give him a serpent? Or if he shall ask an egg, will he offer him a scorpion? If ye then, being evil, know how to give good gifts unto your children: how much more shall your heavenly Father give the Holy Spirit to them that ask him?" (Luke 11:11-13). The *best gift* God gives for guidance out of abductive dead ends is His Spirit of deduction.

# Welcome to Deductland!

By now you are hopefully convinced of the scientific basis for the God Hypothesis. If you are living a life of naturalism, you question every bit of evidence presented to you. Then, you decide whether to follow Ockham's razor—the simplest conclusion or make a more convoluted conclusion based on your personal preference. Such a decision-making process is circular...like the path of processionary caterpillars. It is also myopic and aimless.

In my career, I learned that not everyone wants to be farsighted. Early in my ophthalmology residency, I examined a man with myopia (nearsightedness) who had 20/200 vision. When I showed him what 20/20 vision would be like with prescription lenses, I thought he'd be elated. However, he surprised me by saying that his unaided 20/200 vision was clear and that his aided 20/20 vision was blurry. As frustrating as this experience was for me, it taught me that all I could do was show him what he was missing. He would have to make the choice to forego driving and a host of other activities because of his unwillingness to wear corrective lenses. Similarly, not everyone is willing to sacrifice his or her nearsighted worldview for God's farsighted one.

One of the great learning experiences in life comes from obtaining a passport and visa to visit another country. During our visit abroad, if we break the laws of that county, we are likely to be detained, imprisoned, or deported even though we weren't required to learn the laws of that country in order to enter. However, in order to enter the Kingdom of God, to enjoy the company of a celestial society, we must demonstrate beforehand that we can keep the laws of that society. And so it behooves us, as it did Agatha Christie's island guests, to learn as much as we can about our Host and His Kingdom...and to take advantage of every covenant offered to us for our benefit.

**God's fastest way to fine-tune and add new information is through His covenant path.** You won't be able to prove this to yourself at first; no experiment can. However, evidence and reason will lead you to the most plausible explanation of what you should do. Having reached a certain level of abductive acumen, you are now ready to venture into the land of deductive discovery—Deductland.

Everyone who was ever born is "hardwired" to receive deductive evidence beyond the five senses. In a revelation given to the Prophet Joseph Smith in 1832, the Lord said: "And the Spirit giveth light to every man [and woman] that cometh into the world; and the Spirit enlighteneth every man [and woman] through the world, that hearkeneth to the voice of the Spirit. And every one that hearkeneth to the voice of the Spirit cometh unto God, even the Father. And the Father teacheth him of the covenant which he has renewed and confirmed upon you, which is confirmed upon you for your sakes, and not for your sakes only, but for the sake of the whole world" (Doctrine and Covenants 84:46-48).

Since the Spirit of Christ is offered to everyone, why doesn't everyone receive it? The Lord went on to say: "And the whole world lieth in sin, and groaneth under darkness and under the bondage of sin. And by this you may know they are under the bondage of sin, because they come not unto me. For whoso cometh not unto me is under the bondage of sin. And whoso receiveth not my voice is not acquainted with my voice, and is not of me. And by this you may know the righteous from the wicked, and that the whole world groaneth under sin and darkness even now" (Doctrine and Covenants 84:49-53).

The greatest waste on Earth is not wealth, energy, or resources; it is our living far below our privileges. Even to the Church, the Lord once said: "And your minds in times past have been darkened because of unbelief, and because you have treated lightly the things you have received—Which vanity and unbelief have brought the whole church under condemnation" (Doctrine and Covenants 84:54-55). However, the Lord is merciful! If we are willing to "look unto [Him] in every thought," He has promised us "there I will be also, for I will go before your face. I will be on your right hand and on your left, and my Spirit shall be in your hearts, and mine angels round about you, to bear you up" (Doctrine and Covenants 6:36, 84:88).

If you live in "Abductland," I invite you to obtain a passport and visa for "Deductland," the land of trust, love, and happiness. You'll probably want to stay. If you don't feel comfortable there, keep trying to fit in. It'll be a far happier home than Abductland ever was. With Michelangelo, you'll be able to see yourself as an imprisoned image and say, "In every block of marble, I see a statue...as plainly as though it stood before me [in the mirror] shaped and perfect in attitude and action. I have only to hew away the rough walls that imprison my lovely apparition to reveal it to other eyes as mine already see it."

Each new day will come to you fresh and untouched, like a piece of pure marble, unstained, uncut, and unspoiled and you may carve out of it whatever you please the person you visualize yourself to be. But before you can improve the future, you must improve the present, and before you can improve the present, you must improve your worldview model. For as the sculptor visualizes the statue in the rough, you must see the greatness of yourself before you begin to carve...a greatness after the image of the God of the universe, Father of your spirit, and bestower to you of His divine attributes which lie latent within you.

Imagine living prior to the invention of the compound microscope in AD 1590. Red corpuscles, white corpuscles, and platelets hadn't been discovered. It wasn't until much later that descriptions of these blood cells laid the foundation of the field of hematology. Similarly, in 1843, the Lord revealed: "There is no such thing as immaterial matter. All spirit is matter, but it is more fine or pure, and can only be discerned by purer eyes; We cannot see it; but when our bodies are purified we shall see that it is all matter" (Doctrine and Covenants 131:7-8). Look forward in faith to the day when your eyes will be able to discern the finer matter of the spirit.

There are those who require little or no physical evidence to support their faith. Their familiarity with the language of the Spirit enables them to receive ongoing evidence deductively. These are some of the most admirable people who walk the earth. Deduction is the language Jesus invites us to learn. He once told His disciples: "I have meat to eat that ye know not of" (John 4:32). When His confused disciples asked what He meant, He explained, "My meat is to do the will of him that sent me, and to finish his work" (John 4:34). The meat to which Jesus referred was the deductive evidence that comes to those who walk the covenant path. As they keep their covenants, they "know that it is by [God] that [they] are led" (1 Nephi 17:13).

# Conclusion

Near the end of my ophthalmology residency in the late 1970s, I was introduced to the newly emerging technique of extracapsular cataract surgery ("extracap") that would gradually replace intracapsular cataract surgery ("intracap") as the standard of care in eye surgery. It would take years for ophthalmologists to fully adopt the new technique because the transition involved a steep learning curve. For me it required post-residency training courses to unlearn the old way and learn the new way over many hours of practice on cadaver pig eyes. My mentors had taught me that a good "extracap" is better than the best "intracap." However, a bad "extracap" is worse than the worst "intracap." It became clear to me that I needed to follow very strict guidelines if I wanted better outcomes than I had previously obtained with older techniques. Today, virtually all cataract/lens implant operations are variations of extracap.

While living in Mongolia, I knew a man who described to me his life under communism prior to the fall of the Iron Curtain. During communism he had heard the word "stress" but didn't know what it meant. Life had been relatively stress-free, as far as he was concerned, since "the government pretended to pay him and he pretended to work." When capitalism was first introduced to Mongolia, it stalled because people were not prepared for it, and they suffered tremendously. Over time, as capitalism developed, the negative connotation of stress became positive as the value of initiative and self-reliance was learned and valued. This man learned that good capitalism was better than the best communism. However, according to him, bad capitalism was worse than the worst communism.

Good covenant path Christianity is better than the best of all other worldviews. However, bad Christianity can be worse than the worst of them. Analogous to extracapsular cataract surgery and capitalism, the success of covenant path Christianity lies in its second-mile opportunity, which, if taken, leads to life, but if not taken, leads to destruction. Jesus emphasized the desirability of this "more excellent way" (1 Corinthians 12:31) when He cautioned: "Enter ye in at the strait [narrow, strict] gate: for wide *is* the gate, and broad *is* the way, that leadeth to destruction, and many there be which go in thereat: Because strait *is* the gate, and narrow *is* the way, which leadeth unto life [eternal], and few there be that find it" (Matthew 7:13-14).

**The strait gate and narrow way is the covenant path of Christianity.** Although immortality is a gift to everyone, eternal life in the Kingdom of God is earned by relatively few because of the overwhelming tendency for people to want more latitude than a narrow road can give. Few people are inclined to get off a narrow road at a right angle. Failure begins as soon as they decide to broaden the road...their worldview. The road itself is critical for success. Self-discipline is narrow; broad-mindedness is wide and weak.

Far too many of us are perennial optimists who believe in a happy ending regardless of the road we take or how wide we make it. Broad-mindedness is like the Powder River of Wyoming and Montana, which early inhabitants described as "a mile wide, an inch deep, too thin to plow and too thick to drink." Only a narrow stream can go deep enough to form a torrent with enough power to tear away the mountainside.

It was a narrow road that the Prophet Joseph Smith took in sacrificing "character, reputation, honor, applause, his good name, his home, lands, family, and finally his own life for the truth's sake."[280] His life and words taught: "Let us here observe, that a religion that does not require the sacrifice of all things never has power sufficient to produce the faith necessary unto life and salvation."[281] The source of his teaching was the Lord Himself, who said: "He that loveth father or mother more than me is not worthy of me: and he that loveth son or daughter more than me is not worthy of me. And he that taketh not his cross, and followeth after me, is not worthy of me. He that findeth his life shall lose it: and he that loseth his life for my sake shall find it" (Matthew 10:37-39). That is a narrow road!

How can we love the Lord more than our own family members? Jesus answered this question when He prioritized the two great commandments: "Thou shalt love the Lord thy God with all thy heart, and with all thy soul, and with all thy mind. *This is the first and great commandment.* And the second is like unto it, Thou shalt love thy neighbour as thyself. On these two commandments hang all the law and the prophets" (Matthew 22:37-40) [italics mine]. As the author of eternal families, the Lord authorizes the eternal sealing of a husband and wife along with their children in His Holy Temples. Notwithstanding, no ordinance seals (binds) couples or families solely to each other; they must first be bound (under covenant) to the Lord. No eternal family exists without Him.

And so, the Lord directs each of us to "...seek ye first the kingdom of God, and his righteousness [by planting yourself firmly on His covenant path]; and all these things [family, etc.] shall be added unto you" (Matthew 6:33). We follow His admonition by keeping our eye single [fixed] on laying up for ourselves treasures in heaven (Matthew 6:20-22). Heavenly treasures are stored by bringing souls, beginning with our own, to Christ through missionary and temple work. This is the thing of greatest worth to all of us (Doctrine and Covenants 15:6).

If you have ever had an airplane ride through a violent storm that required an instrument landing, you would have prayed for a narrow-minded pilot. One flash of broad-mindedness might have destroyed the plane and everyone on board. In 1974, a study on critical decision-making was conducted by Paul Slovic, who found that decision accuracy didn't improve by increasing relevant information from 5 pieces of data to 10, 40, or 88. However, one's confidence increased dramatically. It's dangerous to become overconfident with unlimited, useless information from the Internet.

For over thirty years, I lived in a home that was not identified on Google's global positioning system. Although I tried to explain to people coming to my home for the first time that they would get lost by using it, more often than not, they ignored my instructions and followed their Google GPS to an abandoned shack twenty minutes away before calling me to ask how to get to my home. The fact that Google was never notified to update their data is not the point. People often choose to believe what they want to believe regardless of evidence from a motivated source, like I was in directing guests to my home...and like God is in directing His children home to His kingdom.

It is critical to concentrate on those few sources on which you can rely. As Harry Emerson Fosdick said: "The man who swears allegiance to a cause places upon himself limitations stronger than any slave's, because he has given his heart."[282] Success in eternity requires the narrow road of focus and concentration...of seeing oneself together with Christ in everything and everywhere. The Lord beckons us:

"Look unto me in every thought; doubt not, fear not" (Doctrine and Covenants 6:36).

If someone had described to you, prior to your birth, the growth you were going to experience from birth to adulthood, would you have believed it? Perhaps not. Think of a baby lying in the arms of his mother. He has eyes but cannot discern objects, ears but cannot distinguish sounds, and hands perfectly fashioned but helpless. He has legs, but they are unable to bear the weight of his body, much less to walk. His brain and personality are correspondingly unproductive, and yet, within the span of a few short years, what a change takes place! From such a helpless beginning come scientists, engineers, teachers, artists, musicians, congressmen, prophets, etc. Having experienced life for yourself, shouldn't it be easier to have faith in your post-mortal future that has been promised to you by the Lord and all His holy prophets?

Edgar Allen Poe once said, "They who dream by day are cognizant of many things which escape those who dream only by night." You might not administer a universe the same way God administers His. However, you and I don't have a universe. So, the most productive thing we can do is to learn about ours with particular emphasis on a study of our creator. Then, we need to learn how to make the most of our lot; whoever, whatever, wherever, whenever, or however we are, taking advantage of every opportunity from a long-range perspective.

The most fulfilling experience one can have in life is the exhilarating feeling of the personal love of God. No other experience comes close. Once felt, the worst experience one can imagine is losing that love...and hope of ever feeling it again. This concept became indelibly impressed upon me on the last day of spring semester in 1968 when I went to a movie in Salt Lake City with the girl to whom I had just proposed. I wouldn't be seeing her again until school resumes in the fall. The film we saw was *Camelot,* which we saw very little of, spending most of our time gazing into one another's eyes, contemplating our love for each other and the covenants we would be making together with the Lord. When the final scene began, our eyes were drawn to the screen.

King Arthur's wife, Guinevere, had been unfaithful. Despite the king's love for her, the demands of his subjects prevented him from restoring her to her exalted position in the kingdom. After dismissing Lancelot, King Arthur and Guinevere exchange these concluding words:

King Arthur: "You must go too, Jenny."

Guinevere (sobbing): "I know. So, in the past, Arthur, I would look in your eyes and I would find, there, forgiveness. Perhaps, I may in the future…to be there again." Then, losing her composure, she cries, "But now I won't be with you. I won't see it!"

King Arthur: "Good-bye, my love."

Guinevere would always remember the king loved her. However, that knowledge would give her little consolation because her actions had disqualified her from ever seeing his face and feeling his love again. As she departs, the king continues to watch her from a distance and says to her, "My dearest love!" But Guinevere can no longer hear him nor feel the immediate presence of his love. Her actions had not changed the king's feelings for her, but she was unable to see the forgiveness in his eyes, hear it in his voice, nor feel it from his countenance. The symbolism of this scene is powerful imagery of the effect of our actions on our future with our Heavenly King.

As His metaphorical bride, we must first be willing to enter into a covenantal relationship with God and then be faithful to that covenant to qualify for His presence. Jesus said: "Except a man be born of water and *of* the Spirit, he cannot enter into the kingdom of God" (John 3:5). This is the beginning of the covenant path, which, in the Lord's words, is required to enter His Kingdom. What about those who don't have the opportunity for baptism? They are taught the gospel in the post-mortal Spirit World, and their ordinance of baptism is performed by mortals in a temple on their behalf. Baptism is the gateway to all higher ordinances, thus fulfilling the declarations of Peter and Paul that "God is no respecter of persons" (Acts 10:34, Romans 2:11).

# Caution

In 2001, I attended a small, private event that was also attended by actor Charlton Heston, his wife, Lydia, and their son, Fraser. Despite his motion picture fame, Mr. Heston, who preferred to be called Chuck, was unassuming, congenial, and visibly devoted to his wife of fifty-seven years. My wife commented to him that of all of his leading ladies, his wife, Lydia, was the loveliest. The comment brought an ear-to-ear smile to his face.

I mentioned to him my admiration for his character portrayals. He responded, "I never tire of hearing this." Then he asked, "Which movie in particular stands out in your mind?" I wasn't prepared for his question. I thought of his role as Moses in *The Ten Commandments*, Ben-Hur, John the Baptist, Michelangelo, and many others. After a moment, I answered, *El Cid.* He pondered my answer for a few seconds and then said, "That was a good movie." Then we discussed why I had chosen the story of the eleventh-century Spanish hero, El Cid, over all of his other films. It was because of what it taught me about honor.

After defeating two Moorish tribes on the day of his scheduled wedding, Charlton Heston, in the role of Rodrigo Díaz de Vivár, set the tribal leaders free, hoping that it would encourage peace. One of the Moorish kings, who had been fearing the reprisal and death of his sons after his execution, was encouraged with the hope of peace between the Moors and the Christians as a result of Rodrigo's compassion. When Rodrigo asked the Moorish kings, "Do you solemnly pledge never again to attack King Ferdinand's country?" This first king responded, "I do." Then, after being untied, he looked into Rodrigo's eyes and said, "Among our people, we have a word for a warrior with the vision to be just—the courage to be merciful. We call such a man 'El Cid' [the Lord]. I, Moutamín, Emir of Zaragoza, pledge eternal friendship to the Cid of Vivár and allegiance to his sovereign lord, King Ferdinand of Castille. May Allah strike the eyes from my head and the flesh from my bones if I break this pledge, in the name of Allah." Then he knelt in fealty.

As a fifteen-year-old boy at the time, I was deeply moved by the commitment of this Moorish king. I watched him carefully throughout the rest of the movie to see if he would keep his pledge. He did, despite severe tests of his loyalty. The second Moorish king, who was released at the same time, wasn't at all convincing in his vow. While he was being untied, he looked upward and muttered the words," In the name of Allah." However, his eyes and face betrayed his sincerity and, as I suspected, he later broke his pledge.

For freeing the Moors, Rodrigo was charged with treason. His answer to the charges came in the form of a challenge to the death from Count Gormaz, the king's champion and father of Rodrigo's fiancé. Count Gormaz discouraged Rodrigo from defending his honor by saying, "Go home, Rodrigo. No one will think the less of you for not standing up to the king's champion."

Rodrigo then asked Count Gormaz, "Can a man live without honor?"

"No," Gormaz replied. "Now, I can see what I once saw in you to be worthy of my daughter's hand in marriage."

Rodrigo won the sword fight. However, he paid a dear price for defending his honor by having to win back the love of his beloved Chemaine after taking the life of her father.

I have often contemplated Rodrigo's inspired question, "Can a man [or woman] live without honor?" Honor requires heart, but a heart can be hardened. Elder Maxwell describes the process as follows: "Hardness of heart comes first in the form of forgetfulness, for memory is the mother of feeling. When a people can no longer be stirred up to remembrance, they become past feeling. Their hearts become like shells, and finally, stones."[283] "Past feeling" is a scriptural term to depict people who become sufficiently encrusted in their excesses that they kill their capacity to feel. It caused Louis XVI to reportedly say while standing on the scaffold of his guillotine, "I have seen all of this coming for ten years. How was it possible that I never wanted to believe it?"[284]

When I was ten years old, I saw a newly released science fiction movie called *Invasion of the Body Snatchers.* It was about an extraterrestrial invasion in the small, fictitious town of Santa Mira, California. Alien plants had fallen from space and were growing into large seed pods capable of forming exact replicas of nearby human beings. If you fell asleep close to a giant pod, it would form a duplicate of you with your exact physical characteristics, memories, and personality. The real "you" would die, and the only way anyone could distinguish your pod from you was by your lack of human emotion, particularly your inability to love. From this movie, the expression "pod people" arose in the late twentieth century to describe people whose love was superficial.

When pod people took over the majority of Santa Mira, the remaining humans cried out for help to neighboring towns who thought they were all suffering from an "epidemic of mass hysteria." As townspeople continued to be replaced, pod people tried to convince remaining humans to submit to sleep because, in doing so, life loses its frustrating complexity as all emotions and sense of individuality vanish.

By the end of the movie, the last remaining couple tried to keep each other awake while escaping to the next town. They got separated for a few moments, and when they met again and kissed, the man realized, to his horror, that his partner had fallen asleep, and she was now one of them. Alone, he ran away as she sounded the alarm. Aliens chased him to a crowded state highway, where they stopped, knowing no one would believe his story.

The most memorable part of the movie is when he says, "I've been afraid a lot of times in my life. But I didn't know the real meaning of fear until I had kissed Becky. A moment's sleep and the girl I loved was an inhuman enemy bent on my destruction. That moment's sleep was death to Becky's soul."

Why would a low-budget movie that I saw at age ten still have me worked up almost seven decades later? Because throughout my life, I have seen people allow their humanity to drain away without seeming to care about it. They didn't consciously put love and faith out of their mind. They became so open-minded that it just fell out. Once very loving people hardened their hearts, grew callous, and began to defend their pride instead of their honor, it is as though they had fallen asleep and awakened less-caring, less-loving, and less-human. **With all my heart, I urge you to be cautious not to fall asleep spiritually. Doing so will render you immune (hardened) from spiritual promptings.**

Lost Arctic explorers know that as they become fatigued, they are inclined to want to lie down and rest, which is the most dangerous thing they could do. Even snow invites peaceful repose to those who fail to realize that it is an invitation to death. Angelo Patri once said that education is just being afraid at the right time.[285] A little fear can keep us awake and prevent the drowsiness that precedes death from freezing. We need to have what Shakespeare called "the fear that reason leads."

We live in a twilight zone of mortality in which many who walk among us could be characterized as vogue on the outside and vague on the inside. Elder Sterling W. Sill described this state of death as a disability that comes in fractions.[286] We can be dead even though we haven't been buried. Our gravestone might as well be inscribed now in the words: "Dead at 30 buried at 65." Dr. Norman Vincent Peale wrote a book on this subject: *Stay Alive All Your Life.* Jesus was the ultimate example of life. The Apostle John said of Him: "In him was life; and the life was the light of men" (John 1:4). In confirming John's statement, Jesus said: "I am come that they might have [eternal] life, and that they might have it more abundantly" (John 10:10). Our greatest pursuit should be directed toward infusing a greater percentage of eternal life into ourselves.

Pontius Pilate once asked a crowd, "What shall I do...with Jesus?" (Matthew 27:22). He was asking the wrong people, hoping to erase Jesus from his agenda instead of honoring his office to uphold justice. However, trying to appease the crowd didn't work. It never does because a significant relationship exists between Jesus and every person who has ever lived. Jesus is our Mediator (1 Timothy 2:5), our Savior (Luke

2:11), and our Advocate with the Father (1 John 2:1). It would be well for us to ask ourselves the same question Pilate asked the crowd, only in an inspired way: "What shall I do with Jesus?" Our daily answer to this question will determine our honor, our humanness, and our destiny.

# Invitation

By now, you might be thinking to yourself that this book should have been named *Finding a Worldview at the Theater.* If you will indulge me in one more movie scene, I'll conclude by returning to my favorite singer. In the 1950 movie *The Toast of New Orleans,* shrimp fisherman Pepe (Mario Lanza) attends a public vocal recital featuring soprano opera star Suzette (Kathryn Grayson) near his home at Bayou Minou. During her performance, Pepe uninvitedly joins Suzette in her solo of "Be My Love," turning it into an impromptu duet. He sings so beautifully that Suzette's manager, Jacques (David Niven), recruits Pepe to sing in the opera.

However, Pepe's transition takes him through a steep learning curve in social graces. He thinks that if you are a gentleman in New Orleans, "you don't sing unless you're invited...you don't dance unless you know how...and when you want something very much you don't reach out." Pepe's reference to not reaching out was because of his falling in love with Suzette while

Jacques was out of town scheduling a world tour for Pepe and Suzette. When Pepe kissed Suzette, she reciprocated at first, but his awkward aggressiveness in trying to kiss her again prompted her to slap his face. Unbeknown to Pepe, Jacques is engaged to Suzette. Later, when Jacques returns home to New Orleans, a discouraged Pepe informs Jacques of his encounter with Suzette and of his intention to quit the opera:

Pepe: "I thought the whole thing over last night. Bayou Minou is where I belong. I don't fit in around here."

Jacques: "Maybe you're right."

Pepe: "Thanks for everything you tried to do for me. I'm sorry I wasted your time."

Jacques (as Pepe opens the door to leave): "Wait a minute, Pepe. You've got so much to offer the world; I can't let you throw it away because of a personal problem...yours or anyone else's.

Pepe: "Do you think I should stay? The way she feels, she won't even talk."

Jacques: "If I know you, you probably scared the wits out of her."

Pepe: "I never scared anyone else."

Jacques: "You say you don't belong...maybe you don't. I don't know. But you can try. LEARN to belong!"

Pepe: "She wants me to be like everyone else around here...a gentleman. I couldn't do that.... Could I?"

Jacques: "Give it time, Pepe.

Pepe: "She told me yesterday that I'd never change. She said that..."

Jacques: "Whatever she said yesterday, it's possible that she didn't mean it. You'd better stay. We'll know soon enough one way or the other."

Pepe (walking back into the room): "You know something? You're a very smart man!"

Jacques (realizing he might be sacrificing Suzette): "I used to be."

Pepe stays with the opera, becomes a gentleman and a star, and wins Suzette. In the process, he discovers the invaluable reward that comes with persevering to fit in.

Throughout life, we encounter situations, individuals, groups and organizations that make us feel like shrimp fishermen on an opera stage. Our first impulse is to leave, that is, unless there is something or someone we love enough that compels us to stay...to try to fit in. Keeping God's commandments can seem uncomfortable or trivial if we are "past feeling" the anticipatory happiness of a celestial society. Failing to understand the supernal joy of an eternal family, we resist God's spiritual promptings to fit into His Kingdom. In our minds, we either dismiss the idea of a Judgment Day or brace ourselves to vent our displeasure over injustices we suffered in mortality. Pride can be capable of stiff resistance, and when pride doesn't work, there is always fear. We can imagine ourselves hiding "from the face of him that sitteth upon the throne" (Revelation 6:16; Isaiah 2:19). But are these really viable options?

In 2004, Harvard University concluded a seventy-five-year study from 1938 to 2012 on what makes people happy. Harvard psychiatrist Dr. George Vaillant, who led the last part of the study, concluded that there are two pillars of happiness: "One is love. The other is finding a way of coping with life that does not push love away."[287] Think about all the negative emotions we feel that push love away, any one of which is capable of causing us to miscalculate the most dreadful of all unanticipated losses...our love for God.

A covenantal relationship with God introduces us to a unique type of love called *Hesed* in the Hebrew Bible. *Hesed* has no adequate English equivalent. It describes a covenant relationship in which both parties are bound to be loyal and faithful to each other.[288] When we make a covenant with God, we leave neutral ground forever. Like covenantal family love, covenantal love of God grows as it is nurtured. As it develops, it melts away awkwardness. Covenantal love is what the Lord meant when He said: "If ye keep my commandments, ye shall abide in my love; even as I have kept my Father's commandments, and abide in his love" (John 15:10). Abiding in the king's love is what Guinevere forfeited by her banishment.

Some of my most uncomfortable experiences as a shrimp fisherman on the opera stage of life have occurred when I have grieved the spirit of love by speaking or acting "amiss" (James 4:3; Luke 23:41), saying something either irrelevant, inappropriate, or noncontributory for the occasion. Speaking amiss can be unintentional when we don't know what to say but feel the need to say something anyway. I wonder if the scriptures weren't teaching us something about this phenomenon when Peter, James, and John saw Jesus transfigured before their eyes and beheld Moses and Elias appear to them. Peter must have been bewildered as he said to Jesus, "Lord, it is good for us to be here: if thou wilt, let us make here three tabernacles; one for thee, and one for Moses, and one for Elias." Peter's suggestion seemed to fall upon deaf ears when a bright cloud overshadowed them and a voice declared, "This is my beloved Son, in whom I am well pleased; hear ye him" (Matthew 17:4-5).

However, Peter showed no offense over his ignored suggestion but meekly kept trying to fit in. Later, when the Lord began to wash Peter's feet, Peter again spoke amiss by telling the Lord, "Thou shalt never wash my feet." When Jesus answered, "If I wash thee not, thou hast no part with me." Peter responded, "Lord, not my feet only, but also my hands and head." Jesus then assured Peter, "He that is washed needeth not save to wash his feet, but is clean every whit" (John 13:8-10). Peter had spoken and acted amiss, but without guile. Once it was so hard for him to fit in that he "fell down at Jesus' knees, saying, Depart from me; for I am a sinful man, O Lord" (Luke 5:8). Over time, his meekness enabled him to fit in and become a powerful disciple of Christ.

As we seek the promptings of the Holy Ghost, it is given to us what to ask and say... (Doctrine and Covenants 50:30) and saying it is made easier because "there is no fear in love; but perfect love casteth out fear" (1 John 4:18). No personal problem should ever rise to the level of derailing us from our individual role in eternal life, as a star or as a stage hand. Our problem is often a lack of imaginative power for the glorious future that lies ahead. In mortality we see complexity and confusion around us but seem to imagine only simplicity in eternity. The idea that complexity with exquisite order can exist after mortality is beyond our reach.

Atheists cannot imagine a universe in which there is a place for any life beyond mortality. Pantheists imagine a universe in which individuals give up their personality and return to the great ocean of life. Sadducean Jews imagine there is no resurrection, while Pharisaic Jews imagine life everlasting following a "to-be-determined" resurrection. Muslims imagine life everlasting for those who declare Allah as the only god and Muhammed as His messenger. Trinitarian Christians imagine resurrection on an individual basis for believers in Christ.

However, Covenant Saints look forward to immortality for everyone who ever lived. Those who choose to disregard law and commandments qualify for telestial glory and the presence of the Holy Ghost. Those who live honorable lives qualify for terrestrial glory and the society of the Son of God. But those valiant enough to make and keep sacred temple covenants qualify for the highest degree of celestial glory together with their families in the society of the Son and the Father (Doctrine and Covenants 76).

On my worst days, I find myself understanding the thinking of an atheist who beholds only madness in the world and, therefore, concludes that the greatest future happiness lies in the cessation of life after mortality. On my better days, I relate to the pantheist, conceiving life as a state of bliss in which there is no personal identity or individual personality...all life forms, like droplets of water, merging into one great body. However, on my best days, every doubt of mine vanishes as to the reality of a world where there is room for all life, an art gallery of personalities who can express themselves in a safe environment with such a high degree of love that no one is offended. I believe that such an environment can accommodate someone even like me. Only in a world where the Spirit of God radiates powerfully can awkwardness be melted away by Christ-like love.

Have you made the commitment to return to our Father's home? (John 14:2). Are you diligently preparing for your trip now? We've been given sacred scriptures to serve us as an authentic guide, a kind of travel literature by which we may prepare for our magnificent experience beyond mortality. Every doctrine, principle, and commandment is calculated to lead us back to His presence. Since we usually think of death as unpleasant, we might be inclined not to think about it and make inadequate preparations. But lack of preparation doesn't cancel the trip; it just changes the destination. No one plans or prepares to go to prison. People usually go there when they haven't made definite plans to be somewhere else. Similarly, the Lord never gives us directions on how to get into a lower kingdom. We go there only by our own default of not following the directions to the Celestial Kingdom.

I invite you to have faith in a celestial world. Believe the Lord and all His holy prophets. Jesus repeatedly invited us to follow Him. However, that is only part of the invitation. In its entirety, the invitation consists of three parts: 1) Deny yourself, 2) Take up your cross daily, and 3) "follow me" (Luke 9:23). **Whatever your cross is to you, pick it up and follow the Lord Jesus Christ.** If you laid your cross down, pick it up again. If you are bearing your cross while standing still, it will become lighter as you move forward in faith. The Prophet Moroni has invited us to "seek this Jesus of whom the prophets and apostles have written, that the grace of God the Father, and also the Lord Jesus Christ, and the Holy Ghost, which beareth record of them, may be and abide in you forever" (Ether 12:41).

Please don't be offended by those who do not measure up to the standard that you might expect of a disciple. The word "sainthood," as incorrectly inferred to describe a holy person who goes to heaven after death, is not found anywhere in either the Old or New Testament. However, the word "saint" is used over 200 times. It simply means a person who is on the covenant path—a baptized member of the Lord's Church. The title "saint" bears no relationship to a person's degree of righteousness. However, it does connote a greater expectation of righteous living.

Leo Tolstoy once wrote of a priest who was criticized by one of his congregants for not living as resolutely as he should. The critic concluded that the principles the erring preacher taught must, therefore, also be erroneous. In response to that criticism, the priest said: "Look at my life now and compare it to my former life. You will see that I am trying to live out the truth I proclaim." Unable to live up to the high ideals he taught, the priest admits he has failed. But he cries: "Attack me, [if you wish,] I do this myself, but [don't] attack...the path I follow. ...If I know the way home [but] am walking along it drunkenly, is it any less the right way simply because I am staggering from side to side?...Do not gleefully shout, 'Look at him! ...There he is crawling into a bog!' No, do not gloat, but give...your help [to anyone trying to walk the road back to God.]"[289]

Try your best to walk the road back to God yourself, and as Pepe's manager Jacques would say, "Try to fit in with other saints." That necessitates your first becoming a saint by submitting yourself to the ordinances of the covenant path. Thereafter, **Johann Wolfgang von Goethe** (A.D. 1749-1832), widely regarded as the greatest and most influential writer in the German language, has excellent counsel on how to conduct your life. He said that you ought to hear at least one good song every day, read a good poem, see an exquisite picture, and if possible, speak [and hear] a few sensible words... so that worldly cares may not obliterate the sense of the beautiful which God has implanted into the human soul. In other words, seek daily sources that will inspire you.

Among those "few sensible words," I invite you to read a little each day from the Book of Mormon and to ponder carefully its content. If you have studied the Book of Mormon and cannot yet bring yourself to acknowledge it as a testament of Christ, read the Bible with an open mind and questions. As Nephi wrote: "...if ye believe not in these words [Book of Mormon] believe in Christ [Bible]. And if ye shall believe in Christ ye will believe in these words, for they are the words of Christ, and he hath given them unto me; and...Christ will show unto you, with power and great glory, that they are his words" (2 Nephi 33:10-11).

In his last counsel, Mormon urged us to "repent, and be baptized in the name of Jesus, and lay hold upon the gospel of Christ, which shall be set before you, not only in this record but also in the record which shall come unto the Gentiles from the Jews, which record shall come from the Gentiles unto you. For behold, this [the Book of Mormon] is written for the intent that ye may believe that [the Bible]; and if ye believe that ye will believe this also" (Mormon 7:8-9).

Indeed, if you commit yourself to a diligent and thorough study of the Bible, you will ultimately be led to the additional evidence of the Book of Mormon, which will expand your understanding of the Bible. The covenant path is like a funnel, beginning with a wide enough spout for everyone. With patience, all can emerge successfully through the "strait and narrow" [literally, narrow and narrowing] other end by proceeding forward in faith. Ironically, the gospel funnel is liberating, not restrictive; enlightening, not darkening; and individualistic, not sameness.

Mysteriously, the vast majority choose to take the wide, easy road to destruction. They disqualify themselves as "not cut out" for celestial glory by being, in Churchill's words, "timid, tiny, tardy, torpid, tedious, and tentative." So, more than anything else, decide firmly where you want to go. The word "decide" shares an etymological root with "homicide." The Latin root "cide" means to cut or kill. "De" means off. So, when you decide something, you cut off or kill every other choice or possibility. Cut off all other alternatives. If you will do this, it will put you onto the narrow strait. Don't try to widen it with options and alternatives. Changing a decision into an intention guarantees failure.

Wouldn't it be wonderful if this book could have been entitled *And Then There Were All?* God has made it clear that this is His desire, His invitation, and His work. He "inviteth...all to come unto him and partake of his goodness; and he denieth none that come unto him, black and white, bond and free, male and female; and he remembereth the heathen; and all are alike unto God, both Jew and Gentile" (2 Nephi 26:33). His love and forgiveness are universal. However, He cannot separate us from our indifference, ignorance, indecision, and inflexibility. He has left the unfinished business of our development to ourselves:

> "God left the world unfinished, for man to work
> his skill upon.
> He left the oil still in the earth, the electricity still
> in the clouds.

He left the rivers unbridged, the forests unfelled and the cities unbuilt.

God gave to man the challenge of raw materials, not the ease of finished things.

He left the music unsung and the pictures unpainted and the problems unsolved.

That man might know the joys and glories of creation,

God provides the quarries, but He carves the statues only by the hand of man.

God also left the world of men unfinished. He left the lessons unlearned,

the testimonies unformed, the abilities undeveloped,

that man may share in the work and glory of God."[290]

Think about claims as they present themselves to you. Consider their implications on your life, and don't dismiss a whole category over one that you don't like. Ponder each claim individually because "all truth is independent in that sphere in which God has placed it" (Doctrine and Covenants 93:30). Even if you are not conscious about claims, you are nevertheless controlled by the ones you live. Identify them, and don't let thoughtlessness charter your destiny. Taking one road necessitates leaving another "road not taken," as Robert Frost expressed.

Not only is all truth independent "to act for itself, [but] all intelligence also; otherwise, there is no existence" (Doctrine and Covenants 93:30). The implications of this scripture are profound. We have always existed as intelligences. The only form of life in the universe is individual. Graciously, our Heavenly Father can rescue us from being alone. But it doesn't happen from wishful thinking.[291] At sacred altars in His holy temples, He authorizes husband and wife, parents and children, to be joined under the authority of His eternal priesthood in bonds and covenants that will endure forever.

We have come a long way from being mere intelligences to becoming spirit sons and daughters begotten of heavenly parentage, followed by becoming physical sons and daughters begotten of mortal parents. We have a long way to go from our current expanding universe with a dark night sky to a sea of glass and fire in the presence of God (Revelation 15:2; Doctrine and Covenants 130:7), where there is no night (Revelation 22:5).

But, you might say, "I'd hate living on a sea of glass where there is no night!" Words can be mystifying. When my children were little, I would sometimes have a discussion with them that went something like this:

Me: "If you'll be really good and finish your chores, I'll get a surprise for you."

Children: "What is it, Daddy?"

Me: "If I told you, it wouldn't be a surprise. Don't you think I **can** get something for you that you will think is wonderful?"

Children: "Oh, yes, we know you can!"

Me: "Don't you think I **want** to get something you'll really like?"

Children: "Oh, yes, we know you want to."

Me: "Then, please trust me and go do your chores."

Our Heavenly Father loves to surprise us. In the words of the Apostle Paul, "...Eye hath not seen, nor ear heard, neither have entered into the heart of man, the things which God hath prepared for them that love him" (1 Corinthians 2:9).

**My greatest wish for you is to fulfill your destiny by joining those on the covenant path of whom history will be able to one day record, *"And Then There Were Some*...who found that 'which was prepared for them from the foundation of the world, and their joy shall be full forever'"** (2 Nephi 9:18).

# Notes

1. Nightingale, Earl. *Don't Follow the Follower*, https://www.nightingale.com/articles/dont-follow-the-follower/.
2. Platinga, Alvin. "Evolution vs. Naturalism." *Books and Culture*, July-August, 2008.
3. Koons, Robert C. "The General Argument from Intuition." In *Two Dozen (or so) Arguments for God*, edited by Jerry L. Walls and Trent Dougherty, Oxford: Oxford University Press, 2018. pp. 238-57.
4. Darwin, Charles. *The Autobiography of Charles Darwin, 1809-1882*. Edited by Nora Barlow. New York: Norton, 1958. See also Darwin Correspondence Project. "Letter no. 13230." http://www.darwinproject.ac.uk/DCP-LETT-13230.
5. Dawkins, Richard. Interview with Ben Wattenburg. Think Tank, 1996. http://www.pbs.org/thinktank/transcript410.html.
6. Dawkins, Richard. *The God Delusion*. Boston: Houghton Mifflin, 2006.
7. Meyer, Stephen C. *Return of the God Hypothesis.* HarperCollins Publishers, 195 Broadway, New York, NY 10007, 2021. pp. 444.
8. Barrett, Justin. *Born Believers: The Science of Childhood Religion*. New York: Free Press, 2012.
9. Gopnik, Alison. "See Jane Evolve: Picture Books Explain Darwin." *Wall Street Journal*, April 18,

2014. http://www.bu.edu/cdl/files/2014/04/WSJ-Teaching-Tots-Evolution-via-Picture-Books-WSJ.com_.pdf.

10. Pew Research Center. "The Changing Global Religious Landscape." April 5, 2017. https://www.pewforum.org/2017/04/05/the-changing-global-religious-landscape. See also "The Future of World Religions: Population growth Projections, 2010-2050." April 2, 2015. https://www.pewforum.org/2015/04/02/religious-projections-2010-2050.

11. Quoted by Meyer, Stephen C. "What's Wrong with Atheism?"—Science and God." PragerU, 5-Minute Video.

12. Meyer, Stephen C. *Return of the God Hypothesis.* HarperCollins Publishers, 195 Broadway, New York, NY 10007, 2021. pp. 7.

13. Jaki, Stanley. *The Paradox of Olbers' Paradox: A Startling Account of the Scientific Meaning of the Darkness of the Night Sky.* New York: Herder and Herder, 1969.

14. Poe, Edgar Allen. *Eureka: A Prose Poem.* 1848. Andesite Press, 2015.

15. Dicke, Robert H., et al. "Cosmic Black-Body Radiation." *Astrophysical Journal Letters* 142, 1965. pp. 415.

16. Luminet, Jean-Pierre. "Lemaître's Big Bang." Lecture given at "Frontiers of Fundamental Physics 14," Aix Marseille University, Marseille, France, July 15-18, 2014.

https://arxiv.org/ftp/arxiv/papers/1503/1503.08304.pdf. pp. 10.

17. Metaxas, Eric, *Is Atheism Dead?*, Salem Books, 2021, pp.18.

18. Meyer, Stephen C. *Return of the God Hypothesis.* HarperCollins Publishers, 195 Broadway, New York, NY 10007, 2021. pp. 272.

19. Guillen, Michael. *Believing Is Seeing.* Tyndall Refresh, 2021. pp. 15.

20. Meyer, Stephen C. *Return of the God Hypothesis.* HarperCollins Publishers, 195 Broadway, New York, NY 10007, 2021. pp. 125-127.

21. Ellis, George. "Cosmology: The Untestable Multiverse." *Nature* 469, January 20, 2011, pp. 294-5. doi:10.1038/469294a.

22. Hooft, Gerard 't. *In Search of the Ultimate Building Blocks.* Cambridge: Cambridge University Press, 1997. pp. 163-4.

23. Sill, Sterling W. "The Laws of Leadership." *Leadership.* Bookcraft, Inc. Salt Lake City, Utah. 1958. pp. 11-17.

24. Dawkins, Richard. *River Out of Eden: A Darwinian View of Life.* New York: Basic Books, 1995. pp.133.

25. Meyer, Stephen C. *Return of the God Hypothesis.* HarperCollins Publishers, 195 Broadway, New York, NY 10007, 2021. pp. 243-4.

26. Sandage, Allan. "A Scientist Reflects on Religious Belief." *Truth: An Interdisciplinary Journal of Christian Thought* 1, 1985. pp. 53.
27. Hawking, Stephen, and G.F.R. Ellis. *The Large Scale Structure of Space-Time*. Cambridge: Cambridge University Press, 1973. pp. 364.
28. Genesis 1:1-3—Jewish Publication Society Version.
29. Rendsberg, Gary A., *Great World Religions: The Book of Genesis*, Lecture Two, "The First Creation Story"—from the Great Courses—Religion, The Teaching Company, 2006.
30. Lewis, C. S. *The Screwtape Letters*. Westwood, New Jersey: Balbour. 1961. pp. 14.
31. Meyer, Stephen C. *Return of the God Hypothesis.* HarperCollins Publishers, 195 Broadway, New York, NY 10007, 2021. pp. 257.
32. Sill, Sterling W. "Anti-Art." *Principles, Promises, and Powers*. Bookcraft, Inc. Salt Lake City, Utah. 1975. pp. 69.
33. Metaxas, Eric, *Is Atheism Dead?*, Salem Books, 2021, pp. 36.
34. Ibid. pp. 45-50.
35. Chu, Jennifer. "Study pinpoints timing of oxygen's first appearance in Earth's atmosphere." Massachusetts Institute of Technology. PHYS ORG, Earth\Earth Sciences. May 16, 2016. https://phys.org/news/2016-05-oxygen-earth-atmosphere.html

36. Geisler, Norman L. and Frank Turek. "Divine Design." *I Don't Have Enough Faith to Be an Atheist.* Crossway, 2004. pp. 98-106.

37. Polkinghorne, John. "So Finely Tuned a Universe: Of Atoms, Stars, Quanta, & God." *Commonweal*, August 16, 1996. pp. 16.

38. Hawking, Stephen. *A Brief History of Time*. New York. Bantam Books, 1988. pp.126.

39. Metaxas, Eric, *Is Atheism Dead?*, Salem Books, 2021, pp. 44-45.

40. Meyer, Stephen C. *Return of the God Hypothesis.* HarperCollins Publishers, 195 Broadway, New York, NY 10007, 2021. pp. 130-2.

41. Metaxas, Eric, *Is Atheism Dead?*, Salem Books, 2021, pp. 62.

42. Ibid. pp. 64.

43. Ibid. pp. 65-6.

44. Ibid. pp. 63.

45. Ibid. pp. 62-3.

46. Geisler, Norman L. and Frank Turek. "Divine Design." *I Don't Have Enough Faith to Be an Atheist.* Crossway, 2004. pp. 105-6.

47. Metaxas, Eric, *Is Atheism Dead?*, Salem Books, 2021, pp. 58-61.

48. Ibid. pp. 66.

49. Davies, Paul. *New York Times* op-ed. 2007. Quoted by Metaxas, Eric, *Is Atheism Dead?*, Salem Books, 2021, pp. 55-6.

50. Briggs, David. "Science, Religion Are Discovering Commonality in Big Bang Theory." *Los Angeles Times*, May 2, 1992, B6-7. https://www.latimes.com/archives/la-xpm-1992-05-02-me-1350-story.html.
51. Howell, F. Clark. *Early Man*. Time-Life Books. New York, 1965.
52. Lubenow, M.L. *Bones of Contention*. Baker Books. Grand Rapids, Michigan. 2004, pp. 39-40.
53. Rupe, Christopher and Dr. John Sanford. *Contested Bones*. FMS Publications, 2019. pp. 10.
54. Doolittle, W. Ford. "The practice of classification and theory of evolution, and what the demise of Charles Darwin's tree of life hypothesis means for both of them." *Philosophical Transactions of the Royal Society of London* B 364, 2009: 2221-2228.
55. Meyer, Stephen C. *Signature and the Cell, DNA and the Evidence for Intelligent Design.* "Beyond the Reach of Chance." Harper Collins, New York. pp. 219.
56. Eden, Murray. "Inadequacies of Neo-Darwinian Evolution as a Scientific Theory." In *Mathematical Challenges to the Neo-Darwinian Interpretation of Evolution,* edited by P.S. Moorhead and M.M. Kaplan, 5-19. Wistar Institute Symposium Monograph No. 5. New York: Liss, 1967.
57. Sanford, J.C. "Are Random Mutations Good?" *Genetic Entropy*, FMS Publications, 2014. pp. 15-35.

58. Clark, Jay D. "Is Evolution Credible?" *A Personal Search for Understanding Evolution.* Dorrance Publishing Co. Pittsburgh, PA. 2022, pp. 36.

59. Marks, Jonathan. "What is the viewpoint of hemoglobin, and does it matter?" *History and Philosophy of the Life Sciences* Journal 31 (2):241-62, 2009, pp. 246. https://www.ncbi.nlm.nih.gov/pubmed/20210111.

60. Arsuaga, Juan L. *The Neanderthal's Necklace*, NY: Four Walls Eight Windows Publishing, New York, 2002. pp. 3.

61. Tattersall, Ian. *Masters of the Planet: The Search for Our Human Origins*. Palgrave MacMillan, New York, 2012, pp. 226.

62. Bronowski, Jacob. "The Ascent of Man," a television series produced by the BBC and Time-Life Films, 1973.

63. Nibley, Hugh W. "Before Adam," in Hugh W. Nibley, Old Testament and Related Studies, Volume I of Collected Works of Hugh Nibley, edited by John W. Welch, Gary P. Gillum, and Don E. Norton. Salt Lake City: Deseret Book Company; Provo, Utah: Foundation for Ancient Research and Mormon Studies, 1986, pp. 82-83.

64. Hongzhi Li, *Zhuan Falun*. Yih-Chyun Book Co., Ltd. Taipei, Taiwan, 2019. pp. i.

65. Ibid. pp. 40.

66. Haldane, J.B.S. Possible Worlds and Other Essays. Philadelphia: Richard West, 1972. pp. 209.

67. Gafni, Isaiah M., *Great World Religions: Judaism*, course guidebook from the Great Courses—Religion, The Teaching Company, 2003, pp. 5.
68. Cherry, Shai, *Introduction to Judaism*, course guidebook from the Great Courses—Religion, The Teaching Company, 2004, pp. 107-8.
69. Ibid.
70. Ibid. pp. 104.
71. Noble, Thomas F.X., *Popes and the Papacy: A History*, course guidebook from the Great Courses—Religion, The Teaching Company, 2006, pp. 99-102. Professor Noble quotes the Vatican Council as saying "the Church of Christ 'subsists' in the Roman Catholic Church, instead of saying that the Church of Christ *is* the Roman Catholic Church."
72. Gafni, Isaiah M., *Beginnings of Judaism*, course guidebook from the Great Courses—Religion, The Teaching Company, 2008, pp. 99-103.
73. Ibid.
74. Esposito, John L.., *Great World Religions: Islam*, course guidebook from the Great Courses—Religion, The Teaching Company, 2003, pp. 5.
75. Nelson, Russell M. "The Everlasting Covenant," *Liahona*, October, 2022.
76. "Biography according to the Islamic tradition. Muhammed." *Britannica*. https://www.britannica.com/biography/Muhammad/Biography-according-to-the-Islamic-tradition.
77. Esposito, John L.., *Great World Religions: Islam*, course guidebook from the Great Courses—

Religion, The Teaching Company, 2003, pp. 13-17.

78. Ibid. pp. 2.

79. Quran. Chapter 4, Al-Nisā', section 23, v.171.

80. Wikipedia: https://en.wikipedia.org/wiki/Islamic_schools_and_branches

81. O'Reilly, Bill & Martin Dugard. *Killing Jesus*. Henry Holt & Company, LLC. New York, New York. 2013, pp. 1.

82. The Complete Works of Flavius Josephus. *The Antiquities of the Jews*, William Whiston, translator. New Leaf Publishing Group. 2008. Book 18, Chapter 3, pp. 426.

83. O'Reilly, Bill. "No Spin News," The First TV, March 28, 2024. A report from Martin Dugard's on-location research of Jewish and Roman Historical Archives.

84. Allen, Joseph Lovell & Blake Joseph Allen. *Exploring the Lands of the Book of Mormon*. Book of Mormon Tours and Research Institute LLC. 2008. pp. 276, 309.

85. Torquemada, Juan de. *Monaquia Indiana*. Volume 1. San Francisco: A. L. Bancroft, 1983. 3:47.

86. Allen, Joseph Lovell & Blake Joseph Allen. *Exploring the Lands of the Book of Mormon*. Book of Mormon Tours and Research Institute LLC. 2008. pp. 285, 311.

87. Ibid. pp. 263, 311.

88. Ibid. pp. 309-331.

89. Evans, Van C., PhD. *Willka Wasin Wiraqocha: The House of the Lord.* Publisher: Van Evans. 2019, pp. 26.

90. Ibid. pp. 34.

91. Ibid. pp. 33.

92. Ibid. pp. 32.

93. Ibid. pp. 29-32.

94. Ibid. pp. 33.

95. Hansen, L. Taylor. *He Walked The Americas.* Amherst Press, Amherst, Wisconsin. 1963.

96. Stoddard, Mark J. "Did Jesus Visit Russia After His Resurrection? A Newly Restored Painting Points to this Tradition." Meridian Magazine, September 7, 2021. https://latterdaysaintmag.com/did-jesus-visit-russia-after-his-resurrection-a-newly-restored-painting-points-to-this-tradition/

97. Lewis, C.S. *Mere Christianity.* HarperCollins Publishers, 1952. pp. 51-2.

98. Johnson, Luke Timothy, *Great World Religions: Christianity*, course guidebook from the Great Courses—Religion, The Teaching Company, 2003, pp. 21.

99. Peterson, Daniel C. "Are There Any Good Reasons to Believe?" *Deseret News.* 2 February 2018.

100. *Ante-Nicene Fathers*, Volume 1: *The Apostolic Fathers.* "The Epistle of Ignatius to the Philippians." Hendrickson Publishers, 2012. pp. 116. This epistle is labeled "spurious" because

there is no other documentation of it during the first six centuries A.D.

101. *Ante-Nicene Fathers*, Volume 1: *The Apostolic Fathers.* "The First Apology of Justin." Hendrickson Publishers, 2012. pp. 184.
102. *Ante-Nicene Fathers*, Volume 2: "Theophilus to Autolychus." Hendrickson Publishers, 2012. pp. 100-01.
103. Ibid. pp. 105
104. Callister, Tad R. *The Inevitable Apostasy and the Promised Restoration*, Deseret Book Company, 2006, pp. 149-51.
105. Hinckley, Gordon B. "Don't Drop the Ball," *Ensign*, November, 1994, pp.48.
106. *Ante-Nicene Fathers*, Volume 1: *The Apostolic Fathers.* "Irenaeus Againt Heresies." Hendrickson Publishers, 2012. pp. 419.
107. *Ante-Nicene Fathers*, Volume 3: "Against Praxeas." Hendrickson Publishers, 2012. pp. 603.
108. Ibid. pp. 597.
109. Ibid. pp. 599.
110. Ibid. pp. 600.
111. Ibid. pp. 604.
112. Ibid. pp. 606
113. Ibid. pp. 608-9.
114. Ibid. pp. 625.
115. Ibid. pp. 627.
116. Ibid. pp. 623.

117. *Ante-Nicene Fathers*, Volume 5: "Fathers of the Third Century: Hippolytus." Hendrickson Publishers, 2012. preface, pp. vi.

118. *Ante-Nicene Fathers*, Volume 5: Hippolytus: "Against the Heresy of One Noetus." Hendrickson Publishers, 2012. pp. 228.

119. Ibid. pp. 226.

120. *Ante-Nicene Fathers*, Volume 4: "Origen Against Celsus." Hendrickson Publishers, 2012. pp. 643-44.

121. *Ante-Nicene Fathers*, Volume 4: "Origen De Principiis." Hendrickson Publishers, 2012. pp. 284.

122. *Ante-Nicene Fathers*, Volume 6: "Works of Dionysius—Extant Fragments." Hendrickson Publishers, 2012. pp. 92.

123. Ibid. pp. 94.

124. *Ante-Nicene Fathers*, Volume 5: "A Treatise of Novatian Concerning the Trinity." Hendrickson Publishers, 2012. pp. 628, 636.

125. Talmage, James E. *The Great Apostasy*, Seagull Book and Tape, 1993. pp. 74-5.

126. *Ante-Nicene Fathers*, Volume 4: "On Modesty." Hendrickson Publishers, 2012. pp. 74.

127. *Ante-Nicene Fathers*, Volume 5: "The Life and Passion of Cyprian." Hendrickson Publishers, 2012. pp. 270.

128. Talmage, James E. *The Great Apostasy*, Seagull Book and Tape, 1993. pp. 75.

129. *Ante-Nicene Fathers*, Volume 5: "Hippolytus: Elucidations." Hendrickson Publishers, 2012. pp. 154-5.
130. Ibid.
131. Talmage, James E. *The Great Apostasy*, Seagull Book and Tape, 1993. pp. 76.
132. Esposito, John L.., *Great World Religions: Islam*, course guidebook from the Great Courses—Religion, The Teaching Company, 2003, pp. 32; and Johnson, Luke Timothy, *Great World Religions: Christianity*, course guidebook from the Great Courses—Religion, The Teaching Company, 2003, pp. 20.
133. As found in Weber, *History of Philosophy*, 85, as cited in Barker, *Apostasy from the Divine Church*, 230, quoted by Callister, Tad R. *The Inevitable Apostasy and the Promised Restoration*, Deseret Book Company, pp. 111.
134. Hatch, Edwin. *The Influence of Greek Ideas and Usages upon the Christian Church*. 5th ed. Edited by A.M. Fairbairn, Eugene, Oregon: Wipf and Stock Publishers, 2003, pp. 14.
135. Ibid, pp. 133, 207-8.
136. *Ante-Nicene Fathers*, Volume 6: "Peter, Bishop of Alexandria." Hendrickson Publishers, 2012. pp. 257.
137. *Ante-Nicene Fathers*, Volume 6: "Alexander: Elucidations." Hendrickson Publishers, 2012. pp. 303-04.
138. Talmage, James E. *The Great Apostasy*, Seagull Book and Tape, 1993. pp. 101-2.

139. Wikipedia: https://en.wikipedia.org/wiki/Arius.
140. Handwerk, Brian (May 2006). "Constantine the Great Rules". *National Geographic.* Archived from the original on August 26, 2014. Retrieved September 23, 2014.
141. Hanson, Richard Patrick Crosland. *The Search for the Christian Doctrine of God: The Arian Controversy, 318-381*. T. & T. Clark. 1988, pp. 154.
142. Ibid. pp. 855.
143. Ibid. pp. 849-50.
144. Ibid. pp. 846.
145. Schaff, Phillip. *The Seven Ecumenical Councils.* "Excursus on the Word Homousios." https://biblehub.com/library/schaff/the_seven_ecumenical_councils/excursus_on_the_word_homousios.htm#1.
146. Jörg Ulrich. "Nicaea and the West." *Vigiliae Christianae.* 51, no. 1: 10-24. 1997, pp. 15.
147. Hanson, Richard Patrick Crosland. *The Search for the Christian Doctrine of God: The Arian Controversy, 318-381*. T. & T. Clark. 1988, pp. 211.
148. Britannica, 1971 edition, Vol. 6, "Constantine," pp. 386
149. Hanson, Richard Patrick Crosland. *The Search for the Christian Doctrine of God: The Arian Controversy, 318-381*. T. & T. Clark. 1988, pp. 65, 86.
150. Williams, Rowan. *Arius: Heresy and Tradition.* Eerdmans Publishing. 2004, pp. 82.

151. Athanasius (23 January 2010). "Edict by Emperor Constantine against the Arians". *Fourth Century Christianity*. Wisconsin Lutheran College. Archived from the original on 19 August 2011. Retrieved 2 May 2012.

152. Jones, Arnold Hugh Martin (1986). The later Roman Empire, 284-602 : a social economic and administrative survey. Baltimore, MD: Johns Hopkins University Press. ISBN 978-0-8018-3284-0. And MacMullen, Ramsay. *Voting About God by Early Church Councils*. Yale University Press. 2006.

153. Wikipedia: https://en.wikipedia.org/wiki/Arius.

154. Rendsberg, Gary A., *Great World Religions: The Book of Genesis*, "The Second Creation Story," course guidebook from the Great Courses—Religion, The Teaching Company, 2006, pp. 14.

155. Ibid. "On Reading the Book of Genesis," pp. 4.

156. Eusebius (Eusebius Pamphilus). *The Ecclesiastical History of Eusebius Pamphilus.* Translated by Christian Frederick Cruse. Grand Rapids, Mich.: Baker Book House, 1955. pp. 432.

157. Wikipedia: https://en.wikipedia.org/wiki/Catholic_Church

158. Wikipedia: https://en.wikipedia.org/wiki/Eastern_Orthodox_Church

159. *Ante-Nicene Fathers*, Volume 5: "Elucidations." Hendrickson Publishers, 2012. pp. 561.

160. *Ante-Nicene Fathers*, Volume 3: "Elucidations." Hendrickson Publishers, 2012. pp. 426.

161. Ibid. "On Prescription Against Heretics." pp. 258.
162. Ibid. "Tertullian Against Marcion." pp. 286.
163. Callister, Tad R. *The Inevitable Apostasy and the Promised Restoration*, Deseret Book Company, 2006, pp. 59-60.
164. Noble, Thomas F.X., *Popes and the Papacy: A History*, course guidebook from the Great Courses—Religion, The Teaching Company, 2006, pp. 9.
165. *Ante-Nicene Fathers*, Volume 5: "The Epistles of Cyprian." Hendrickson Publishers, 2012. pp. 394-396.
166. Ibid. pp. 388.
167. *Ante-Nicene Fathers*, Volume 5: "The Seventh Council of Carthage Under Cyprian." Hendrickson Publishers, 2012. pp. 565.
168. Talmage, James E. *The Great Apostasy*, Seagull Book and Tape, 1993. pp. 118; Callister, Tad R. *The Blueprint of Christ's Church*. Deseret Book Company, 2015, pp. 157.
169. *Ante-Nicene Fathers*, Volume 5: "Introductory Notice to Hippolytus." Hendrickson Publishers, 2012. pp. 3-5.
170. Ibid.
171. *Ante-Nicene Fathers*, Volume 8: "Elucidations." Hendrickson Publishers, 2012. pp. 642.
172. Durant, Will. *The Story of Civilization: The Age of Faith*. New York: Simon & Schuster, 1950, pp. 525-26.
173. *Ante-Nicene Fathers*, Volume 8: "Elucidations." Hendrickson Publishers, 2012. pp. 642-3.

174. Sullivan, Francis A. *From Apostles to Bishops: The Development of the Episcopacy in the Early Church*. New York: The Newman Press, 2001, pp. 14.

175. *Ante-Nicene Fathers*, Volume 1: "Epistle of Ignatius to the Romans." Hendrickson Publishers, 2012. pp. 75.

176. Sullivan, Francis A. *From Apostles to Bishops: The Development of the Episcopacy in the Early Church*. New York: The Newman Press, 2001, pp. 15-16.

177. Noble, Thomas F.X., *Popes and the Papacy: A History*, course guidebook from the Great Courses—Religion, The Teaching Company, 2006, pp. 99-102.

178. Van Passen, Pierre. *A Crown of Fire: The Life and Times of Girolamo Savonarola*. New York: Charles Scribner's Sons, 1960. pp. xviii.

179. Durant, Will. *The Story of Civilization: The Age of Faith*. New York: Simon & Schuster, 1950, pp. 381.

180. Talmage, James E. *The Great Apostasy*, Seagull Book and Tape, 1993. pp. 154-5.

181. Wesley, John. *The Works of John Wesley*. Volume VII, 3rd edition. Peabody, Massachusetts: Hendrickson Publishers, 1986. pp. 89: 26-7.

182. Durant, Will. *The Story of Civilization, Part VI: The Reformation*. New York: Simon & Schuster, 1957, pp. 16-17.

183. *Ante-Nicene Fathers*, Volume 7: "Constitutions of the Holy Apostles." Hendrickson Publishers, 2012. pp. 410.

184. Ibid. pp. 480.

185. Mosheim, Johann Lorenz von. *Ecclesiastical History, Century IV*, Part II, chapter 3, 1753, pp. 16. Quoted in Talmage, James E. *The Great Apostasy*, Seagull Book and Tape, 1993. pp. 107.

186. *Ante-Nicene Fathers*, Volume 3: "On Prescription Against Heretics." Hendrickson Publishers, 2012. pp. 262.

187. https://www.livescience.com/christianity-denominations.html.

188. Wikipedia: https://en.wikipedia.org/wiki/Evangelicalism

189. Sill, Sterling W. "The Land of the Book." *The Best of Sterling W. Sill*. Bookcraft, Inc. Salt Lake City, Utah. 1983. pp. 170.

190. Cousins, Norman, ed. *"In God We Trust": The Religious Beliefs and Ideas of the American Founding Fathers*. New York: Harper & Brothers, 1958. pp. 156.

191. Barrett, Ivan J. *Joseph Smith and the Restoration*. Brigham Young University Press. Provo, Utah. 1968. pp. 30-31.

192. Smith, Joseph Fielding. Latter-day Apostle training of newly called missionaries which the author attended at the Salt Lake City Mission Home in October, 1965.

193. Porter, Larry C. *Reverend George Lane—Good "Gifts," Much "Grace," and Marked "Usefulness."* Brigham Young University Religious Studies Center. 2012. https://rsc.byu.edu/exploring-first-vision/reverend-george-lane-good-gifts-much-grace-marked-usefulness.

194. Nelson, Russell M. *Teachings of Russell M. Nelson*, "Doctrine." Deseret Book Company, Salt Lake City, Utah. 2018. pp. 90.

195. Sill, Sterling W. "What Are You Up To?" *What Doth It Profit?* Bookcraft, 1965, pp. 322.

196. Sill, Sterling W. "The Sorting Table." *The Quest for Excellence.* Bookcraft, 1967, pp. 247.

197. Sill, Sterling W. "Blessing Number Four." *What Doth It Profit?* Bookcraft, 1965, pp. 44.

198. Ibid, pp. 43-44.

199. Sill, Sterling W. "Joan of Arc." *What Doth It Profit?* Bookcraft, 1965, pp. 153.

200. Sill, Sterling W. "The Second Mile." *The Law of the Harvest.* Bookcraft, 1963, pp. 280-81.

201. Sill, Sterling W. "If Trouble Comes." What Doth It Profit? Bookcraft, 1965, pp. 139-40.

202. Sill, Sterling W. "Simon and the Cross." The Law of the Harvest. Bookcraft, 1963, pp. 301-7.

203. Smith, Joseph. Lectures on Faith. Salt Lake City: Deseret Book, 1985. lecture 6, number 4.

204. Maxwell, Neal A. Meek and Lowly. Deseret Book Company, Salt Lake City, Utah. 1987. pp. ix.

205. Maxwell, Neal A. “Irony.” *The Neal A. Maxwell Quote Book*. Bookcraft, Inc. Salt Lake City, Utah. 1997. pp. 171-72.

206. Maxwell, Neal A. “Looking at Leadership.” *A More Excellent Way*. Deseret Book Company, Salt Lake City, Utah. 1967. pp. 23-24.

207. Maxwell, Neal A. “Eternal, Intelligent, Independent.” *That Ye May Believe*. Bookcraft, Inc. Salt Lake City, Utah. 1992. pp. 21.

208. Maxwell, Neal A. “Self-Pity.” *The Neal A. Maxwell Quote Book*. Bookcraft, Inc. Salt Lake City, Utah. 1997. pp. 311.

209. Maxwell, Neal A. “Humbleness of Mind.” *Meek and Lowly*. Deseret Book Company, Salt Lake City, Utah. 1987. pp. 48.

210. Maxwell, Neal A. “Leading in Meekness.” *Meek and Lowly*. Deseret Book Company, Salt Lake City, Utah. 1987. pp. 27.

211. Maxwell, Neal A. “Willing to Submit.” *Not My Will, But Thine*. Bookcraft, Inc. Salt Lake City, Utah. 1988. pp. 105.

212. Ibid. pp. 95-96.

213. Maxwell, Neal A. “Humbleness of Mind.” *Meek and Lowly*. Deseret Book Company, Salt Lake City, Utah. 1987. pp. 48.

214. Maxwell, Neal A. “Leading in Meekness.” *Meek and Lowly*. Deseret Book Company, Salt Lake City, Utah. 1987. pp. 27-28.

215. Maxwell, Neal A. “Endure It Well.” *But for a Small Moment*. Bookcraft, Inc. Salt Lake City, Utah. 1986. pp. 117-18.

216. Maxwell, Neal A. "Leading in Meekness." *Meek and Lowly*. Deseret Book Company, Salt Lake City, Utah. 1987. pp. 29.

217. Ibid. pp. 30-32.

218. Maxwell, Neal A. "The Fellowship of His Sufferings." *All These Things Shall Give Thee Experience*. Deseret Book Company, Salt Lake City, Utah. 1979. pp. 28-29.

219. Maxwell, Neal A. "Humbleness of Mind." *Meek and Lowly*. Deseret Book Company, Salt Lake City, Utah. 1987. pp. 36.

220. Maxwell, Neal A. "Pursuing Consecration." *If Thou Endure It Well*. Bookcraft, Inc. Salt Lake City, Utah. 1996. pp. 49-50.

221. Parshall, Ardis E. "George Bernard Shaw on Mormon Polygamy." 13 January 2009. From a coast to coast radio broadcast entitled "The Future of Political Science in America," given April 11, 1933, at New York Metropolitan Opera. This was Shaw's only major address during his only visit to the United States. Four years later, he gave permission for his remarks to be reprinted in the July 1937 issue of the *Improvement ERA*.

222. Daniel 2:44; "The Church of Jesus Christ Today." *Gospel Principles*. The Church of Jesus Christ of Latter-day Saints, 1997, pp. 114.

223. Reeve, W. Paul. *Religion of a Different Color: Race and the Mormon Struggle for Whiteness*. Oxford University Press, 2015, pp. 215-19.

224. Maxwell, Neal A. "Faith in Gospel Ordinances." *Lord Increase Our Faith*. Bookcraft, 1994, pp. 76.

225. Maxwell, Neal A. "Humbleness of Mind." *Meek and Lowly*. Deseret Book Company, Salt Lake City, Utah. 1987. pp. 37, 47-48.

226. Maxwell, Neal A. "Blessed Are the Meek." *Meek and Lowly*. Deseret Book Company, Salt Lake City, Utah. 1987. pp. 102.

227. Sill, Sterling W. "Joseph Smith" *The Glory of the Sun,* Bookcraft, 1961, pp. 134.

228. "The First Vision." *Church History in the Fulness of Times Student Manual*. The Church of Jesus Christ of Latter-day Saints, 2003, pp. 34-5.

229. Andrus, Hyrum L. and Helen Mae. *They Knew the Prophet—Personal Accounts From Over 100 People Who Knew Joseph Smith*. Covenant Communications, 2004, pp. 1-2.

230. Hales, Brian C. quoting Richard L. Bushman in "Joseph Smith's Sexual Polyandry and the Emperor's New Clothes: On Closer Inspection, What Do We Find?" FairMormon Conference, 2012.

231. Oaks, Dallin H. and Joseph I. Bentley. "Joseph Smith and Legal Process: In the Wake of the Steamboat *Nauvoo*." *BYU Law Review*, 1976, pp. 735.

232. Maxwell, Neal A. "All Hell is Moved." *BYU Speeches*. 8 November 1977. Devotional.

233. Arrington, Leonard J. *Brigham Young: American Moses*. University of Illinois Press, 1986, pp. 110.

234. "Trial of Elder Rigdon." *Times and Seasons.* 15 September 1844, pp. 651.
235. Welch, John W. "Impressions of a Prophet." *The Joseph Smith Papers — Television Documentary Series*, Season 2, Disc 1, Episode 3. Larry H. Miller Communications, 2010.
236. Clark, Jay D. "Who was Joseph Smith?" *Spiritual Evolution—One Week at a Time*. Amazon Publishing. 2021, pp. 311-21.
237. Barney, Ronald O. "Impressions of a Prophet." *The Joseph Smith Papers — Television Documentary Series*, Season 2, Disc 1, Episode 3. Larry H. Miller Communications, 2010.
238. Turley, Richard E. Ibid.
239. Maxwell, Neal A. "On Letting Go of the World." *Wherefore, Ye Must Press Forward.* Deseret Book, 1977, pp. 20-2.
240. Quincy, Josiah. *Figures from the Past.* Boston: Robert Brothers, 1883, pp. 376.
241. Church of Jesus Christ of Latter-day Saints Gospel Topics Essays—Book of Mormon and DNA Studies: https://www.churchofjesuschrist.org/study/manual/gospel-topics-essays/book-of-mormon-and-dna-studies?lang=eng.
242. Oaks, Dallin H. "Book of Mormon and DNA Studies." https://www.churchofjesuschrist.org/study/manual/gospel-topics/book-of-mormon-and-dna-studies?lang=eng.

243. Clark, John, Wade Ardern, and Matthew Roper. "Debating the Foundations of Mormonism: The Book of Mormon and Archaeology." FAIR Conference, 2005. In 2019, Matthew Roper updated the list to include 205 publicly available claims of anachronisms in the Book of Mormon. His research concluded that 141 claims (69%) had been disproven, 26 (13%) were trending, and 38 (18%) were not disproven; Matt Roper and Kirk Magleby. "Time Vindicates the Prophet." FAIR Conference, 2019.

244. Anderson, Richard Lloyd. *Investigating the Book of Mormon Witnesses.* Deseret Book Company, 1981.

245. Callister, Tad R. *A Case for the Book of Mormon.* Deseret Book Company, 2019.

246. Potter, George and Richard Wellington. *Lehi in the Wilderness—81 New, Documented Evidences that the Book of Mormon is a True History*. Cedar Fort, Inc., Springville, Utah. 2003. Since its publication, 23 additional evidences have been discovered, increasing the total to 104.

247. Ibid. pp. 3,19.

248. Ibid. pp. 5.

249. Nibley, Hugh. *An Approach to the Book of Mormon*. Deseret Book Company, Salt Lake City, Utah. 1988. pp. 256.

250. Potter, George and Richard Wellington. *Lehi in the Wilderness—81 New, Documented Evidences that the Book of Mormon is a True*

*History*. Cedar Fort, Inc., Springville, Utah. 2003. pp. 34-35.

251. Ibid. pp. xi.

252. Nibley, Hugh. *An Approach to the Book of Mormon*. Deseret Book Company, Salt Lake City, Utah. 1988. pp. 264.

253. Ibid. pp. 253.

254. Potter, George and Richard Wellington. *Lehi in the Wilderness—81 New, Documented Evidences that the Book of Mormon is a True History*. Cedar Fort, Inc., Springville, Utah. 2003. pp. 41-49.

255. Neom.com: https://www.neom.com/ar-sa/regions/siranna?utm_source=linkedin&utm_medium=paid_social&utm_campaign=an~neom_bu~goa_cn~goa_yr~2023_pt~li_ch~paid-social_ca~video-views_mk~sa_ff~ep3&utm_term=video&utm_content=siranna_hero_15_videoviews_pro_int_ep3&li_fat_id=23790f56-c74f-47ca-bd27-a438524f3738.

256. Quran. Chapter 2, Al-Baqarah, section 14, v.115-16.

257. Potter, George and Richard Wellington. *Lehi in the Wilderness—81 New, Documented Evidences that the Book of Mormon is a True History*. Cedar Fort, Inc., Springville, Utah. 2003. pp. 74.

258. Ibid. pp. 99-100 (quoting notable English archer H. Walrond).

259. Ibid. pp. 116 (on display in the Salalah Museum of National Heritage and Culture, September, 1999).

260. Newton, Lynne S. and Juris Zarins. *Dhofar Through the Ages: An Ecological, Archeological and Historical Landscape*. Archaeopress. 2019. pp. xv-xvi.

261. Potter, George and Richard Wellington. *Lehi in the Wilderness—81 New, Documented Evidences that the Book of Mormon is a True History*. Cedar Fort, Inc., Springville, Utah. 2003. pp. 130.

262. Ibid. 130-33.

263. Shahri, Ali. *The Language of Aad*. Dubai: National Packaging & Printing Est., 2000. pp. 25.

264. Potter, George. Discovering the Amazing Jaredites. Cedar Fort, Inc., Springville, Utah. 2003. pp. 19-20.

265. McConkie, Bruce R. *Mormon Doctrine*. Bookcraft, Salt Lake City. 1966. pp. 463 (referencing *Juvenile Instructor*, vol. 27, pp. 282 and *Improvement Era*, vol. 8, pp. 704-705).

266. Forster, Rev. Charles B. D. *The Historical Geography of Arabia.* London: Darf Publishers Ltd. 1984. pp. 90.

267. Shahri, Ali. *The Language of Aad*. Dubai: National Packaging & Printing Est., 2000. pp. 31.

268. Potter, George and Richard Wellington. *Lehi in the Wilderness—81 New, Documented Evidences that the Book of Mormon is a True*

*History*. Cedar Fort, Inc., Springville, Utah. 2003. pp. 140.

269. Ibid. pp. 146
270. Ibid. pp. 128
271. Improvement Era, February, 1939, volume 42, pp. 94.
272. Maxwell, Neal A. "On Letting Go of the World." *Wherefore, Ye Must Press Forward.* Deseret Book, 1977, pp. 20-2.
273. Callister, Tad R. *The Blueprint of Christ's Church.* Deseret Book Company, 2015, pp. 3-21.
274. Fosdick, Harry Emerson, ed. *Martin Luther.* New York: Random House, 1956. pp. 174-75.
275. Talmage, James E. *The Great Apostasy*, Seagull Book and Tape, 1993. pp. 158.
276. *History of the Church* - volume 3, chapter 26: "Adam and the Presidency of the Priesthood," pp. 386. https://byustudies.byu.edu/history-of-the-church-volumes-1-7/.
277. Maxwell, Neal A. "All Hell is Moved." *BYU Speeches.* 8 November 1977. Devotional.
278. Maxwell, Neal A. "On Letting Go of the World." *Wherefore, Ye Must Press Forward.* Deseret Book, 1977, pp. 1.
279. Sill, Sterling W. "Forward." *The Way of Success.* Bookcraft, Inc. Salt Lake City, Utah. 1964. pp. 5.
280. Benson, Ezra Taft, "This Is a Day of Sacrifice," *Ensign*, May, 1979. pp. 32.
281. Smith, Joseph. *Lectures on Faith*. Salt Lake City: Deseret Book, 1985. lecture 6, number 7.

282. Sill, Sterling W. "Strait Is the Gate." *Leadership, Volume II*. Bookcraft, Inc. Salt Lake City, Utah. 1960. pp. 303.

283. Maxwell, Neal A. "To My Dear Omner, with Concern but Undiminished Love, Greetings!" *Of One Heart*. Deseret Book Company, Salt Lake City, Utah. 1975. pp. 56.

284. Maxwell, Neal A. "Discipleship in Our Day." *A Time to Choose.* Deseret Book, 1972, pp. 14.

285. Sill, Sterling W. "The Point of No Return." *Leadership, Volume II*. Bookcraft, Inc. Salt Lake City, Utah. 1960. pp. 238.

286. Sill, Sterling W. "The One Business of Life." *Making the Most of Yourself*. Bookcraft, Inc. Salt Lake City, Utah. 1971. pp. 8-9.

287. "Church News Viewpoint: Happiness = Love." *Deseret News.* 13 October 2016.

288. Nelson, Russell M. "The Everlasting Covenant," *Liahona*, October, 2022.

289. "The New Way," *Leo Tolstoy: Spiritual Writings,* sel. Charles E. Moore (2006), 81–82. Quoted by Holland, Jeffrey R. in General Conference, Be Ye Therefore Perfect—Eventually, October, 2017.

290. Sill, Sterling W. "Unfinished Business" - adapted from Dr. Allen Stockdale. "The Alphabet of Inspiration." *Leadership Volume II*. Bookcraft, Inc. Salt Lake City, Utah. 1960. pp. 177-78.

291. Nelson, Russell M. "The Temple and Your Spiritual Foundation," *Liahona*, November, 2021.

# About the Author

Jay D. Clark, MD, grew up in Los Angeles, where he attended military school as a boy. After serving as a missionary in Brazil for the Church of Jesus Christ of Latter-day Saints, he attended Brigham Young University, where he met and married Pat Hoge of Blackfoot, Idaho. They graduated together in 1970, after which Jay went on to medical school and post-graduate residency training. He became board-certified in ophthalmology and founded Utah's first Medicare-certified eye surgery center. With Pat as Jay's surgical assistant and companion, they served as humanitarian and proselyting missionaries on four continents. Their greatest loves are the Lord and His temples, family, country, service, inspirational learning, music, and scuba diving.

Printed in the USA
CPSIA information can be obtained
at www.ICGtesting.com
LVHW021957101024
793017LV00001B/1

9 781917 505208

December, 2024

Dear Hank & Sara,

Merry Christmas! We miss not being your neighbors. With great esteem for your contributions to building faith in a world in which so many youth are asking why, we hope you'll enjoy reading about our adventures following Lehi's Trail in the Arabian Peninsula.

With our love, admiration and best wishes,

Jay & Pat

jaypatclark@gmail.com